NAPOLEON IN AMERICA

THE REVOLUTIONARY AGE
Francis D. Cogliano, Christa Breault Dierksheide,
Eliga H. Gould, and Patrick Griffin, Editors

Napoleon in America

Bonaparte and the Rhetoric of US Empire

Mark F. Ehlers

UNIVERSITY OF VIRGINIA PRESS
Charlottesville and London

The University of Virginia Press is situated on the traditional lands of the Monacan Nation, and the Commonwealth of Virginia was and is home to many other Indigenous people. We pay our respect to all of them, past and present. We also honor the enslaved African and African American people who built the University of Virginia, and we recognize their descendants. We commit to fostering voices from these communities through our publications and to deepening our collective understanding of their histories and contributions.

University of Virginia Press
© 2025 by the Rector and Visitors of the University of Virginia
All rights reserved
Printed in the United States of America on acid-free paper

First published 2025

9 8 7 6 5 4 3 2 1

LIBRARY OF CONGRESS CATALOGING-IN-PUBLICATION DATA

Names: Ehlers, Mark F., author.
Title: Napoleon in America : Bonaparte and the rhetoric of US empire / Mark F. Ehlers.
Description: Charlottesville : University of Virginia Press, 2025. | Series: The revolutionary age | Includes bibliographical references and index.
Identifiers: LCCN 2025006450 (print) | LCCN 2025006451 (ebook) | ISBN 9780813953533 hardback | ISBN 9780813953540 trade paperback | ISBN 9780813953557 ebook
Subjects: LCSH: Napoleon I, Emperor of the French, 1769-1821—Influence | Bonapartism—United States—History—19th century | United States—Territorial expansion | United States—History—19th century | BISAC: HISTORY / United States / 19th Century | HISTORY / Wars & Conflicts / Napoleonic Wars
Classification: LCC E179.5 .E45 2025 (print) | LCC E179.5 (ebook) | DDC 973.5—dc23/eng/20250708
LC record available at https://lccn.loc.gov/2025006450
LC ebook record available at https://lccn.loc.gov/2025006451

Cover art: Map of Louisiana, Samuel Lewis and Aaron Arrowsmith, 1805 (Library of Congress, Geography and Map Division, http://hdl.loc.gov /loc.gmd/g4050.ct000654); shadow, seleznev_photos/envato.com; colors, LiliiaRudchenko/envato.com
Cover design: Elke Barter

To Dad

CONTENTS

List of Illustrations	ix
Acknowledgments	xi
Introduction: The American Proteus	1
1. Boundaries: The Mississippi Crisis	11
2. Cost: The Louisiana Purchase	40
3. Allies: Florida and the War of 1812	68
4. Democracy: Waterloo to Andrew Jackson	108
5. Glory: The Mexican War	145
Conclusion: Bonaparte's Dream	181
Notes	187
Bibliography	205
Index	219

ILLUSTRATIONS

1. Charles Brockden Brown   34
2. The Louisiana Purchase   65
3. The Floridas   71
4. "The Prairie Dog Sickened at the Sting of the Hornet"   75
5. "Napoleon's Return from Elba"   115
6. Walter Scott   132
7. "Napoleon Crossing the Alps"   134
8. "The Model of a Republican President"   143
9. "Three Views of Napoleon"   146
10. William Ellery Channing   153

ACKNOWLEDGMENTS

If I have learned anything during the process of completing this project, it is that while writing may be a solitary endeavor, turning the words on the page into a book is a process that incurs many debts.

This book began as a dissertation at Louisiana State University. Thus, first and foremost and above all, I must thank Nancy Isenberg and Andrew Burstein. Together they guided this project from its inception to its final completion—even after their well-earned retirements from academia. They offered not only feedback on the content and the writing, but also unfailingly insightful advice and council on every step of the publication process. I am deeply thankful to have had such wonderful mentors.

During my research process, the staff members at the American Antiquarian Society were both patient and knowledgeable—even when I had to retrace my research steps after a computer disaster. They pointed me down a number of rabbit holes that proved incredibly helpful to my project. Similarly, the staff at James Madison's Montpelier, especially Hilarie Hicks, went far above and beyond my expectations when I innocently inquired if they had any information on the Napoleon-related paraphernalia in their collection.

Along the way from research to publication, I've had the opportunity to work within a number of academic communities that have all played a role in making this work better. Within the LSU history department, I was able learn, teach, write, and commiserate alongside incredible peers such as David Brokaw, Andrew Wollard, Zach Isenhower, and Kristine Grinnis. At West Point, my fellow AMDIV instructors, Eric Davis, Danny Sjursen, Andy Forney, and Shauna Hann, were unfailingly helpful and kept me both focused on writing and well supplied with coffee. Most recently, the students and faculty at Sandy Spring Friends School have been curious and endlessly kind as I worked through the process of turning my many drafts into a manuscript. I'm incredibly thankful to have found such supportive academic homes.

Thank you to the acquisitions and editorial teams at UVA Press—especially Nadine Zimmerli, for shepherding the manuscript from proposal to publication. I'm also thankful for the peer reviewers who offered both support and extremely helpful suggestions for improving the project. Everyone I worked with was extraordinarily competent and helpful in guiding me through the publication process, and I've emerged at the other end with a far better piece of writing.

All this being said, the manuscript would still be a meandering mess without the hours that my partner and editor Kerri Hunt spent critiquing my drafts, discussing my ideas, and offering feedback on how to tighten up my arguments or expand my analyses.

And finally, to my budding historian Anna, thanks for believing that your dad could write a book that you would want to read someday.

INTRODUCTION

The American Proteus

On the evening of August 4, 1832, twenty-nine-year-old John H. Latrobe sat down to pen a long letter to a friend. In this missive, the young lawyer and inventor described his recent visit to see the aging James Madison at his Montpelier estate in Orange County, Virginia. After entering the stately Georgian-style manor house, he had been ushered into Madison's drawing room by a servant and encouraged to have a look around while he waited for his audience with the former president. Based on his letter, Latrobe had clearly been fascinated by the eclectic collection surrounding him, and he described parts of it in great detail. In particular, he noted two statues of Napoleon Bonaparte. The first, he wrote, was carefully placed under a looking glass. It was a beautiful bronze piece of Napoleon in exile on Elba, with an allegorical figure of Icarus upon the pedestal. The other, placed on the mantle, was a satirical piece. It was a statue of the French monarch Louis XVIII, which, when opened, playfully displayed the figure of Napoleon inside—recalling Bonaparte's unceremonious dethroning of the Bourbon king during the emperor's brief return to power in 1815.[1]

Perhaps if Latrobe had spent more time in Madison's drawing room before being whisked away for his meeting, he would have noticed other Napoleonic paraphernalia as well. Madison's correspondence and estate inventories reveal that, in addition to the items Latrobe mentioned, the former president also possessed an alabaster statute of Napoleon crossing the Alps, several Napoleonic engravings of varying quality, a series of Napoleon medals commemorating the general's many victories, as well as at least three biographies of Bonaparte. Most wonderous of all was the full-length portrait of the emperor Napoleon which, according to a visitor in 1834, hung prominently over the mantel in the Montpelier drawing room.[2]

Though the two never met, the lives of James Madison and Napoleon Bonaparte were intertwined in the first decades of the nineteenth century through webs of imperialism and state expansion. Madison served ably as Thomas Jefferson's secretary of state and oversaw the transfer of the Louisiana territory from Napoleon to the United States in 1803. As the fourth president, Madison directed the American occupation of Florida to prevent the troubled region from falling into the hands of the French emperor. In 1812, at the height of Napoleon's power, Madison sought a declaration of war against Bonaparte's chief rival, Great Britain, thus initiating an unfortunate act of cobelligerency that his political opponents never let him forget. Both men ended their political careers within a year of each other and went into retirement: Napoleon as an exiled emperor on St. Helena, Madison as a senior statesman at Montpelier. Though it seems unlikely that Napoleon thought much of Madison in his exile, from the range of Napoleon-related items in Montpelier it seems quite likely that Madison spent a good deal of time trying to understand the life and legacy of his contemporary.

Madison, however, was only one of millions of Americans who found themselves trying to understand Bonaparte between the French Revolution and the American Civil War. On the Niagara frontier during the first decade of the nineteenth century, for example, young Eber Howe remembered the excitement generated by the postman bringing the local paper and "with what avidity the family circle would gather round to hear my father read the wonderful doings of that great human butcher, [Napoleon]." Bonaparte's death in 1821 only added to the American fascination with his life and legacy. Napoleon's name and image appeared in paintings, lithographs, books, cartoons, wax figures, speeches, toasts, busts, cake decorations, and countless other items that graced the advertisement sections of early American newspapers. By 1830 even modest families living on the fringes of American settlement usually owned a Bible, a hymnbook, an almanac, and biographies of Washington and Bonaparte. Families that could not afford books accessed the life of Napoleon through libraries. According to literary historian Scott Casper, Americans checked out biographies of the French general more than any other type of book during the mid-nineteenth century.[3]

Some of this was simple hero worship; some was that morbid fascination with the lives of the rich and famous that continues in our own day. But often enough, the French emperor was used consciously by Americans as a rhetorical device to justify or to challenge national policy—especially when it came to American imperial expansion. In this work, I explain how the American public's rhetorical construction of Napoleon first as a political figure and then a historical figure shaped an emerging and evolving sense of American imperial identity between about 1800 and 1850. To do this, I take close look at the rhetoric surrounding the Mississippi Crisis of 1802–3, the ensuing Louisiana Purchase, the acquisition—or conquest—of Florida, and finally the Mexican American War, which ended in 1848.

In a simplistic way, Americans often saw similarities between continental expansion in the Old and the New Worlds. Both the United States and Bonaparte's France were republics (or at least started that way), and both actively expanded beyond their borders during the first decades of the nineteenth century. Even after the expansion of Bonaparte's France was halted prematurely at the Battle of Waterloo in 1815, Americans continued to use him to debate the merits of an imperial republic. In other words, they asked if a nation could retain its republican principles and still engage in military conquest. This discourse, carried on in print media and appearing in cultural ephemera, reflected a broader societal debate about the nature of American expansion. In the Early Republic, Napoleon's name carried multiple meanings. Both as a political actor and as a powerful symbol of imperial values, Bonaparte proved rhetorically useful to two competing accounts of the rationale for and the meaning of the imperial project in the United States. One rationale justified expansion as vital to protect American sovereignty and liberty from Bonaparte's own imperialism; the other saw the republican empire of the United States as a benevolent force of history and used the Bonapartist model of empire as a yardstick against which American imperialism could be measured. At the same time, references to the French emperor also provided a framework for anti-imperialist arguments that highlighted the similarities between aggressive and undemocratic Napoleonic imperialism and American expansion.

Understanding the role that Napoleon played in the early American discourse of empire helps explain how Americans came to construct and to understand their particular imperial identity. It shows how Napoleon and his empire functioned as an example that was accessible across both class and regional boundaries. This made him an important point of reference for Americans as they debated the central questions of empire. How and where were the boundaries of nation and empire—both geographic and demographic—to be drawn? How could republican liberty and natural rights be squared with the inherent domination and national othering implied by the project of empire? Under what conditions was violence justified in the imperial project? The fundamental questions surrounding the formation of an imperial identity were not only those of the American political elite, nor were they simply a top-down process; they were all debated and negotiated vigorously in the American press—which served as a meeting point for literate Americans of all classes. Because Napoleon could serve as a common cultural touchpoint for their arguments, understanding how Americans viewed Napoleon and his empire is critical to understanding how Americans imagined their own empire.[4]

At the same time, examining how Americans understood the imperial image of Bonaparte also helps us better understand the anti-imperial response to the emerging imperial identity of the United States. Through the twentieth century, scholars tended to see imperial expansion as a nearly hegemonic force within nineteenth-century American society that was easily explained by the ubiquitous phrase "manifest destiny." Only recently have scholars come to question the homogenous imperial identity implied by this phrase. While there is no question that the ideology of imperial expansion was an extremely powerful force for unity within the Early Republic, it was never absolute. Those opposed to the forming imperial identity of the United States used widespread American rejection of Napoleon's violence in Europe to build a powerful rhetorical arsenal that highlighted the hypocrisy of American imperial ambitions. Anti-imperialists could and did maintain a logically coherent and (sometimes) principled argument against the very idea of empire by relying on the negative imperial example provided by Napoleon.[5]

Early American Visions of Empire

Americans began their dialogue about empire almost as soon as they emerged from their War for Independence. It may seem surprising that Americans who owed their political existence to the rejection of the British empire should immediately seek to define themselves in imperial terms. In fact, in their revolution, Americans had not rejected empire itself but merely what they saw as the corrupted version of empire that the British monarch and Parliament embodied. For most Americans of the Early Republic, there was nothing inherently inconsistent with being an imperial nation, the question was how such a system should properly function and to what end. This question, which was caught up in contrasting visions of the American future and the very nature of the American union, led to the emergence of an irrevocable political split by the mid-1790s. The political ideologies of the two factions—Federalists and Jeffersonians—that dominated this era of American politics shaped two rival conceptions of imperial expansion.[6]

Federalists generally looked east toward Europe and sought to fashion the United States into a great commercial and economic empire that would be respected around the globe. This was particularly important in the chaotic and dangerous world that emerged from the French Revolution. They saw Great Britain as the best example of a liberal imperial system that the world had yet seen—one that championed the economic freedom of its citizens but, when well administered, had enough checks in the system to prevent it from becoming a tyrannical despotism. When it came to expansion, Federalists envisioned a stable central government that could efficiently administer its imperial holdings and provide a sense of national identity for the peoples within its holdings. For Federalists, it was critical that physical expansion be tied to economic expansion—land simply for the sake of it was useless and could even be dangerous to the political unity of an imperial republic if it was extended beyond the ability of the central government to impart a common sense of identity. They preferred cautious expansion into regions that had a specific commercial or strategic purpose. Control of the Mississippi River's mouth, for example, was vital to export valuable American products from Ohio and Kentucky to Europe.[7]

At the other end of the American political spectrum were the Jeffersonians. They envisioned a sprawling agricultural empire of land-owning farmers who tilled the fertile American soil far from the money and corruption of large cities. The availability of cheap western land was thus absolutely critical to this vision for the American future. This was to be an empire with no metropole—an empire of equal states held together by common culture, not by the force of a powerful central government. For the Jeffersonians, the failure of the British empire was in its failure to recognize the political equality of Britons in the provinces. Their solution was to not have an imperial metropole at all. The Jeffersonians' preferred method of expansion was what later scholars would call settler colonialism. Geographic expansion would be through "natural" means, which, the Jeffersonians believed, had the value of Newtonian-like inevitability, as opposed to the man-made violence of military conquest. In the mind of Jeffersonians, as the sparsely populated Native peoples in possession of fertile but untapped western lands inexorability passed away, their place would naturally and peacefully be taken by American settlers. These vigorous Americans would bring agriculture and civilization to untamed lands before their sons and daughters would head west again and repeat the process on a new western frontier.[8]

Given their conceptions of empire and union, Americans found that they could not avoid Europe as the wars of the French Revolution raged during the last decade of the eighteenth century. The Federalist vision for the future required Americans to become enmeshed in a highly profitable world of Atlantic trade whereas the Jeffersonian vision had Americans bumping up against the still expansive, if decaying, European colonies in the Americas—especially along the Gulf Coast and the lower Mississippi River. Every foreign policy choice that the first four presidential administrations made was interpreted to benefit either one or the other of the major belligerents as they battled for supremacy in Europe. Ultimately, the question that faced the first generation of Americans was whether the revolutionary disorder of France or the aristocratic order of Great Britain was more of an ideological threat to the infant United States and its embryonic empire. On this answer would hang the future of American expansion during the first fifteen years of the nineteenth century.

Newspapers as Political Weapons

Whether they identified as Jeffersonians or as Federalists, Americans in the Early Republic relied on newspapers to make and spread their arguments for and against national expansion, and it is from this rich source that I draw most of the evidence for my work. When considering the place of newspapers as a historical source for the intellectual currents of the early American republic, it is important to understand their purpose. One historian has noted aptly, "the newspaper press was the political system's central institution, not simply an atmosphere in which politics took place." Newspapers were the vital link between parties and their constituents, and thus newspaper editors were powerful political agents. On the one hand, editors saw themselves as the democratic voice of "the people" since many Americans were excluded from the franchise by property restrictions during the first few decades of the nineteenth century. On the other hand, in a political world that eschewed overt campaigning, editors were also the means by which political organizations could reach the American people. Newspapers thus both reflected and shaped public opinion, and the line between opinion and news piece was considerably more blurred than it is today.[9]

Newspapers usually featured highly partisan news stories or lengthy excerpts of presidential or congressional speeches that were followed by several columns of commentary. Some of these pieces might be generated by the editor of the paper, but others would be in the form of pseudonymously authored letters to the editor. These were usually from local or sometimes even national party leaders who attempted to maintain the fiction that the elite of American society did not engage in unseemly political wrangling with their social inferiors. These commentaries could have a very large circulation, and they served as the crucial link between party organizations in different parts of the country. Often pieces printed in one of the major party newspapers in New York or Philadelphia would be picked up and reprinted in other, smaller papers across the nation, or they might be printed as independent pamphlets and circulated separately. Well-received commentary pieces might be printed in a dozen different newspapers from Kentucky to Maine over the course of a few weeks or months. It was not uncommon for opposing newspapers to print their own commentaries that attempted to refute the opposition's widely republished pieces. In this way, the American public witnessed vibrant debates about national expansion taking place in print before their eyes.[10]

Napoleon and the Early Republic

One bit of news that both Federalists and Jeffersonians followed with particular interest was the rise of Napoleon Bonaparte. Most Americans first became aware of the Corsican-born general in 1796 when he was put in command of the French republican army charged with clearing the Austrians out of their strongholds in northern Italy. Within weeks, newspapers were full of Bonaparte's thrilling dispatches from the front lines. By the end of the year, one Federalist newspaper from Baltimore noted with some concern the degree to which "the public mind in America is wrought up to a high state of anxiety" over Napoleon's series of stunning victories in Italy. In October 1797, Bonaparte's Italian campaign came to a successful conclusion with the Austrians forced to sign the Treaty of Campo-Formio. The successful general was reassigned to northern France where a 120,000-man army was assembled for the invasion of Britain itself. A young American senator from Tennessee named Andrew Jackson watched developments from Europe breathlessly. "Should Boneparte make a landing on the English shore," Jackson wrote to a friend, "Tyranny will be Humbled, a throne crushed and a republick will spring from the wreck—and millions of distressed people restored to [the rights of man by the] conquering arm [of Bonaparte]."[11]

Despite an official declaration of neutrality from the United States with respect to the French Revolutionary Wars, almost immediately Americans came to starkly different conclusions about what the career of Bonaparte meant. Jeffersonians, such as Andrew Jackson, initially hailed Napoleon as a brilliant republican general whose victories spread the promise of liberty and freedom to those oppressed by despotic European monarchies. As part of the traditional Independence Day toasts made by the New York Democratic society in 1797, twenty-two cheers were made in support of "Gen. Buonaparte and the brave officers and soldiers of the French armies," who were engaged in "securing the liberty, peace and happiness of mankind." Federalists, on the other hand, urged caution. They detested the bloody social and political chaos unleashed by the French Revolution and liked it even less when it became apparent that Bonaparte's spectacular victories provided France the means to spread the revolution to its neighbors, whether they wanted it or not.[12]

The revolution, with Bonaparte at its head, soon spread beyond Europe. When it became clear that an invasion of Britain was unlikely to succeed, the Directory ordered Napoleon to take command of an army setting out for Ottoman Egypt. Not only would this threaten British economic influence in the region, but it might allow the French to put pressure on British interests as far away as India. It also had the advantage of removing the popular young general from France, where he might become a political liability. The Directory government saw no downside to the plan. Bonaparte himself was elated, for it gave him to the opportunity to follow in the footsteps of great conquerors such as Alexander the Great. In May 1798, the fleet set sail. Malta was reduced after a brief siege, and the French army landed at Alexandria in July 1798. Despite the harsh climate, which claimed a number of his soldiers, Napoleon's forces won several early dramatic victories. The tide soon turned against Bonaparte, however. In August Bonaparte's fleet was destroyed by the British in Aboukir Bay, and in October the Egyptian population in Cairo rose in revolt against the French occupiers. A winter offensive into Syria met with little success, and the campaign was marred by bloody atrocities on both sides and the deadly outbreak of plague within the French army. Realizing that no relief could be possible with his fleet destroyed, Bonaparte abandoned what remained of his army in Alexandria and returned to France in August 1799.[13]

The Egyptian campaign was only marginally successful from a military perspective, but it did help Napoleon in at least one way. It ensured that his American reputation was not tarnished by the souring of Franco-American relations that occurred in the last years of the eighteenth century. Irritated by the ratification of the Anglo-American Jay Treaty and in desperate need of money to fight its interminable wars, in late 1796 the French Directory rebuffed the American ambassador and ordered its navy to seize American merchant ships and their crews on the high seas. In response, the newly elected president, John Adams, dispatched three envoys to seek a resolution to the emerging crisis. France, however, needed money. The three Americans were met by French agents referred to as X, Y, and Z, who demanded a $250,000 bribe and a loan to France of $12 million before any negotiations could begin. Astonished, the Americans refused—"no, no, not a sixpence," retorted the South Carolinian Charles Pinkney, once he was certain that there was no diplomatic way forward. The XYZ Affair provoked a furious American response. A habitually tightfisted Congress voted to construct a fleet of modern warships and made plans to expand its insignificant national army to fifty thousand men—still rather small by European standards, but far larger than any force the United States had fielded during the Revolution. "Millions for defense, not one cent in tribute!" went the slogan that was trumpeted by Federalist papers and partisans throughout the country. Over the next two years, the American and French navies engaged in a desultory conflict called the Quasi-War. Federalist political infighting between the more conciliatory Adams faction and the belligerent Hamilton wing of the party, however, prevented the war crisis from expanding far beyond some occasional, though furious, ship-to-ship duels and the capture of numerous merchant vessels.[14]

For many Americans, it came as welcome news that Napoleon had abandoned his army in Egypt, returned to France, and engineered a coup that toppled the hated Directory in December 1799. In its place, Bonaparte established a government of three executives with himself as First Consul and wielding nearly all real political power. In the spring of 1800, Bonaparte, who was eager to redeem his military reputation, took command of a French army that crossed the Alps to deal with an Austrian force that had reoccupied some of the territories seized by the French during Napoleon's first campaign there in 1796. With war in Europe and political concerns in France occupying his attention, the First Consul had little interest in sparring with a minor power on the other side of the Atlantic. Shortly after assuming the Consul's office, Napoleon adopted a more conciliatory stance toward the United States. This led to the Convention of 1800 that ended the half-hearted naval conflict between the two nations in September of that year. Most Americans breathed a sigh of relief. Troubling to at least some, however, was the nagging sense that with the ascension of Bonaparte, France had become a republic in name only. While some die-hard Jeffersonians continued to hope that Bonaparte's near dictatorial powers as First Consul would be only temporary, most Americans expressed relief that they, at least, were separated from Bonaparte by the waters of the Atlantic Ocean.[15]

1

Boundaries

The Mississippi Crisis

During the first few months of 1803, an anonymous author published a long pamphlet sporting a grandiose title, "An Address to the Government of the United States on the Cession of the Louisiana Territory to the French and on the Late Breach of Treaty by the Spaniards, including the Translation of a Memorial on the War of St. Domingo, and the Cession of the Mississippi to France." The author—the novelist and essayist Charles Brockden Brown—claimed to have translated a secret communiqué from a "French Counseller of State" to the First Consul of the Republic, Napoleon Bonaparte. In the "deciphered" document, Brown, as the French diplomat, argued persuasively that Bonaparte ought to immediately occupy the Louisiana Territory, which had recently been begrudgingly ceded to him by his Spanish allies. After completing the translation of this imagined foreign intelligence, Brown made an urgent appeal to his own government in the remainder of the pamphlet. With French military occupation of the Louisiana Territory apparently inevitable, he argued for a preemptive American military occupation of the territory before Bonaparte could officially take possession of the area. Yes, he admitted, this would mean a foreign war waged against Spain. Yet, he argued, the danger of allowing Bonaparte to militarize and define the natural western boundary of the United States was worth the political consequences of war.[1]

Brown's pamphlet was not a single militant voice in the wilderness. He was only one of many influential American voices calling for military action to seize New Orleans in the spring of 1803. The story of how the infant United States almost came to blows with Spain for control of New Orleans and ultimately ended up buying the entire Louisiana territory from Napoleon Bonaparte represents the first chapter in a long history of American imperial expansion. The Louisiana Purchase is usually fondly remembered as the first opportunity of an embryonic nation to burst through the boundaries defined by the Treaty of Paris in 1783. Yet, as Brown's appeal to his government shows, the road to what most Americans remember as the greatest land deal in US history was not a simple or peaceful one. It involved fear and hyper-partisan political bickering that almost developed into America's first foreign war involving land forces.

The debate over American military action to seize New Orleans, which Brown encapsulated in his pamphlet, also introduced a common thread into the greater national discussion over imperial expansion that would tie together American thought on the subject for the next half century—Napoleon Bonaparte. During the Mississippi Crisis of 1802–3, Napoleon entered the national debate over the imperial identity of the United States. His image as a dangerous political actor whose own voracious imperial appetites worked outside natural and international law led Americans to consider embracing their own aggressive imperial measures and established an early tradition of defensive imperial expansion within the American consciousness.[2]

The Boundaries of Louisiana

To understand American imperialism during the first half of the nineteenth century, and the role that Napoleon played in the American debate over their imperial identity, we must start at the same place Charles Brockden Brown did in his pamphlet—with the land of Louisiana and the lines that Europeans drew across it. Where, exactly, Louisiana was on the map in 1803 was difficult to say. No Europeans had traversed it in its entirety, and the maps of the region were vague and reflected the geographic interpretations of at least three different imperial powers. It was generally accepted by the imperial states of Europe that Louisiana was the territory dominated by the by great Mississippi River and its tributaries west to the Rocky Mountains—at least some 827,000 square miles. On some eighteenth-century maps, though, Louisiana included the Missouri River system or even the entire Gulf Coast and Florida. These amorphous geographic boundaries and the arbitrary lines European monarchs drew across the continent would later play a large role in American debates over the natural limits of Louisiana.[3]

Louisiana was no stranger to the byzantine world of imperial politics by the time that Bonaparte turned his gaze there at the end of the eighteenth century. The region was initially bypassed by the Spanish during the sixteenth century in favor of establishing far more commercially viable colonies in the silver-producing regions of Mexico and occupying a few strategic outposts in Florida, which, by their reckoning, ran the entire length of the Gulf Coast to the Mississippi River. Moving south from their possessions in Canada, the French claimed the Mississippi delta at the end of the seventeenth century. Compared to the far more lucrative sugar-producing islands in the Caribbean, however, Louisiana remained an undesirable, backward wilderness. Ultimately, the French managed to do little more than fortify the mouth of the Mississippi River at New Orleans and establish string of fur-trading posts around the junction of the Ohio and the Mississippi Rivers around present-day St. Louis.[4]

During the eighteenth century, the entire Gulf Coast became an imperial football in a long series of wars between European empires. The end of the Seven Years' War in 1763 led to a complex territorial reshuffling of North America: French Louisiana was ceded to Spain, and French Canada was turned over Great Britain. At the same time, Spain ceded its possessions in Florida to Great Britain. But within a dozen years, the British imperial bureaucracy pushed its thirteen original mainland North American colonies into open revolt. Seeking allies, the infant American republic sought recognition and support from Britain's old enemies of France and Spain. Looking to avenge their embarrassment at the hands of the British during the Seven Years' War, both powers eventually entered the war on the side of the Americans. The treaties that ended this British civil war turned international conflict affirmed the independence of the colonies and Spanish control of both Florida and Louisiana. The Treaty of Paris (1783) defined the new nation's boundaries as all territory west to the middle of the Mississippi River, south of Canada and north of Florida, though the exact northern boundary of Spanish Florida was left unclear.[5]

The Mississippi River and its tributaries loomed large in the minds of the newly independent Americans, the Spanish, and the French. In an age when the only way to transport goods to market economically was via water routes, Americans living west of the Appalachian Mountains depended upon the free flow of cargo down the Ohio to the Mississippi and then through New Orleans to the Gulf of Mexico. For its part, Spain eyed nervously the thousands of Americans who began to flock into the nebulous Florida border regions. This unease resulted in several treaties between Spain and the United States. The most important of these, Pickney's Treaty of 1795, clarified the boundary between the United States and Florida as the thirty-first parallel of latitude, and both sides agreed to allow each other unimpeded access to the Mississippi River. The treaty also provided Americans a "right of deposit" in New Orleans, which allowed westerners to transport and store their goods in New Orleans without having to pay a tax to the Spanish empire. Meanwhile, France had not lost interest in its former colony of Louisiana. In 1794, the Directory government quietly opened negations with Spain for the retrocession of the territory, but for years the Spanish government proved remarkably intractable on the issue. Bonaparte, however, would not be dissuaded so easily.[6]

The Retrocession

When Napoleon overthrew the Directory in 1799 and established a three-man Consulate government with himself as First Consul, he inherited a long-established French desire to rebuild its western empire. He quietly redoubled pressure on his ally Spain to retrocede Louisiana to France in exchange for territory in Italy. While Spain had resisted such moves from the Directory for years, under enormous political and military pressure from Napoleon, Spain backed down. Not unhappy to be rid of the financial drain on its economy and happy to use a newly invigorated France as a buffer between New Mexico and the United States, the Spanish government secretly acceded to Napoleon's demands in October 1800 after securing a verbal agreement that the French consul would allow no third party to possess Louisiana. Well aware of the firestorm that the retrocession would cause in the United States, both powers attempted to keep the deal secret until Bonaparte had the ability to solidify his control of the region.[7]

Eager to realize his dream of re-creating a North American empire, Napoleon concluded his wars in Europe—at least temporarily. The Peace of Lunéville pacified Austria in February 1801; then, eight months later, he ended hostilities with the British in the Peace of Amiens. The result of these treaties was a greatly enlarged French state. It also freed France from fear of the British navy. In January 1802, Americans read that a large French expeditionary force under the command of Napoleon's brother-in-law, Charles Leclerc, was on its way to North America to assert the First Consul's control over his western empire. This action confirmed the worst fears of many Americans—especially the more Franco-phobic Federalists. Rumors of the Spanish retrocession of Louisiana to France had been circulating in diplomatic circles since the end of March and in the American press since at least June, but the sailing of the French fleet for the Americas left no doubt in the minds of the American public that they would have a new neighbor on their western border. President Thomas Jefferson and his secretary of state, James Madison, immediately initiated diplomatic efforts to find out the exact extent of the retrocession and to see if Napoleon would be willing to sell the all-important port of New Orleans. The delicate negotiations that followed took over a year and have been well chronicled in other places. Jefferson was willing to wait for diplomacy to work, but not all of his countrymen were so patient, and they quickly adopted a vocabulary to express their concerns.[8]

At the heart of American unease with the retrocession of Louisiana was the inability to predict how Napoleon would define France's natural boundaries—also called "natural frontiers." The Enlightenment concept of national borders being defined by human reason and nature (mountain ranges, oceans, and rivers, for example) became part of the French discourse during the halcyon days of the sixteenth century, though French military reverses during the eighteenth century called the idea into question. As early as 1793, the French revolutionary leader Danton revived the idea. It was Napoleon Bonaparte, however, who finally made these limits a reality through his dramatic victories over the Austrians in the Wars of the First and Second Coalitions (1792–98 and 1799–1802). In the early nineteenth century, "natural boundaries" were not exactly a definable term in international relations, but one that European states accepted as a self-evident and benign foundation of foreign policy nevertheless. The Treaty of Lunéville and Peace of Amiens brought the idea of "natural boundaries" or "natural frontiers" to the front of American discourse about expansion. The treaties extended the borders of France to the Rhine and created French client states in Northern Italy, Holland, and Switzerland. The uneasy peace and its connection to the rise of Napoleon showed a new threat to the European balance of power and provided Americans with a new development that required them to engage in a broader debate about legitimate expansion.[9]

These ideas about imperial boundaries defined by the natural environment developed in tension with a second model of statecraft centered on the idea of a "balance of power" between states. The balance of power argument went back to the theorist Emmerich Vattel—a Swiss political philosopher who published his immensely influential diplomatic treatise, *The Law of Nations,* in 1758. Vattel argued that peaceful relations between nations relied on maintaining a relative balance between independent states theoretically equal in political and economic power. Such a system served as a bulwark to the threat of a naturally despotic "universal monarchy," because the acquisition of additional power by one state would lead to a reaction among the other states to restore balance to the international system. Peace among nations was predicated not on the rationality of the natural world but on the Enlightenment idea of rational self-interest among rival states. When Vattel wrote in the mid-eighteenth century of a "universal monarchy," he was thinking of Charles V or Louis XIV. After 1800, Americans increasingly associated the threat of "universal monarchy" with Napoleon. Over the next decades, American discourse around expansion swung between these two systems, sometimes coalescing around one model and sometimes the other, and sometimes trying to view the United States as an exception altogether from the old rules of European power politics.[10]

Americans took note of the new, extended French borders created by the Treaty of Lunéville and Peace of Amiens, and their reactions were mixed. An editorial from South Carolina happily commented that Bonaparte had no further cause for war as France had reached its "natural limits." The author and, at least officially, the French government defined these limits as that territory bounded by "the Rhine, the Pyrannese [Pyrenees], the Alps, the Mediterranean and the Atlantic." This author articulated the belief of most Americans by making peace contingent on a nation extending to its natural boundaries, but not beyond them. It was reasonable and beneficial for the French empire to extend to the boundaries defined by nature because, once accomplished, this would prevent the need for further conflict by removing any further justification for aggression.[11]

Other Americans were not so sure, and their unease revealed concerns about Bonaparte's understanding of France's natural frontiers. One American wrote a satirical commentary on the peace negotiations. The author likened the carving up of Europe to a family dinner and painted a vivid word picture of the scene that ensued. Bonaparte, as the most successful power broker, sat at the head of the table and ate first. The whole European family knew him as a "monstrous pie eater." After all, at the "banquet of Campo Formio, whole Italian fricassees and all the Flanders' bacon liked not to have satisfied him." His enormous appetite was compounded by his apparent fasting of late in Egypt—a sly jab at Napoleon's failures there. The author warned the Russian emperor, who sat across from the First Consul, to keep a wary eye, lest Bonaparte "claim a little more than his share." This observer raised the issue of imperial "appetites," something that might not be contained by natural boundaries. Nations might be greedy, driven by other impulses, beyond the enlightened principle of natural frontiers. Reason, Americans began to realize, could fail when confronted by an imperialist such as Bonaparte. Americans' fear of Napoleon's expansionist appetites for the Western Hemisphere grew steadily as they waited for news from the French fleet.[12]

It was not just Bonaparte's imperial "appetites" that worried Americans; it was that these unnatural ambitions were combined with the means to achieve them in the person of the First Consul. Gone were the defensive wars of the early 1790s when Republican France was fighting for its very survival against the collected monarchies of Europe. For an increasing number of Americans, Bonaparte's wars no longer represented the preservation of republican liberty, but rather aggressive and irrational imperial conquest. As early as 1798, the *Otsego Herald* identified Napoleon as that "infamous general, commonly called The Butcher." That same year, the editor of the Baltimore *Federal Gazette* wrote that in the ongoing European wars France relied on its triumphant veterans, and "the renowned Bonaparte, who, unsatisfied with empire already obtained through seas of blood, pants for universal dominion." In 1801, the *Virginia Argus* noted of Bonaparte's wars, "the quantity of property and blood which have been expended . . . would have been sufficient for founding a colony more populous and powerful than the United States collectively." The editor of the *Argus* thus drew a clear contrast between colonial expansion and the bloody warfare of imperial conquest. By the time the crisis over New Orleans emerged in 1802, most Americans had come to associate Bonaparte with bloody imperial conquest that stretched the limits of widely recognized international custom and reason.[13]

Coriolanus and America's Natural Boundaries

In early 1802, American expansionists began invoking the name of Napoleon and the idea of natural boundaries within the context of Louisiana. One of the first and most eloquent arguments was made by William Stephens Smith. Born in New York City to a middle-class family, Smith graduated from Princeton and briefly studied law before joining the Continental Army. He witnessed most of the great battles of the American War for Independence and fought under many of the most famous commanders. He ended the war as a lieutenant colonel supervising the British evacuation of his hometown. The aftermath of the war appears to have left Smith bored and looking for a sense of purpose. He briefly served on the American legation to Great Britain, where he met and married the daughter of John Adams in 1786—thus becoming a staunch Federalist by default. He returned to the United States in 1788 and held a variety of minor federal positions and dabbled in western land speculation, none of which provided a very secure financial future. For a few months, he was deeply involved with the aborted expansion of the national army during the Quasi-War with France, the first project for which he showed any real enthusiasm since the War for Independence. The election of Thomas Jefferson in 1800 found Smith out of political favor, bored, in financial straits, and wishing nostalgically for his days of military glory. Given his background, it is unremarkable that he cast his eyes westward.[14]

This was the context in which Smith entered the expansion debate. In January 1802, he penned an incredibly popular article that eventually ran in several widely read New York and New England papers under the classical pseudonym "Coriolanus." Smith warned his readers that with the accession of Bonaparte the geopolitical situation in the Americas had dramatically changed. All of the First Consul's military and diplomatic maneuvering demonstrated a policy of expanding France to its "ancient limits" rather than its natural boundaries. In other words, said Coriolanus, Napoleon intended to repossess all of the territories lost by the French monarchy in previous wars. As evidence, Coriolanus pointed to the French repossession of Guiana with "expanded and almost limitless boundaries," as well as the French occupation of the Rhine valley and the transalpine regions of Italy.[15]

Smith inserted a new element into the American discourse of expansion with this part of the essay. Instead of leading France to its divinely appointed and thus legitimate "natural" boundaries, Smith suggested that Napoleon was ambitiously expanding his empire beyond this sphere to France's "ancient limits." To Americans of the early nineteenth century, the concept of a nation's "ancient limits" was ill-defined but generally understood to be the intellectual opposite of a nation's natural boundaries. To most people who thought about such things, the term seems to have meant the most expansive territorial limits ever claimed and administered by a given nation. In the American mind, where natural boundaries were based on reason and geography and were self-evident, ancient limits were based on ill-defined, arbitrary lines drawn by power-hungry monarchs and their minions. As such they were dangerous and usually contested. For Smith, this is what Napoleon threatened to bring to the Western Hemisphere with control of Louisiana.

With this concerning trend established, he turned his attention to Napoleonic designs in Louisiana. "In the possession of Spain," he observed somewhat disingenuously, "Louisiana was a clearly defined territory." He meant here that Spain defined Louisiana by its natural boundaries. Under the "all grasping hand" of the First Consul, however, "its limits are undefined." A survey of history, he argued, showed that if Napoleon continued his policy of extending France to its "ancient limits," then he would apply the same principle to North America. Smith predicted that with control of these areas, Napoleon would soon detach the trans-Appalachian region from the union by promising free passage to western settlers shipping their goods along the Mississippi. Smith expected his audience to remember that the "ancient limits" of France included areas as far east as the Appalachian Mountains within living memory. After painting this dire picture, Smith provided the remedy. He recommended that a force of western militia move down the Mississippi to preemptively seize Spanish territory along the river before Napoleon could officially take control of it. This would demonstrate to Napoleon and the world that if the "conqueror of Europe" sought to interfere with the "just career of a free and enlightened people," Americans would assert their rights. Exactly what "rights" Napoleon was infringing upon Smith hinted at in the last part of the article.[16]

Coriolanus ended his essay with a strident defense of aggressive imperialism to counter Bonaparte's attempt to impose France's "ancient limits" in the Americas. "All empire," he noted, "is traveling from east to west." Thus, he postulated, empire would naturally achieve its greatest height in the United States. There would soon come a time, he continued, when America would include uncounted peoples and lands west of the Mississippi. That river, he contended, was "never designed as the western boundary of the union." God—or nature—had never intended the "best part of his earth" to be populated by subjects of a French "usurper." Smith's America, in other words, had far more expansive natural boundaries than those imagined by the diplomats who had drawn up the Treaty of Paris. Nature's god himself had designed the American nation to be different than Napoleon's France. In time, Coriolanus predicted, all European-held dominions in the Americas would become part of an immense, "free and sovereign empire." An American empire, he imagined, that would "unfold the doors of liberty" to millions yet unborn. His decidedly pro-expansionist position rejected the balance-of-power politics that constrained European states and redefined the divinely appointed natural boundaries of the United States to encompass the entire American continent.[17]

The Coriolanus essay demonstrates a combination of two emerging rationales for American expansion that were rhetorically knotted together by the dangerous actions of Bonaparte. On the one hand, the essay posited an irresistible, divinely sanctioned, westward movement of Americans across the continent to seek out the country's true natural boundaries west of the Mississippi River. In the eyes of Coriolanus, the expansion of this American empire would be a benefit to all mankind—what later Americans and American historians would term "manifest destiny." Yet, Coriolanus argued that this natural and beneficial expansion of the United States was profoundly threatened by Bonaparte's dangerous claim to the "ancient limits" of France. Thus, Coriolanus reasoned that aggressive military action in the present was required to defend the future liberal empire of the United States. Smith's Coriolanus essay was the first to apply these justifications for imperial expansion to the context of Napoleon and Louisiana, but the essay must be read in the context of the other arguments circulating in 1802 and 1803. Smith's article gained even traction later in late 1802 when his warnings about Bonaparte's threat to the United States became even more real due to an escalating crisis over the fate of New Orleans.

Crisis and Response

American concerns about Louisiana surged dramatically in mid-1802 as the long-anticipated French military presence in the Caribbean became a reality. This military threat combined with ill-timed news coming from both

France and Spanish New Orleans resulted in urgent American discussion about how to secure their western borders. In February, the French army that had left Europe in the wake of the Peace of Amiens and that had caused such consternation among Americans suddenly landed, not in Louisiana, but in the French Caribbean possession of Saint-Domingue.

Saint-Domingue, now modern Haiti, was the crown jewel in the French colonial system of North America. It produced the valuable luxury commodities of sugar and coffee at the price of a grotesquely oppressive slave system. Taking advantage of the French Revolution in Europe, a massive slave uprising began in 1791 that toppled the white regime. After several bloody and chaotic years of civil war that involved fighting back military intervention from both the British and the Spanish, the rebels established a new Black power structure under the charismatic leadership of Toussaint L'Ouverture, which claimed nominal allegiance to the French empire but functioned as a self-governing colony. For Napoleon, bringing Saint-Domingue back under direct colonial control was the key to the reestablishment of his American empire. Indeed, Napoleon largely saw Louisiana as a granary for his far more precious Caribbean colony. At first, things seemed to go quite well. Taking advantage of internal divisions among the Black leadership, the French commander (and Napoleon's brother-in-law) Charles Leclerc made steady progress in the reconquest of the island. By the end of May 1802, he had arrested L'Ouverture. With Saint-Domingue seemingly coming back under French control, most Americans anticipated that the French expeditionary force's next move would be north to New Orleans in order to officially receive the newest part of their empire from the Spanish.[18]

Equally troubling to many Americans was the publication and wide circulation of an article from the semi-official Bonapartist newspaper, *Gazette de France*, in June. According to the article, "the idea of re-attaching Louisiana to the domain of France is perhaps, of all political conceptions, the wisest and most important." Noting the rapid population and economic growth of the American republic, the *Gazette* asserted that a European barrier was needed to prevent the expansion of a people "whom nature has promised the empire of half the world." If unchecked, the French author opined, Americans would soon spread from "the North to the South, cover Mexico, the West-Indies [and] Canada." Spain was too weak to prevent Americans from spilling over of their "present limits." The article stated unequivocally that only a reinvigorated French colony in Louisiana could curtail American expansion to natural boundaries that encompassed the entire hemisphere.[19]

Read within the context of American assumptions about natural borders, the torrent of belligerent commentary that followed the publication of this article should come as no surprise. Most Americans agreed with the *Gazette*'s dim assessment about the ability of Spain to hem in American expansion. That was the point, of course. Under Spain, the colony was sparsely populated and weakly held. Under the Jeffersonian theory of natural expansion, American citizens would simply move in to fill the vacuum left by the decrepit Spanish empire and come to dominate the area through natural increase. For those Americans of a Jeffersonian persuasion, this had the twin attraction of being "natural" expansion—as opposed to conquest, and not expanding the power of the central government through the creation of a permanent colonial bureaucracy. To many Americans, the *Gazette* (presumably with the nod of Napoleon) was suggesting that France impede the legitimate, natural process of American expansion with the arbitrary and irrational "ancient limits" of France.[20]

The words in the *Gazette* article combined with the presence of a veteran French army only a few hundred miles from New Orleans in Saint-Domingue made Bonaparte's threat to American expansion very real. Then in October 1802, the headstrong Spanish intendant of New Orleans exacerbated an already tense situation when he revoked the American right of deposit promised by the Pinckney Treaty of 1795. With western commerce choked off at the stroke of a pen, easterners began to wonder how long residents of Kentucky and Tennessee would remain in the union if their government proved unable to protect their economic rights. Suspicious Americans immediately (but incorrectly) saw the nefarious hand of Bonaparte behind the port closure and a plot to detach the frontier states from the eastern seaboard. Though Bonaparte had nothing to do with the port closure, the fears of these Americans were not entirely without merit. In early 1803, for example, Francis Flournoy, a Kentucky farmer writing under the penname "A Western American," suggested ominously that "the interests of France, Spain and Western America would go hand in hand." When Americans looked west, they increasingly saw Bonaparte and his legions not only preventing the expansion of their empire but actually dismembering it.[21]

The perception of Bonaparte as a militant imperialist combined with his army only a few hundred miles from New Orleans pushed Americans to frankly discuss a much more aggressive style of imperialism. The debate over American expansion that occurred in the wake of the publication of the *Gazette de France* article and the closure of New Orleans to American shipping was furious. In December 1802, the original Coriolanus letter was reprinted in various newspapers across New England. It was soon followed by two others that were so popular that the editor of New York's *Morning Chronicle* had to make excuses when he could not publish them fast enough to keep up with demand. By mid-January 1803, eager readers were buying pamphlets of the collected letters of Coriolanus for 50 cents at their local bookstore.[22]

With demands for an aggressive response to Napoleon at a fevered pitch, anti-imperialists finally entered the public debate. One anonymous author launched a blistering rebuttal of Coriolanus in the January 13, 1803, edition of the *American Citizen*. As he did, he established a new trend in the discourse of expansion—one that used Napoleon's imperial image as a negative symbol of violent, lawless aggression. The author began by commending Coriolanus for his "fine painting of the universal domination at which the first Consul aspires." He applauded Coriolanus's harsh rebuke of Napoleon's "aggrandizement" at the expense of "independent empires." Coriolanus was no doubt correct, the author continued, when he claimed that the peace and prosperity of nations depended on their ability to "remain satisfied within their limits." However, the author reasoned, it was just as important for the United States to constrain its own expansion to the natural boundary provided by the Mississippi as it was for France to remain on the west bank of the Rhine. By building on generally accepted American ideas about the inherent benefits of natural boundaries and the dangers of expansion beyond those boundaries, the author set his readers up to take Coriolanus to task in the next section of his article.[23]

Coriolanus had "marked out a path for the United States," wrote the *American Citizen*, "which he censures when trodden by the First Consul." He made this point by considering Coriolanus's description of the means and the justification for American imperialism through the European context of Bonaparte. Coriolanus's grand vision of an American empire containing "millions of souls *west of the Mississippi*," would undoubtably require a war of conquest in the manner of Bonaparte, wrote the author. He was particularly disturbed by Coriolanus's flimsy justification for such a war: the vague notion that since all empire traveled from east to west, the seat of the greatest empire would undoubtedly be in the United States. To the author, this view was nothing other than Bonaparte-like doublespeak to justify American seizure of New Orleans and the Floridas.[24]

The author then took on Coriolanus's suggestion that the God of nature had never intended the Mississippi to be the western boundary of the United States. The *American Citizen* pointed out that this was no different than the evolving French sense of their own divinely appointed "natural boundaries" in Europe: first the Rhine and then the Netherlands. The author applied the same standard to Coriolanus's imperial vision. If not the Mississippi, where exactly, the author wondered, did Coriolanus see the natural boundaries of the United States? The mines of Mexico? The Isthmus of Panama? Cape Horn? If Americans rejected the obvious natural boundary of the Mississippi River, the author explained, they could justify aggressive imperialism anywhere in the Americas, just as Napoleon justified his own imperial expansion in Europe and elsewhere. Rationality thus provided the only real check on aggressive expansion, and if this was jettisoned, the United States would be no better than Napoleon.[25]

Even worse, said the author, was Coriolanus's cynical and Napoleonesque claim that this imperial aggrandizement would be for the benefit for the conquered. The Coriolanus essay had envisioned the empire of the United States throwing open the "doors of liberty" to those whom it conquered. "Just so," the *American Citizen* author noted with thinly veiled snark, "Bonaparte went to Egypt to *unfold the doors of liberty and happiness* to the Turk; and, if we believe him, his benign incursion was perfectly in conformity to the *God of nature*." By directly comparing Coriolanus's rhetoric about an American "empire of liberty" to the widely acknowledged cynicism of Bonaparte's imperial proclamations in Egypt, the *American Citizen* article hoped to paint William Smith's expansionist vison as hollow and hypocritical.[26]

The *American Citizen* article marked the beginning of a new trend in the American discourse of empire. Instead of justifying aggressive expansion to prevent the spread of Napoleonic influence in the Americas, the author applied the example of Bonaparte in Europe as a moral yardstick to measure American imperialism. This comparison was effective because it relied on the common understanding among virtually all Americans that Napoleon's imperial identity was a negative example that worked outside the both the bounds of nature and the law of nations. By pointing out the uncomfortable similarities between American and Napoleonic expansion, it called the entire American imperial identity into question and forced imperialists to refine their arguments, which they did over the coming months.

Imperialists Triumphant

It is difficult to know for certain to what extent the sentiments expressed in the *American Citizen* article found their mark, but it is suggestive that imperialists seem largely to have abandoned their claim of a grand liberal imperial vision for the United States for the duration of the Mississippi Crisis. Nevertheless, the article failed to address the basic question of Bonaparte's military and political influence in Louisiana. This unpleasant prospect weighed heavily on the minds of Americans. For an increasing number of them, allowing Napoleon to gain a foothold in the Americas was an unacceptable risk to their liberty and national security. Imperialists effectively harnessed these fears over the second half of 1802 to whip up support for aggressive American expansion in the Gulf Coast.

Many imperialists based their arguments on the infamous *Gazette de France* article published earlier in the year that had advocated establishing an armed border along the Mississippi. Americans expected Napoleon to use his soldiers in Saint-Domingue to eventually set up a military colony in Louisiana as a buffer to contain American natural expansion. Few, however, believed that Louisiana was the limit of Napoleon's ambition in North America. One writer in the *United States Oracle* used history as a guide. French conduct over the past thirteen years, he suggested, indicated that once Bonaparte had a foothold in Louisiana, it would only be a matter of time before he would find some excuse to provoke a war with the United States. Does Napoleon, the editor asked, "not affect a jealousy of the power and ambition of United States?" Americans only need look to the poor "inoffensive nations" of Europe, he noted, to find what awaited those nations who became victims of Bonaparte's imperial conquests. Another commenter warned that Bonaparte's "gigantic schemes" of empire in the Americas were to be carried out by "generals the most enterprising and experienced" and armies that were "inured to battle and accustomed to victory."[27]

Americans did not only need to worry about restless and experienced French armies on their western borders. For many, the most dangerous part of having Napoleon controlling the western bank of the Mississippi was that a few well-placed forts and imperial decrees could effectively shut down all American commerce west of the Appalachian Mountains. Bonaparte's object, according to the *United States Oracle* author, was to "fetter the commerce of our western and southern territory." With this economic leverage, Napoleon could dismember the United States without a battle. Americans believed they had already seen a taste of this with the Spanish closure of New Orleans in 1802. An article first published in the ubiquitous *American Citizen* worried that by shutting down trade on the Mississippi, Napoleon could pursue a "subtle policy" of economic pressure by which he could induce westerners to "shake off their allegiance and become subjects of the 'Great Nation.'" This author did not fear open warfare with Bonaparte, but he did fear the proximity of a nation so "dreaded for its subtle intrigues." Imperialists would come to expand and refine this rhetoric, which saw Napoleon as a dangerous purveyor of international subterfuge over the course of the next decade whenever they could plausibly see a French threat to American expansion.[28]

The *Oracle's* editor also worried about another type of "subtle intrigue" by which Napoleon intended to fetter the expansion of the United States. The last quarter of the article passed along the rumor that Napoleon had paid particular attention to detaching the allegiance of Indigenous nations of the Mississippi Valley from the benevolent oversight of the United States—even to the extent of inviting some of their representatives to Paris. The government of the United States, the author insisted, merely sought to teach these "savages" to be "good neighbors, and to enable them more effectually to avoid the frauds and cheats, too often practiced on them which have ever been fruitful sources of war." That, of course, was the danger—Napoleon had need of the "friendship and alliance" of the Indigenous peoples in order to support his imperial schemes in Louisiana and would use whatever frauds necessary to turn them against the United States. An article in *The Balance* from June of 1802 struck a similar chord. The French colony in Louisiana, an unnamed but supposedly highly placed source insisted, was to be a military colony made up of 150,000 surrendered Black rebels from the Saint-Domingue conflict reenforced by alliances with friendly Native peoples. Such fears played into American assumptions about race. People of African descent and Indigenous nations were simply putty in the hands of the white men who shaped them either for good or for evil. For both editors, in the hands of an American empire, the west would be a place that advanced civilization. In the hands of Napoleon, however, it would be a place that hatched nefarious plots and violence in order to prevent the otherwise natural advance of the American empire.[29]

The imperialists who penned the articles above believed they had history on their side by the spring of 1803. During the Wars of the French Revolution, alliances shifted with dizzying regularity, and secret deals based on supposed "ancient limits" (such as that which led to the Louisiana retrocession) were frighteningly commonplace. In addition, 1802–3 saw Napoleon completely redraw the map of Europe for the first of several times during his reign to fit new definitions of France's "ancient limits" that always seemed to favor his interests. Americans watched nervously as the Piedmont region of Italy was unceremoniously annexed to France so that Napoleon's Great Republic could control the vital passes through the Swiss Alps. Farther north, the ancient Holy Roman Empire was reorganized in a manner that supported Bonaparte's national aims. With such breathtaking changes occurring to the ancient borders of Europe, it seems little wonder that expansionists worried that having Bonaparte as a western neighbor might very well break up the American union entirely.[30]

Whether the threat came from Bonaparte's armies or from his "subtle intrigues," at the heart of this imperial rhetoric were near frantic concerns about how Napoleon interpreted France's boundaries—both ancient and natural—in the Americas. Prior to the Louisiana retrocession, Americans had largely assumed that it was beneficial for empires to spread to their natural limits. In the winter and spring of 1803, however, newspapers began running articles that suggested the natural frontiers of empire were not nearly as self-evident as Americans had once thought and that highlighted the dangers of France's "ancient limits" in North America.

Several newspapers reprinted an old article from a 1797 edition of the *New York Journal* in which the author had expressed the belief that it was "the right of Republics to correct the errors of their former Kings." The 1797 author had made this comment within the context of French expansion in Europe. With the French poised to occupy Louisiana, however, the article was used as a cudgel. "I have no French maps," an author identifying himself as "Sidney" wrote sarcastically, "nor can I, at this moment, precisely ascertain the limits of the former claims of the French Kings." However, Sidney continued, he was certain that those claims "included nearly one half the present territory of the United States." After reading the same 1797 article and noting that the original author believed that France had been unjustly deprived of Canada, A.B.C. wondered "how far the United States would be affected, if the First Consul of the French Republic should apply a prompt corrective of the procedure."[31]

Undefined French boundaries based on "ancient limits" in the Americas were not the only fear that Americans had. Other Americans worried about how Napoleon would twist the supposedly self-evident language of natural boundaries. An article published in a London paper attracted extensive comment from the editor of the *Alexandria Advertiser*. The London article purported to quote from a French travel narrative in which the author maintained that "the natural limits of *Louisiana* extend to the sources of the *Mississippi* and *Missouri*." Understandably, this caused the editor a great deal of consternation since describing the natural limits of Louisiana in this manner indicated that Kentucky and Tennessee were both part of Bonaparte's claim to Louisiana because the Tennessee and the Ohio Rivers both fed into the Mississippi. According to the *Advertiser*, the London article then suggested that Bonaparte would undoubtedly interpret the Spanish retrocession as including the "utmost extent of [Louisiana's] natural limits."[32]

The imperialist arguments that developed in late 1802 and in 1803 demonstrate a shifting rhetorical emphasis as expansionists attempted to take advantage of the new context provided by the closing of New Orleans, French imperial propaganda, and, most importantly, the situation in Saint-Domingue. Where Coriolanus saw the great threat posed by Bonaparte to a future American empire of liberty, the new expansionist rhetoric argued that Napoleon's actions constituted a direct and immediate threat to the national security of the United States. Where Coriolanus argued that the United States was uniquely free of the boundaries that constrained European powers, the new writers painted the American republic as fragile and subject to the same political and economic dangers that Europe had endured at the hands of Bonaparte. Increasingly it seemed that the only way to avoid the sad example of Napoleonic Europe, was to prevent Napoleon from gaining a foothold in North America.

The Ross Resolutions

The meeting of the seventh Congress at the end of 1802 brought vigorous debates about expansion—both American and French—to the national capital. The American public eagerly followed these debates through their local newspapers. Despite the fact that Jeffersonians controlled both houses of Congress, Federalists fought for an immediate military action to resolve the Mississippi crisis. Their rhetoric both echoed ideas about boundaries already simmering in many parts of the country and expanded upon them. One of the first of the outspoken critics of the Jeffersonian "wait and see" approach was forty-one-year-old Federalist senator James Ross of Pennsylvania. The former lawyer had served in Congress for almost a decade and had been president pro-tempore of the Senate during the fifth Congress. In what would be one of his last acts as a public official, Ross introduced a bill that authorized the president to call out as many as fifty thousand militia from Mississippi and neighboring territories and appropriated five million dollars to finance this call-up. The specific purpose of this army was to seize New Orleans from the Spanish before Napoleon's armies arrived. Even though this measure was narrowly defeated in the Senate on a strictly party-line vote, on February 25, 1803, a Jeffersonian-led bill that authorized the president to call out and fund eighty thousand militia but omitted the language of a preemptive military strike on New Orleans easily passed. The debate over the Ross resolutions and the Jeffersonian successor bill in Congress led to discussion out of Congress over the expediency of aggressive expansion, which reached a fevered pitch in the spring of 1803. In this debate, expansionists found themselves refining their arguments to both account for new geopolitical realities and to address old concerns about the nature of America's own natural frontiers.[33]

Ross defended his measures as a defensive necessity brought about by the new geopolitical realties of dealing with Bonaparte. He warned that after current negotiations with the First Consul inevitably failed, westerners would never forget who allowed such a "powerful and ambitious" despot to take control of the west and would likely strike the best deal they could with Napoleon at the expense of their eastern brothers. Perhaps, he continued ominously, they might even seize the territory themselves and then establish a separate, rival empire. Ross claimed he was not only thinking about the present situation. He was also concerned about the future of the United States. In his mind, nations had to have defensible frontiers, and the Spanish had provided the United States a golden opportunity to legitimately seize what had been denied her by earlier treaties. "The possession of the country on the east bank of the Mississippi," he told his colleagues, "will give a compactness, an irresistible strength to the United States."

Owning this real estate would render the nation increasingly powerful in "all future wars" and force European governments to treat the United States with more respect than ever before. It is interesting to note that the word "natural" does not appear in Ross's speech—or at least in the newspaper versions that remain today. For Ross, then, expansion had moved beyond natural boundaries and was a matter of military expediency and pragmatism brought on by the unnatural territorial appetites of the First Counsel.[34]

New York senator Gouverneur Morris advocated adoption of the Ross resolutions in a popular speech that made its way into numerous newspapers. Morris was no lightweight in politics, and when he spoke, his constituents listened. He had served in the New York provincial congress, the Continental Congress, and briefly as an officer in the New York militia, and he had drafted the preamble to the Constitution. He had also served as minister to France during the initial chaos of the French Revolution. Morris was less concerned with future wars and more with what he saw as current political reality. Dealing with Bonaparte, he argued, required strong action. The legitimacy of the usurper Bonaparte was tied to military success. "Impelled by imperious circumstances, he rules in Europe," Morris explained, "and he will rule here also unless you set a bound to his power." Bonaparte's France had to expand or wither, he argued. Bonaparte had nowhere left to expand in Europe; therefore he had to expand in the Americas. French control of strategic coastal locations such as New Orleans and Florida was "dangerous to other nations, but fatal to us." Thus, for Morris, like Ross, American expansion was partly a pragmatic response to the future threats to national security given that Bonaparte saw French expansion as essentially "boundless." Yet, at the same time, Morris conceived of Florida and New Orleans as a "natural and necessary part of our Empire."[35]

With this established, Morris turned back to the means of obtaining them. Morris wondered at Jefferson's attempt at diplomatically resolving the crisis. "On what grounds do you mean to treat?" he asked his colleagues with more than a hint of sarcasm. Napoleon, he pointed out to the Congress, "wants power. You have no power. He wants dominion. You have no dominion." No, he argued, when dealing with such men as Napoleon, the only question worth asking was "how many battalions have they?" Despite the "pacific nature" of the United States, expansion to Morris was a defensive necessity driven by the character of Napoleonic power and imperialism, which, at least in this case, happily corresponded to what were already America's natural boundaries.[36]

Americans outside of Congress repeated the basic argument of pragmatic, aggressive expansion to the country's "natural boundaries" to counter Napoleonic power and intrigue throughout the spring and into the summer of 1803. One particularly popular piece purported to be an extract of a letter from a "gentleman at Natchez." He bristled at what he saw as the disrespect the "reptile Spaniards" showed toward Americans in New Orleans and denounced the president's insistence on going through all the "ceremonies and etiquette of the courts of . . . Bonaparte." He, like Morris, saw expansion in pragmatic means justified by the very real military danger of Napoleon. "I say start and [drive] them with the spring flood, and then negotiate," he wrote. "We can now get the whole province without the loss of one drop of blood." "Let the French get here," he warned, "'twill be otherwise." Not only did this "gentlemen" take a pragmatic view of expansion, but he also provided a pragmatic view of the relative military balance between the French, the Spanish, and the Americans.[37]

In another article, an author writing as "Pericles" warned that because Bonaparte sought to expand France to its "ancient limits," his policy demonstrated a "manifest and great danger" to the union. "Pericles" was none other than Alexander Hamilton, one of the leading Federalist luminaries. Hamilton's article is particularly instructive since he, unlike most Federalists, had once been sympathetic to Napoleon. As late as April 1801 he gave a popular speech in which he eloquently defended Bonaparte's toppling of the Directory by arguing that the radical excesses of the French Revolution could only be held in check by the strong arm of the First Consul. But that was 1801, and by 1803 the times and the geopolitical landscape had changed. He, like Morris and the "gentleman" from Natchez, counseled seizing Florida and New Orleans in order to negotiate with Bonaparte from a position of strength. He warned that Bonaparte would never negotiate to sell New Orleans or Florida, and therefore Americans would have to fight for it in any case. Taking New Orleans from the Spanish before Bonaparte's veterans arrived from Saint-Domingue and fortified the place only made sense. In the end, according to many Americans, a preemptive, defensive strike in the name of natural frontiers would cost less blood, treasure, and honor in the long run.[38]

There were differences between what these aggressive expansionists saw as the ultimate goal of a military strike on Louisiana. Ross, for example—the ultimate pragmatist—only wanted to fight for New Orleans and the east bank of the Mississippi. Pericles and Morris, on the other hand, saw all of Florida as within the natural boundaries of the United States. Underlying all their arguments was a fear that Bonaparte's occupation of Louisiana would bring the intrigue and warfare of Napoleonic Europe to the Americas. This they saw as the inevitable result of states expanding beyond their natural borders. In some ways, the debate perhaps also shows the small success of arguments such as that made by the *American Citizen*, which denounced Coriolanus and demanded Americans consider what their own natural boundaries really were.

Few Americans made the fear of Bonaparte's political intrigue and warfare as explicitly plain as an author purporting to speak for "Ten Thousand Freemen of Connecticut," in March 1803, which was published next to a copy of the Sidney article in which the author discussed the concerning fluidity of France's ancient limits. Let Bonaparte set up a military colony in Louisiana, he warned, "and one of two things must invariably take place." In one case, under economic and military pressure from Bonaparte, the western states would shift their allegiance from the eastern United States and become mere colonies of France. In such a situation, eventually an economic rivalry would lead to an "interminable war with the eastern states." If this first scenario did not come to pass, then the author expected the west to seize New Orleans without the sanction of the US government and thus drag the United States into a war with France for which it was ill-prepared. The threat from Bonaparte's navy would compel the United States into an alliance with Great Britain and thus trigger a Napoleonic war of cataclysmic proportions on the North American continent. The reason the threat of Bonaparte held so much power over so many Americans in 1803 was that they were familiar with the results of a decade of revolutionary warfare and intrigue in Europe and their preconceived notions of what came to pass when nations either did not expand to their natural boundaries or expanded beyond them.[39]

Such pragmatic rhetoric illustrates that pro-expansionists had refined their arguments by 1803. Coriolanus had argued for aggressive military expansion backed by a divine mandate to spread republicanism across the continent. Pericles and Ross took a different rhetorical approach, arguing that American expansion was a national security concern. This shows that the Mississippi Crisis should be best understood as a shifting of the contested discourse of expansion due to the actions of Napoleon. In general, Americans did agree on the necessity of obtaining New Orleans, though not necessarily all of Louisiana. The public debate in the newspapers revealed that crucial issues were not settled. Not only were the means of expansion contested, but many disagreed over what the natural boundaries of the United States actually were. Where Americans did seem to agree was on the construction of an imperial identity based on their understanding of national security.

Charles Brockden Brown and American Expansion

No one put all the expansionist fears about Bonaparte together as coherently and as creatively as Charles Brockden Brown. Later regarded as one of America's first novelists of note, in the spring of 1803 Brown was a marginally successful author and the editor of two literary magazines. At the height of the Mississippi Crisis, he anonymously authored a pamphlet that was successful enough to be republished in several editions throughout the United States. This pamphlet, sporting the grand title *An Address to the Government of the United States on the Cession of Louisiana to the French and on the Late Breach of Treaty by the Spanish* explicitly used the specter of Bonaparte to reimagine imperialism within an American context. Brown's pamphlet redefined American assumptions about natural boundaries and combined this with the political image of Napoleon to rationalize an American empire that encompassed the entire continent.[40]

Most of the lengthy pamphlet purported to be Brown's translation of a confidential communiqué from a minor French diplomat to Napoleon on the subject of Louisiana. The imagined diplomat opened his memorandum by professing to be an enthusiastic supporter of empire and of Bonaparte. He claimed to be concerned, however, about the means of extending French imperial influence now that the First Consul had expanded French borders in Europe to their natural boundaries of the Rhine, the Pyrenees, and the Alps through his great victories. In particular, the diplomat had become alarmed at the recent invasion of Saint-Domingue, which, he proceeded to explain, was outside the natural bounds of the French empire.[41]

Brown's diplomat spent the first part of his pamphlet explaining to Bonaparte the folly of further attempts to bring Saint-Domingue back into the

FIG. 1. The novelist Charles Brockden Brown was one of many Americans who demanded a military resolution to the question of Louisiana during the Mississippi Crisis of 1802–3. (New York Public Library)

French orbit. Imperial conquest was futile, according to Brown—even for one so gifted in the military arts as Bonaparte. "Alas, there is something in the nature of this warfare which makes courage and numbers avail nothing," he warned the First Consul. "It is not men with whom alone our troops must contend.... Our troops are destined to fight against nature; to contend with the elements." Brown's diplomat went on to explain what he meant by this: "The atmosphere of this island, salutary to a native of the soil, and to men imported from congenial climates, breaths pestilence and death, upon the stranger from Europe." For Brown's diplomat, the very climate itself was an indicator that the island was not, by nature, French. At the same time, the diplomat also indicated that the people living there showed the island not to be French. The French were "strangers"—foreigners—to Saint-Domingue unlike those, both "native" and "imported" who were used to such a pestilential climate. For Brown's diplomat, both the geography and the people excluded Saint-Domingue from France's natural boundaries, and thus attempts to recapture the island were nothing but a drain on French blood and treasure.[42]

Brown's diplomat drew a clear contrast between imperial conquest and colonization. Indeed, he spent several pages explaining to the First Consul that the reason France had lost the initial race for colonization in North America to the British was because Louis XIV had spent too much blood and treasure on irrational European continental conquest instead of on a rational policy toward the Americas. According to the diplomat, France's "stupid rage of ambition could see nothing desirable but what our neighbors already possessed." "Imagine, then," he encouraged Bonaparte, "that the thousands sent to perish under the walls of a German fortress, the arms, the ammunition, the tools, the various apparatus provided for such an expedition, had been sent to America." Indeed, he continued, "Had the minister Richelieu applied one year's subsidy of Gustavus, or the treasures expended in one siege or one campaign in Flanders, in founding a settlement on the Delaware or Chesapeake all that part world which is now English, would have been French." Wars and victories, he concluded, "may rob millions of their happiness and independence; millions they may easily destroy; but they cannot call into existence; they cannot compel to change their language, manners, or religion." Like most Americans of his time, Brown drew a sharp distinction between bloody, ambitious conquest and rational national expansion to natural boundaries through colonization.[43]

If nature and reason precluded the conquest of Saint-Domingue, however, Brown's diplomat had an alternative in mind: the colonization of Louisiana. The diplomat took time to carefully explain why Louisiana, unlike Saint-Domingue, was within the natural limits of Bonaparte's empire. His argument was predicated on the idea that the western half of the North American continent was an empty, but fertile, wilderness and one that was ripe for commercial exploitation. If the area was empty, then simple introduction of French colonists in the form of military veterans and their families would make the area French by default. The few people who populated the area around New Orleans were tired of imbecilic Spanish rule, continued the diplomat. And, after all, he reasoned, they had been Spanish for less than a generation and could easily be made to remember their original allegiance. Even the geography of Louisiana seemed to indicate that it was a natural part of the French empire. The diplomat extoled the virtues of the "American Nile" and insisted that whole area was dominated by a large temperate zone "most favorable to the perfection of the animal and vegetable nature," with no geographic natural boundary to the west save the Pacific Ocean. This climate—natural to Frenchmen—was a far cry from the pestilential hellhole that made Saint-Domingue foreign ground. With French military colonists supported by friendly geography and wise imperial policy, Louisiana could soon be indisputably and intractably French.[44]

With an idyllic Louisiana ripe for colonization firmly established within the natural bounds of the French empire, Brown's diplomat moved on to explain the great political benefit to French possession of this territory—that of stunting the imperial growth of the United States. "It will," he wrote in italics to emphasize his point, "admit into their vitals a formidable and active people, whose interests are incompatible, in every point with their own; whose enterprises will inevitably interfere and jar with theirs; whose neighborhood will cramp all their movements; circumscribe their future progress to narrow and ignominious bounds; and make incessant inroads on their harmony and independence." Americans would certainly oppose such a move by Bonaparte, said the diplomat, but there was little that the United States could actually do about it. Americans, he claimed, were too politically divided and too accustomed to an apathetic method of imperialism to take any real steps to prevent the French occupation of Louisiana.[45]

Most of Brown's ideas were not entirely new. The strength of the pamphlet was that he applied older ideas to the new context of Napoleon in order to demand action. Brown's pamphlet subtlety provided a rational explanation for considering all of Louisiana rather than just New Orleans as within America's natural boundaries. At the same time, Brown hinted that natural frontiers were, even if provided by nature, in practice, not entirely rational and that they could be contested. His conception of borders was made from geography and demography. In the older mode of thinking, if Louisiana's borders naturally fell into the French empire, then there was little Americans could do but accept it. However, the pamphlet made it clear that whatever it was that made Louisiana naturally French could equally apply to the natural boundaries of the United States. The climate, for example, was as equally healthy for an American as for a Frenchman. If the Louisiana territory was an empty vessel waiting to be filled by French colonists, Brown felt that it could equally be colonized by an influx of

Americans—a theory of expansion long accepted by Jeffersonians. "America is ours . . . therefore Louisiana is ours," Brown insisted—speaking in the last part of his pamphlet again as an American.[46]

If natural borders were not exactly self-evident and could be modified by colonization, then it fell to governments to work out these borders through wise policy. The underlying theme of Brown's entire pamphlet was that empires do not develop naturally, though their borders might be defined by nature. "We have a *right* to the possession," Brown told his readers bluntly. "The interests of the human race demand from us the exertion of this right." But, as the word "exertion" implied, empires had to be planned, and those plans had to be carried out by governments—sometimes through armed conflict—as Napoleon showed quite clearly. Jeffersonians, then, could not simply sit back and wait for the American empire to develop naturally, argued Brown in the last part of his pamphlet. For too long, he criticized, the American government had "looked on in apathy while European powers toss[ed] about amongst themselves the property which God and nature have made ours." This may have worked, he admitted, so long as the decrepit Spanish empire was holding onto Louisiana, but Napoleonic rule in Louisiana was different.[47]

Napoleon was not simply a case study in active imperialism for Brown. As the pamphlet indicated, he was also the entire reason that the United States had to reimagine their methods of empire building. Bonaparte's was a vigorous, ambitious, one-man rule, and Americans were already painfully aware that he had an army in the Caribbean that could quickly turn the west bank of the Mississippi into an impregnable fortress. For Brown, the case of Louisiana showed that natural boundaries and national security went hand in hand when applied to the dangerous Napoleonic political context that threatened to curtail their own imperial expansion. The United States in control of the Louisiana territory meant peace, whereas French control meant war and the evils that attended armed conflict. To introduce a violent neighbor such as Bonaparte—who led a people who "measured their success on the ruin of their neighbors"—onto the continent would invariably lead to an "insuperable mound" to American progress as well as sow the seeds of "faction and rebellion." Brown ended his pamphlet with a rousing appeal to Congress for aggressive imperialism. "The iron is now hot," he exhorted the representatives, "command us to rise as one man, and STRIKE."[48]

Damn Sugar, Damn Colonies

Writing in the winter and spring of 1803, Brown and other militant imperialists could not have known how radically the geopolitical situation had changed by April. For months, the American diplomatic delegation in Paris had no luck in achieving Jefferson's goals of obtaining New Orleans and Florida for the United States. As Senator Morris had correctly assessed, the American government possessed very little that interested the First Consul, and American military might was no match to that of French. What no one had counted on, however, was the stunning reversal of fortune that beset the French expeditionary force in Saint-Domingue during the second half of 1802. When the Black population found that Napoleon had given secret orders to reestablish the old power structures (including slavery) on the island, they rose up against the French forces in the summer of 1802. In the guerrilla war that followed, both sides seemed eager to outdo each other in terms of ghastly violence. Even more deadly than the insurgency was the yellow fever epidemic that decimated the French army during the fall and winter months. Despite the belated arrival of reinforcements in early 1803, it became increasingly clear that the survivors would not be able to bring the island back under French control.[49]

As Bonaparte received the disastrous reports out of Saint-Domingue, he is supposed to have growled, "Damn sugar, damn coffee, damn colonies." Even if the quote is apocryphal, the attitude it conveyed was not. Saint-Domingue was a lost cause and with it died Bonaparte's American dream. Though he was clearly disappointed, he quickly sought to turn the situation to his favor. After all, Napoleon was nothing if not a pragmatist. Bonaparte knew that Americans were already dominating the economic life in New Orleans and violently hostile to the idea of a French neighbor. Bonaparte also had European concerns on his mind. He knew that another war was imminent in Europe and that he needed quick cash more than he needed sugar. Furthermore, Bonaparte reasoned that when war erupted in Europe, the British navy would make French control of North American colonies impossible, and that neutral American control of Louisiana would be far better than surrendering the province to his British enemies. Offering Louisiana to the United States had the benefit of drawing the Americans into the French orbit—or at least away from Great Britain in the coming war. In early April, Bonaparte notified his foreign minister and his closest advisers that he planned to sell the entire territory of Louisiana to the United States.[50]

Between 1801 and 1803, the Mississippi Crisis introduced Napoleon into the American discourse on imperial expansion. Bonaparte's image as an irrational and dangerous imperialist forced Americans to confront their ideas about natural frontiers of the United States as well their ideas about the very nature of imperial expansion. The imminent threat of Bonaparte as a western neighbor led to the emergence of an American imperial identity that accepted imperial expansion as a defensive natural security measure. Napoleon also provided a new vocabulary for anti-expansionists during the Mississippi Crisis. These Americans began to use Napoleon as an example of violent, irrational, and lawless imperial expansion, and they argued that a military solution to the crisis would make the United States no different than an increasingly despotic Bonaparte. Though they were ultimately unsuccessful, anti-expansionists managed to force their opponents to refine their arguments and increasingly to define the nature and limits of American expansion. These new arguments would be tested and stretched even further when the Americans finally had to confront the realities of what to actually do with the Louisiana territory once they had obtained it from Napoleon.

2

Cost

The Louisiana Purchase

On June 30, 1803, Boston's *Independent Chronicle* broke the news. Within a week, reports had reached Charleston, and by the end of July even those in the far reaches of Kentucky knew. The First Consul of France had offered to cede not only New Orleans but the entire territory of Louisiana to the United States. "This is a proud day for our nation," gushed the editor of one Federalist-leaning newspaper, "Louisiana is ours!" Yet, the treaty still had to be ratified by the Senate and money for the Purchase allocated by the House of Representatives. Then too, there was the question of exactly how this new territory would be administered. Changing his tone dramatically, the editor urged caution on the part of the policymakers in Washington. "Let them not be too hasty," he warned. "Let us see with what stipulations the cession of that country is clogged." In particular, the editor wanted to know exactly what price Bonaparte had extracted for his North American empire and, just as important, how the cession agreement would affect American foreign policy with regard to Europe. This was an extremely relevant question in mid-1803 since printed next to this column was another that proclaimed the renewal of war between Great Britain and Napoleon's France.[1]

The occupation of Louisiana was neither easy nor uncontroversial. It raised a host of basic questions about American expansion and the administration of empire that the fledgling government of the United States was not immediately prepared to answer. In attempting to find solutions to these problems, Americans continued to turn to the most successful imperialist they knew: Napoleon Bonaparte. The debates over the Louisiana Purchase

Treaty and the occupation of Louisiana saw both continuity and change in the way Bonaparte was used in the discourse of American empire. At first, Federalists pointed to Bonaparte as a treacherous and illegitimate political actor—one whom the United States should not trust in international diplomacy. This built on the already established rhetoric they had used to great effect during the Mississippi Crisis, which posited Napoleon as a grave threat to American national security. Once the treaty was approved, however, and debate shifted to the imperial administration of Louisiana, a new discourse of American expansion emerged. This new rhetoric used Napoleon as a symbolic negative example of oppressive imperial rule. Federalists cast the American occupation of Louisiana as little better than Napoleon's undemocratic and rapacious administration of Europe. Jeffersonians, on the other hand, contrasted peaceful American expansion in Louisiana favorably with the violent expansion of Napoleon's empire. By the end of these debates, Americans had largely accepted Napoleonic imperialism as the moral and ideological yardstick against which to measure their own decisions about expansion. Ultimately, Napoleon's negative imperial identity of illiberal oppression and violence allowed Americans to claim a new, positive imperial identity for themselves.

It is critical to remember that the American occupation of Louisiana took place within the context of the Napoleonic Wars in Europe. As the *Independent Chronicle* article quoted above showed, Americans followed both events with equally great interest. Following the Peace of Amiens in 1802, the French position in Europe was formidable. The extended French republic stretched from the Rhine River in the north, through the annexed territories of Luxemburg, Belgium, and the Rhineland and across the Alps into Nice, Savoy and Piedmont. Beyond this, Bonaparte dominated the foreign and domestic policies of a chain of "sister republics," which included the Netherlands and Switzerland, as well as the Italian, Ligurian (Genoese), and Cisalpine Republics. Bonaparte could also count on Spain as an ally (if a somewhat unwilling one) as well as friendly relations with some of the powerful states in the eastern Holy Roman Empire, most notably Bavaria.[2]

While Napoleon strengthened his hand in Europe, his archrival Great Britain worked to rally the anti-Bonapartist empires on the continent. Just as Americans were learning of the Louisiana Purchase in June 1803, the War of the Third Coalition (1803–6) broke out when Bonaparte aggressively backed Britain into an impossible diplomatic position over the island of Malta. Yet, while the Royal Navy ruled the seas, the British needed continental alliances to be successful against the French Grande Armée. To paraphrase the memorable words of historian Charles Esdaile: the British whale had gone to war with the French elephant. For the first two years of the war, the two powers mostly glowered at each other from opposite sides of the English Channel. However, by mid-1805 the British—thanks largely to the heavy-handed foreign policy of Bonaparte—had cobbled together an anti-French alliance that included Austria, Naples, Sweden, and, most surprisingly, Russia. The international stage was thus set for the opening round of a titanic clash of empires that would last with only short interruptions until 1815.[3]

The Treaty Debate

By mid-1803, the Federalists were a divided and decidedly minority party. However, from their urban strongholds in New England they provided an extremely vocal opposition to what they saw as (borrowing a phrase usually associated with Napoleon in 1803) the Jeffersonian "usurpation" of the national government. Per the terms of the Louisiana treaty, both governments had to ratify the document within six months of receiving it. Though Congress was out of session and not set to reconvene until November, Jefferson called for a special session scheduled to open in October to debate the treaty and allocate the money required to actually purchase the territory. Though the odds were long against them, the anti-treaty Federalists were determined not to simply roll over. Through the summer and into the fall of 1803, they turned their rhetorical guns on the Louisiana treaty through the newspapers. Their objections, while varied, ultimately came back to the central problem of American national security that had served them so well during the Mississippi Crisis the year before.[4]

To understand the nature of the criticisms leveled by the anti-treaty faction, it is critical to understand that by mid-1802 Americans were increasingly coming to understand Bonaparte not as the defender of international republicanism, but as its betrayer. This was made quite clear to most Americans when Bonaparte was affirmed as First Consul for life by a nationwide French plebiscite in August 1802. While the election had a democratic veneer, few Americans were convinced. As early as May 1802 the *South Carolina State Gazette* wrote, "The people of France declared that they would never rest till they had destroyed despotism till they had secured their liberty, and established a republican government. Yet, do they now appear contented and happy under the most despotic government in Europe." In this new government, the *Gazette* went on, there "exists not a legislature, nor the voice of the people," but only "swords of a republican army" that would establish "republican tyrants" to oversee a republican empire. Ultimately, wrote the *Gazette,* the French had simply exchanged masters—"the house of Bourbon to the house of Bonaparte." Such sentiments were echoed by many other Americans. The Federalist editor of the New York *Palladium* crowed in October that even the most steadfast of Jeffersonians were at last coming to realize that "Bonaparte is a despot; and the French the most degraded of slaves." Americans had long recognized the ambitions and the military genius of Bonaparte, but by the end of 1802, most Americans had also come understand Bonaparte as a military despot: a dangerous, duplicitous and aggressive political actor who only recognized principles such as liberty so long as they served his ends.[5]

While many Americans were disappointed with what they saw as Napoleon's betrayal of French liberty, what was even more concerning to them was what they interpreted as Bonaparte's betrayal of France's fellow European republics. As early as 1796, for example, the pro-Federalist New York–based paper *The Minerva* had brought up issues that Americans found themselves facing less than a decade later in the occupation of Louisiana. Confronted by Bonaparte's successful campaigns in Italy, *The Minerva* lamented that this conquest was done in the name of republicanism. Calling attention to an order of Bonaparte's that threatened to burn the homes of any Italians who did not submit to his "republican" rule, the editor groaned, "This is the gentle language of republicanism." In another article published a few days later the same editor bewailed Bonaparte's economic exploitation of the Italian republics. He could understand the abuse of the native population as an unfortunate side effect of war, but, "to give these operations an air of honor and generosity," Bonaparte had played the hypocrite and pretended "to *conquer* the people into *freedom."* This maligning of republicanism was the worst tragedy of the conflict, according to *The Minerva.* This statement cut to the heart of Federalists' fears when it came to dealing with Napoleon—unwitting allies quickly became client states of the French empire. For Federalists, this represented a betrayal of republican values and self-government and explained why any political dealing with

Bonaparte was unwise and undermined the very ideological foundations of the United States.[6]

Probably the most common critique of the treaty was its cost. Anti-treaty Federalists immediately expressed concern over the amount of money required to purchase Louisiana. The price agreed upon was $15 million—$11.25 million to purchase the land outright and an additional $3.75 million to buy off American claims against the French government. This was an astronomical sum for the fledgling United States, which, though in the midst of an economic expansion thanks to a revival of trade during the French Revolutionary Wars, had only just emerged from under the public debt previously owed to France for their assistance during the American War for Independence. Indeed, it was larger than the entire government's revenues for 1803, which totaled only $11 million. Even so, the hefty price tag was not the anti-treaty faction's main complaint. Those who focused on the monetary aspects of the deal appeared far more concerned with the ideological implications of spending the money than on the sum itself.[7]

The best example of this position ran in a series of five widely reprinted articles originally published in Boston's *Columbian Centinel* by an author writing under the pseudonym "Fabricius." Even the Jeffersonian enemies of Fabricius took note of his arguments. Next to one of the reprinted columns, an adulatory editor added the comment, "Fabricius delights as well as instructs. His numbers are copied with avidity into many of the most intelligent papers—and it adds to his honor that he has attracted the notice of some of the jacobin miller-flies." In his essays, Fabricius expressed disbelief that the United States would pay an exorbitant sum for what he saw as a vindication of American rights. He professed to have no problem paying to protect the economic interests of westerners. "Let us cheerfully spend our blood and money for them," he wrote. "It is right that we should do it when necessary, without inquiring or regarding HOW MUCH." It did not follow, however, that the Louisiana Purchase "was a fit end or a right mean to be chosen" when protecting American national security from the likes of Bonaparte. After all, he continued, Americans had been wronged by the Spanish violations of the Pinckney Treaty. "It is a glorious thing," he wrote sarcastically, "for a nation to suffer injuries and then *buy* redress—to be kicked and then pay damages." How the United States responded to such a threat would have important diplomatic ramifications far into the future.[8]

New Orleans could have and should have been obtained by military force, Fabricius insisted. The Kentucky militia—some eighty thousand of them—had been ready to move, Fabricius sighed wistfully, recalling the debates over the Ross Resolutions. They could have made short work of the New Orleans garrison and vindicated American territorial rights to the world. More importantly, it would have prevented Americans from having to involve themselves politically and diplomatically with Napoleon. Fabricius could only think of one reason why New Orleans had not been seized immediately, and that was the Jefferson administration's servile fear of the despot Bonaparte. He was thoroughly disgusted by the idea of a free republic engaged in diplomatic negotiation with the likes of Napoleon and drew a vivid picture of Ambassador James Monroe "crawling like a reptile at the First Consul's feet." Any American who was not ashamed by this servile image, he suggested, ought to "send to Algiers or Botany Bay, and ask the honor of an act of citizenship." These were powerful images in the early American mind. Fabricius was likening American citizenship to the status of slaves held by the pirate empire of the Barbary Coast and the convicts that inhabited the British penal colony in Australia. Paying a great deal of money for a territory that the United States could have had for nothing, argued Fabricius, was nothing more than "tribute" and brought the United States into "common cause" with the French empire just as they were going to war with Great Britain. As discussed in a later chapter, likening the United States to a tributary state of Napoleonic France proved a rhetorical device that gained increasing power as the decade continued.[9]

Others against the treaty were a bit easier on the administration. Instead of seeing Jefferson groveling at the feet of Bonaparte, they saw a naive philosopher president hopelessly outwitted by the hard-nosed political and military scheming of the First Consul. Ideological opponents had long cast Jefferson as an idealist whose policies sounded genuinely republican but were doomed to failure in the real, dangerous world of nineteenth-century politics. In terms of imperial identity, this was the difference between Jefferson's idealized "empire of liberty" of yeoman farmers that spanned the continent and the reality of having to govern such an empire. Until he was president, however, these visions had been more amusing than dangerous. In a series of essays that ran in a wide variety of papers from June to October 1803, an author writing under the appropriate pseudonym "Calculator," laid out the case against the purchase in economic terms that painted the administration as being hopelessly outclassed by Napoleon at the negotiating table and the dangers that would result.

For Calculator, like Fabricius, the timing of the Louisiana Purchase demonstrated the naivete of Jefferson and his followers when confronted by Napoleon. They were so blinded by an irrational ideological need for expansion, he argued, that they forgot basic laws of economics and diplomacy. According to Calculator, "it cannot escape notice that the purchase of Louisiana was negotiated at a juncture the most favorable which could possibly happen for obtaining that wilderness on cheap terms." Everyone knew that Bonaparte was planning to renew his war with England, Calculator pointed out (somewhat disingenuously), and without an effective navy he could not have long maintained his hold on Louisiana. "The territory he put on sale," wrote Calculator, "he was effectually barred from possessing; and was also in the utmost danger of losing." Thus, Calculator concluded, "This circumstance tends to increase the public astonishment at the enormous price which has been pledged." In other words, Bonaparte had sold the land on a buyer's market, and the ambassadors should have taken advantage of that fact in their negotiations. Instead, they had allowed Bonaparte to hoodwink the administration by playing to their naive Jeffersonian ideology of expansion at any cost. In so doing, they forced the United States to put its national security at risk by dealing politically with Bonaparte.[10]

Calculator's other objection to the Purchase was the type of land that Napoleon had sold the United States, sight unseen. This line of attack recalled the natural boundary arguments of the previous year. Quoting heavily from a copy of the document that American ambassador Robert Livingston had presented to Bonaparte, which described the folly of maintaining a colony in Louisiana, Calculator described Louisiana as a vast "western wilderness." It contained no "mines of gold or silver" and would take years and untold amounts of money to make profitable. Why, Calculator asked, should the United States pay an exorbitant sum for a piece of property that American ambassadors had just told Bonaparte was utterly worthless? The very geography of Louisiana itself made it unassimilable into the American empire and hence a danger to the fabric of the republic. Nature itself precluded such annexation.[11]

Calculator summarized this argument in his last article. Louisiana, he concluded, was a foreign territory because it lay beyond the "vast body of water which till very lately has been considered as the ultimate limits of the

United States." Why then, he asked, should Americans transgress this clear "ordination of nature" into a barren wilderness that was obviously foreign to the United States. Indeed, for Calculator, the Mississippi River appeared to be the very voice of the Divine, "which has seemingly said, 'Hitherto ye shall come, and no further.'" This critique of the treaty was also addressed by others. Fabricius, who had an acerbic comment for nearly every aspect of Louisiana, agreed with this assessment. He memorably called the territory an "untrodden waste for owls to hoot and wolves to howl in." It was, he continued, the "realm of alligators and catamounts." By extension then, nature had made it not the realm of Americans. It was, in fact, a realm beyond the natural boundaries of the United States. This line of attack turned on its head the argument of Charles Brocken Brown outlined in the last chapter. By applying the same standards that Brown had used to show that Haiti was outside the natural limits of the French empire, Calculator and Fabricius claimed to show that Louisiana was beyond the natural limits of the United States.[12]

What then were the costs of such unnatural expansion into a foreign wilderness? There were the monetary costs, of course, but there were also political ones. In the autumn of 1804, numerous Federalist papers reprinted an article originally from London that neatly shows the continuing political role of natural boundaries in the late stage of the debate on Louisiana. Like most Americans, the assumption of the British author was that only nations keeping to their natural limits could restore order in the chaotic world created by Bonaparte. The author suggested that before the Purchase, the Mississippi had provided an "unequivocal boundary" to both Spain and the United States, but with that natural frontier transgressed, only an "imaginary" boundary remained. For Americans lured by the riches of Mexico and Peru and with no natural border to arrest their movement, what would stop aggressive American expansion into those places? The article suspected that the selling of Louisiana would ultimately lead to the "total loss [for] Spain of its South American dominion." Even worse, the article continued, the nations of Europe could not sit idly by and watch this happen. Unchecked expansion by the United States, the article concluded, would thus also probably lead United States into war eventually with Great Britain, France, or both. This inevitable conclusion was straight from the thought of Swiss political theorist Emmerich Vattel and his notions of the international balance of power. The emergence of the United States as a great imperial power could only result in the violent reaction of other powers to restore the status quo. By reprinting this article, Federalists suggested in no uncertain terms that transgressing America's natural boundaries would lead to real-world consequences that threatened national security. This put the largely theoretical exercise of natural frontiers into a stark geopolitical reality governed by a balance of power.[13]

The pro-treaty Jeffersonians, on the other hand, celebrated America's freedom from the artificial limits that had constrained the country in the past. In "An Address to All the Monarchists," an author writing under the pseudonym "The Old Soldier" roundly condemned the Federalists for their opposition to the Louisiana Purchase Treaty. In his closing he brought up the idea of boundaries by extolling the virtues of the new, sprawling American empire:

> When I consider the almost boundless extent of the United States, including the all important acquisition of Louisiana, a territory stretching from sea to sea, or from the great river, Mississippi, to the ends of the earth, and from near the tropic of cancer . . . to the polar circle; when I consider the sublime grandeur, magnificence and potency of a monarch commanding such an unbridled kingdom, and sole sovereign of such an immense territory, in comparison of who the emperor of China and the Great Lama of Tibet dwindle into subalterns, Bonaparte and the Kings of Europe are very little things.

The contrast between these two positions is instructive. For many Federalists, crossing the natural boundary of the Mississippi would lead to the United States becoming enmeshed in an endless series of border disputes with European powers, which would threaten American national security. For the Jeffersonians, however, the extent of America's boundless empire proved its greatness in comparison to the rest of the world. With its suggestion of a boundless American empire, this type of rhetoric recalled the argument made by Coriolanus in 1802 and imagined a United States unconstrained by the Vattelian balance-of-power politics that governed Europe. In the end, however, arguments about borders became less important once the treaty was actually received by Congress. Natural boundaries took a backseat to the more practical problem of doing business with such a dangerous political actor as Bonaparte.[14]

Treaty Objections

In September and October, the Spanish minister in Washington attempted to protest the treaty on the grounds that French troops still occupied the Italian province promised to Spain as part of the original retrocession. In other words, Napoleon had sold the territory under false pretenses. The Jefferson administration ignored the petition, but this almost became a serious hiccup in the process of taking possession. Federalists in the House of Representatives briefly attempted to hold up further votes until copies of the Treaty of San Ildefonso could be obtained to verify that Napoleon did, indeed, have a legitimate title to Louisiana. Apparently even administration supporters in Congress had qualms, for the resolution requiring the copies of the treaty was voted down by only two votes even though Jeffersonians enjoyed a three-to-one majority in the House. Based on the newspaper accounts, the public did not get wind of these events until November when Federalist congressmen started to write home to their constituents, but when they did, it resulted in another rhetorical salvo from the anti-treaty faction that continued to make the case that political and diplomatic dealings with Bonaparte could only come at the cost of American security.[15]

Some interpreted the episode as further evidence of the Jefferson administration's naivete in dealing with Bonaparte. For example, an anti-treaty writer identifying himself only as "N" wrote a satirical piece in a New Hampshire paper that criticized the Jefferson administration's lack of forethought when it came to imperial matters. The national debt might well be a "mortal canker" on the young country, "N" opined, but a great deal was a great deal when it came to western real estate. It was a shame that the United States had such "shortsighted rulers," he wrote sardonically. For "a few trifling millions more, Bonaparte would have added . . . the exhaustless mines of Peru and Potosi, and with them a tract of the country, in value above all price." Of course, both these regions were deep within the Spanish New World empire. No matter, said "N." Now was the time to buy, he pointed out, since once all of Europe was at the foot of Bonaparte, he might not be willing to make such excellent bargains. The point of the piece, of course, was that Bonaparte would be happy to sell anything, no matter who actually owned the legal title or the political consequences, to the starry-eyed Jeffersonians.[16]

For "N" the American response to the Spanish objection showed more about Jefferson's naive willingness to blindly follow his expansionist ideology, but for other writers it showed just how corrupt the United States had become in dealing with Bonaparte. One furious letter posted in a New England paper called Napoleon the "arch-swindler" who had stolen Louisiana from his Spanish allies. "I view," he went on, "the U. States as no better than confederates with a gang of thieves—and as receivers of stolen goods." Another widely circulated letter made a similar point. "The Spanish minister's remonstrance," the anonymous author wrote, "is treated with as much contempt as Bonaparte would treat a remonstrance from the Landamman of Switzerland." The anti-treaty faction had struck a chord—though not quite hard enough to derail American expansion. By directly linking American expansionist policy to the morally ambiguous imperial policies of Bonaparte, suddenly the Louisiana Purchase did not look like such a triumphant affair. The event shows just how flexible the rhetoric of Napoleon had already become by 1803—even among similarly minded factions.[17]

Pro-treaty partisans felt the need to respond to this accusation. They bypassed the moral ambiguousness of the deal and focused directly on the legal aspects—like the Federalists, they treated Napoleon as an unscrupulous political actor, but as one who had to be dealt with to eliminate his influence on the continent. The editor of the *Charleston Courier* put it in simple terms for his readers: "What then has the government of the United States, a *bona fide* purchaser, to do with conditions on which the province was sold to France?" He continued by making an analogy that his readers would be familiar with. "If I buy a horse from Titus, which Caius had sold and delivered to him, taking his bond or note as a security for the payment of the stipulated price, what should we say, if Caius, finding his security to be worthless, should come to me and beg of me not to buy the horse?" The legal answer was simple, if perhaps hard on poor Caius. "We should be apt to tell him that he had now nothing to do with the horse and that if he was displeased with his bargain, he had only to upbraid his own folly in giving credit to whom he ought to have known better than to trust." If we transferred this situation to Louisiana, the author was saying that it was Spain's own fault for doing business with an unsavory character like Bonaparte. Understandably, the author neglected to explain the wisdom or the ethics of the United States doing business with the same questionable character. Presumably, it was worth the chance to rid North America of Bonaparte's own imperial ambitions.[18]

There were also rumblings from anti-treaty types about the legal ramifications of making real estate deals with Bonaparte's government. Most of these revolved around the question of the consulship's legitimacy. Since Bonaparte had come to power in a coup, some anti-treaty authors asked, was his government really the legitimate government of France? If it was not, did the treaty hold any legal standing? The easiest answer to these questions was provided by Senator James Jackson, a long-serving English-born senator and one-time governor of Georgia. In a speech that was reprinted in Jeffersonian papers ranging from his home in Georgia to Vermont, Jackson explained the consulate was, indeed, the legal government of France. Jackson argued that no matter what misgivings he had personally of the French government, "Bonaparte by the consent of the nation is placed at its head." Jackson here referred to the mostly legitimate plebiscite that had named Bonaparte "First Consul for life" in August 1802. "No nation," Jackson continued, "had the right to interfere with rule or police of another." The acts of Bonaparte, then, were the genuine acts of the nation of France. Jackson, like other pro-treaty advocates, thus simply ignored the question of whether Americans should deal with Bonaparte by simply saying that they could deal with him in order to establish the American empire.[19]

Other Americans, however, disagreed with Jackson's assessment of Bonaparte's legitimacy. This, then, led to the uncomfortable question of whether the government of the United States could, or should, make legitimate treaties with his government. As before, expansionists tended to quietly sidestep the second half of the question and focus simply on the legal reality of the situation. One congressional speech that made its way into the *Aurora General Advertiser*—probably the mostly widely read American newspaper of the time—was that of Representative James Elliot, a first-term congressman from the politically divided state of Vermont. Elliot attempted to thread the needle of legality when it came to Bonaparte. "I believe," he began, "there is not within these walls an admirer of the present government of France." But, he continued, "we all know the distinction between a king or government de jure and de facto. If Bonaparte be not the rightful ruler of the French republic, he is the present possessor of the powers of government, and can bind the nation by treaties." This meant, he argued, that even if Bonaparte died before the ratified treaty made it back to France, it would still be binding upon the French people.[20]

What these speeches in response to the Spanish objections to the treaty indicate is that the rhetorical battleground of empire had shifted again. It had, for the moment, moved away from the older arguments of expansion based primarily on national security and toward the ideological conception of a republican American empire of liberty. At first glance it is surprising how few Federalists refused to support the treaty given that it provided Americans a chance to rid themselves of the dangers posed by Napoleon's North American imperialism, and how few Jeffersonians defended the treaty in the same terms. What they were debating, then, was becoming less an imperial identity based on national security, but one based on republican principles. For Federalists, the idea of dealing politically with a corrupt despot like Bonaparte would undermine the entire idea of a republican empire. This is why they could, almost in the same breath, support aggressive military expansion to remove the threat of Bonaparte from North America and yet decry unseemly diplomatic wrangling with Bonaparte that appeared, to them, to be the hallmark of Jeffersonian expansion.

Despite the heated rhetorical battle in the press, the final outcome was hardly in doubt. Congress reflected the growing Jeffersonian influence in the nation, and the Louisiana vote showed it. With remarkably little debate on the floor, the Senate voted to accept the treaty a mere two days after receiving it by a margin of twenty-four to seven. One New Hampshire Federalist griped, "The Senate have taken less time to deliberate on this great treaty than they allowed themselves on the most trivial Indian contract." Only one Federalist, Jonathon Dayton of New Jersey, crossed the aisle.[21]

The heated debate in the press over the treaty reveals some important insights into the ideological thought behind American expansion and anti-expansion during the first decade of the nineteenth century. Arguments over expansion were a genuine ideological battle even when it did not directly involve military force. Many historians have simply dismissed opposition to the treaty as insignificant when compared to the larger sweep of American expansion, or as simply political sour grapes from a minority political faction. But those Americans who opposed the treaty and their arguments ought to be taken seriously. While they lost the debate, their arguments established a rhetoric of anti-imperialism that provided the basis for an anti-expansionist tradition within the United States that echoes down to the present day. The underlying focus of the opposition's most lasting arguments was not based on simple political partisanship. More often than not, the opposition presented genuine and principled ideological concerns about a self-governing republic dealing with the likes of Napoleon. The oft-repeated claim that "the United States does not negotiate with terrorists" is a modern incarnation of the same attitude. The fact that the far more numerous pro-treaty faction felt that they had to respond to this argument demonstrates that linking Bonaparte to American expansion contained a great deal of rhetorical and ideological power.[22]

Opposition to Occupation

Accepting the Louisiana Treaty, however, was only the first step on the American road to empire. On October 26, 1803, the Senate passed the legislation that allowed for the formal occupation and administration of Louisiana. Two days later the House of Representatives followed suit and forwarded a bill to the Senate allocating the funds needed to purchase the territory. With that, the question of whether or not the United States would be an empire was settled for good, but this only opened up new questions about the administration of that empire. The language of the bill allowing for the occupation of Louisiana resulted in a vigorous debate among Americans about what their new empire should look like. How Louisiana was administered would be key to the future of American expansion. As one senator put it succinctly, "The U.S. in time will have many colonies—therefore precedents are important." In the debate that followed, Federalists used fears of Napoleon as a danger to American security and the symbolic image of an undemocratic, oppressive Bonapartist empire to contest the Jeffersonian plans for occupation.[23]

To understand the debate over the occupation of Louisiana that follows, it is important to understand how Americans understood Bonaparte's imperial domains. Initially, many Americans, especially Jeffersonians, saw Bonaparte as a liberator striking off the oppressive chains of monarchy. In 1796, one Philadelphia newspaper printed the following glowing editorial about Napoleon's occupation of Italy:

> If anything short of omnipotent power, can restore to the effeminate sons of Italy, the virtues of their illustrious predecessors, it must be the humane, dignified, and endearing treatment of Buonaparte. Did he speak the language of proud and unfeeling victory, he might say,

"creatures of superstition and folly, victims of indolence and error, submit to the sway of a conqueror, determined to hold you up to the universe as an awful example of merited punishment! The chains you have forged for others, shall now be riveted on you!"—but with the heroic magnanimity, inspired by the spirit of rational and enlightened freedom, he announces, "that all shall exercise their rights under the shield of virtue, that every one who acknowledges a God shall worship him in the manner his conscience dictates!"—Frenchmen! If these are your arms, victory is yours forever!

For optimistic Jeffersonians at the start of Napoleon's career, Bonaparte seemed to be creating an empire of liberty that spread the promise of liberal, republican government to oppressed peoples.[24]

By 1802, however, most Americans had a very different understanding of what Napoleonic imperialism meant to those unfortunate enough to fall victim to it. The acerbic Massachusetts Federalist Fisher Ames pointed this out in a series of widely reprinted public letters in October 1802. Ames began by drawing parallels between the imperialism of classical Rome and Bonaparte's imperialism, under which, he wrote, "the civilized world is first to bleed, and then to sweat in chains." Ames consciously drew on the imagery of slavery as he described the imperial project of Bonaparte. Under the rapacious imperial eye of Napoleon, he wrote, the nominally independent little republics of Europe "are nothing; they are slaves, paid by titles to freedom for hewing wood and drawing water." They are, he continued, nothing but "new recruits" for the wars of the French republic. These unfortunate imperial possessions of France, he went on, "are made to obey, like slaves, and yet to say and to swear, on occasion that they are sovereign and independent, as may best suit the ambitious policy of France." As this passage shows, perhaps nothing about the imperial republic of Bonaparte irritated Ames more than its hypocrisy. Bonaparte had treated his sister republics, said Ames, "not as associates, but as victims." He went down a long list of Napoleon's imperial victims: Venice had been sold to the Austrian emperor in a cynical diplomatic deal, Holland had been drained of economic resources at the point of French bayonets, and Switzerland had been drained of its youth "to be food for gunpowder." All of this to support nothing more than the vainglorious military ambitions of Bonaparte. For Ames, and many other Americans, by 1802 Bonaparte's imperialism meant precisely the opposite of what it had meant to so many five years earlier. Instead of freedom it brought subjection under the veneer of liberty and rendered entire populations into the subjects and slaves of a French military despot masquerading as a savior of liberalism.[25]

As they looked at the Purchase Treaty in the autumn of 1803, both Federalists and Jeffersonians had concerns about how it would shape the occupation of Louisiana, and this unease would encourage them to adopt measures at odds with their own liberal imperial values. The clause that caused the most angst was in the third article of the treaty and had allegedly been written by Bonaparte himself. It proclaimed that "the inhabitants of the ceded territory shall be incorporated in the Union of the United States, and admitted as soon as possible . . . to the enjoyment of all the rights, advantages, and immunities, of citizens of the United States." Some Americans smelled a rat. The always cantankerous Senator William Plumer wondered, "What could induce Bonaparte to insist on this people's [sic] being incorporated into the Union? He has never discovered a strong attachment to the rights of any nation, or to that of any individual." Plumer's fears reveal that it was not only the geographic extension of the United States that gave so much concern to Americans, but also the demographic expansion that the Purchase represented. This was an unexpected twist to the problem of demographic boundaries articulated by Charles Brockden Brown in his pamphlet on the Mississippi Crisis. Brown had argued that the population of Haiti made the island un-French, but he had portrayed Louisiana as essentially empty. Calculator and Fabricius took the same approach in their opposition to the Purchase when they described Louisiana as a vast wilderness. However, Americans soon realized such portrayals were a fiction. In fact, the purchase of Louisiana was not simply an expansion of the geographic boundaries of the United States: it also represented the potential for national expansion.[26]

Read literally, Article III of the Purchase Treaty appeared to require that *all* inhabitants of Louisiana become citizens of the United States. This caused many Americans, both Jeffersonian and Federalists, grave concern. The people of Louisiana were, as one newspaper put it, a strange amalgamation of "red-white, black, [and] black and white." Would they become citizens? The terms of the treaty seemed to suggest that they would. In the early nineteenth century, the idea of the "nation" as a concept undergirding a state was only beginning to take on its modern connotations and thus was both extremely malleable and extremely worrisome for many Americans. Race was part of the equation, and it would play a larger role as time went on, but it was only a part. To many native-born Americans, even Louisianans of European decent seemed simply too foreign in language, religious customs, and political systems to ever be assimilated into the United States. "Can it be conceived," asked one writer rhetorically, "that these people, bred in despotism, will suddenly be fitted for self government and republicanism?" These demographic worries had their roots in American perceptions of Bonaparte as a dangerous threat to national security.[27]

Many commentators wondered if the crafty Napoleon had once again fooled the naive Jefferson administration. One writer complained that allowing "people of different nations, distinguished by dissimilar manners, various habits, strong prejudices, and fixed sentiments of attachments to several countries" to enjoy the benefits of incorporation into the American nation "must soon produce a dissolution of the union." This, as some writers pointed out, would only help Bonaparte in the long run by providing a ready ally for him in the Western Hemisphere. Others wondered if Napoleon had deliberately inserted the third article, knowing that the United States could not fulfill this part of the document and thus giving France a reason to "justly abrogate the whole treaty" and reclaim Louisiana without paying back the $15 million. Nothing seemed impossible for the wily Napoleon in the first decade of the nineteenth century.[28]

Even Bonaparte himself—or at least his minions—made this charge more believable. In the widely published farewell to the people of Louisiana, the French commissioner in New Orleans, Pierre Laussat, proudly announced that the First Consul congratulated the people of the territory on their "peaceful emancipation." Bonaparte, he said, would always think on the inhabitants of Louisiana as his brothers. "Your children will become our children," he explained, "and our children will become yours." Bonaparte, Laussat continued, wished to "perpetuate the ties which unite the French of Louisiana with the Frenchmen of Europe," and he hoped that the sight of the French flag would "never cease to gladden [their] hearts." More than that, however, Laussat repeatedly reminded the inhabitants of Louisiana of Bonaparte's insistence that they be incorporated into the American nation as soon as possible in order that their liberty, property, and religion be protected.[29]

Words like these greatly worried an author in *The Repertory*. "In the face of the World," he wrote, Bonaparte had officially encouraged the

Louisianans to remember their "common origin" as Frenchmen. According to the First Consul, the author continued, "The people of Louisiana ... will always be attached to the interests of France." Thus, "a band of Frenchmen is to be incorporated into our Union, and to remain, after incorporation, still Frenchmen, still attached to the interest of France." Yet, the author marveled, "this threatened danger stirs no fear, the insult stirs no anger." Another disgusted author wrote that Napoleon was obviously counting on the "cameleon" inhabitants of Louisiana to gain a "preponderance" of influence at "the national councils." The fear was that Bonaparte knew that they would always maintain their "eternal love and gratitude" for France. Thus, as new states were carved out of Louisiana and gained congressional representation, eventually the emperor would have a union of allies ready to do his bidding. Significantly, Julien Vernet's recent work on the transfer of Louisiana to the United States shows that, prior to the official handover, Laussat did indeed deliberately set up a pro-French municipal council in New Orleans in an attempt to maintain French influence in the region. Sometimes, rhetoric is reality.[30]

What then was to be done with the "cameleon" inhabitants of Louisiana? If the people of Louisiana were truly foreign, then should they then be treated not as part of the nation, but as imperial subjects? More than a few Americans proposed solutions that sounded more like what Napoleon would impose on a defeated foreign foe than what one would expect as part of an "empire of liberty." These solutions represented some rare bipartisanship between Federalists and Jeffersonians. "I have always thought," mused Federalist Gouverneur Morris (who had been of the loudest advocates for a preemptive military strike on New Orleans) "that when we should acquire Canada and Louisiana, it would be proper to govern them as provinces, and allow them no voice in our councils." Jeffersonian senator George Campbell of Tennessee explained to his congressional colleagues that he considered the Louisianans as standing in "nearly the relation to us as if they were a conquered country." Then there was the novelist and militant expansionist, Charles Brockden Brown, who was ready to treat Louisiana's few "present inhabitants as vassals" if need be, until they could be supplanted by American settlers. Factions from both ends of the political spectrum seemed to agree that bringing those from outside America's natural demographic boundaries—especially Napoleon's former subjects—into the American empire would require imperial oversight to ensure their loyalty.[31]

The inhabitants of Louisiana were also concerned about the rather unrepublican system with which their new imperial rulers threatened to saddle them. In a document presented to Congress in the winter of 1804–5, Louisianans questioned the legitimacy of the American occupation. The document, titled "A Remonstrance of the People of Louisiana against the Political System Adopted by Congress for Them," appealed to the history of the United States to support their inclusion into the American system of republican government. They briefly referenced Article III of the Purchase Treaty, but, realizing its controversial nature, they carefully framed most of their argument on the inalienable rights of mankind implied in the Declaration of Independence and in the US Constitution. "Do political axioms on the Atlantic become problems when transferred to the shores of the Mississippi?" they asked. By rhetorically divorcing ideology from geographical place, they called the whole idea of empire into question. By speaking the same political language, they encouraged the Congress to see them as within the natural boundaries of the United States—as fit members of the American nation. The Louisianans concluded by hoping that the nation that had been formed on the principle that "governors were intended for the governed and not the governed for the governors" would not be "deaf to their just complaints." They wanted nothing to do with American imperialism.[32]

Even as they used the language of liberalism to confront the ideology of empire in the "Remonstrance," some Louisianans were not above using the American fear of the wily Bonaparte to their own advantage. A US official sent to Louisiana in 1804 warned the US government that if the demands made in the "Remonstrance" were not met, there were Louisianians "who speak seriously of appealing to France & requesting the first Consul to give them aid." A few months later, no less than the governor of Louisiana, William Claiborne, told Secretary of State James Madison that he believed the "Remonstrance" was tinged with "foreign influence," since "the most sincere Admirers of Bonaparte are among the Memorialists." As historian Peter Kastor has pointed out, these actions were not serious threats but were made to force the government of the United States to take their demands seriously. Yet, their appearance in the official record shows that Louisianans were quite capable of effectively harnessing the power of Napoleon into their rhetoric to define their own sense of the American empire and their place within it.[33]

Many native-born Americans scoffed at the "Remonstrance," and some used it as an opportunity to justify an imperial administration of the new territory that seemed in conflict with their republican principles. The *Republican Watchtower* printed a particularly vicious satirical response to the petition in which the author posed as a Louisiana "Creole." In the original document the authors had conspicuously avoided unnecessary references to the promises made in Article III and made no reference at all to Bonaparte, instead seeking to situate themselves politically within the American natural boundaries of liberalism. But in the mock "Remonstrance," the First Consul entered the argument in the first paragraph. "You promise de citizen Bonaparte dat you shall take us into one state," the "Creole" wrote in an oblique reference to Article III. Of course, the "Creole" continued, it was not the Louisianans who had actually wanted to leave the French empire; it was the Americans who "give fifteen million dollar for his [Bonaparte's] permission for dat." Territory might be transferred by treaty, but not loyalty.[34]

The mock "Remonstrance" justified the exercise of American imperial power in Louisiana in several ways. Importantly, it was composed in a pidgin dialect with obvious racial overtones. This had the effect of flattening Louisiana's complex ethnic makeup into a simplistic and servile caricature. The "Creole" repeatedly displays his incapability of self-government through a slavish loyalty to his imperial master Bonaparte rather than to the principle of republican liberty. In May 1804, Napoleon was declared hereditary emperor of the French by the French Senate. But even this final betrayal of the revolution appears to be entirely lost on Napoleon's servile subject. The "Creole's" use of the term of political equality, "citizen Bonaparte," even after the new emperor began exercising his dictatorial powers, demonstrates that the "Creole" is so entirely enthralled with an individual that he is entirely unaware that he is the subject—and not the citizen—of the imperial system. By tying the Louisianian loyalty to a military despot rather than to the idea of liberty, the author cleverly tapped into already established doubts that many Americans had about the administration of their new empire. The mock "Remonstrance" painted Louisianans like the "Creole" as servile subjects of French militarism and thus justified the aggressive and repressive imperial measures adopted by the Jefferson administration in Louisiana.[35]

The Administration of Louisiana

Ultimately, the overwhelmingly pro-administration Congress agreed—at least to a certain extent—with those who agitated for a less than republican solution for Louisiana. Both the act authorizing the occupation of Louisiana and the act creating the territorial government gave the executive branch sweeping authority to administer the new region and severely limited any popular participation in government. According to the occupation document, the president was authorized to "employ any part of the army and navy of the United States," as well as the militia, to enforce the transfer. Presidential supporters saw this threat of force as particularly important, given that Spain had threatened to contest the occupation and still occupied the territory even though it had been (in theory at least) ceded to France. Then, of course, there was no guarantee that the "cameleon" inhabitants of Louisiana had any interest in becoming part of the United States. The act also gave the president the unilateral authority to exercise all "military, civil and judicial powers" in Louisiana until such time as Congress could make other arrangements, for which no timeline was given.[36]

Five months later the Congress passed the statute creating the territorial government of Louisiana. They created a governor, who would be appointed by the president and serve at his pleasure. The governor would be assisted by a council of the thirteen "most fit and discreet persons of the territory." These too would be appointed by the president, as would the judges who would see to the judicial needs of the territory and the officers of the territorial militia. In fact, virtually every civil, military, and judicial officer of the new territory would be appointed by the president of the United States. Significantly, there would be no legislature. Not everyone was happy with the outcome, of course. One Federalist senator glowered, "This is a Colonial system of government." He was not being complementary. Concerns about both the expansion of executive power and the undemocratic occupation of Louisiana led to new rhetorical comparisons between the imperial policies of the United States and those of Napoleon.[37]

In response to the creation of the territorial government, the opposition launched a counterattack that tied the American occupation of Louisiana directly to Bonaparte as a negative, illiberal symbol of imperialism rather than as a danger to American national security. In March 1804, the editor of

Boston's *Repertory* vented at what he saw as the potential for tyranny contained in the act creating the territorial government. "IT IS A DESPOTISM," he wrote using all capitals and italics to emphasize his point. "Never, before, have we seen a system of government, constructed by any association of men, among whom *there was not one of the people to be governed!*" The editor then tied the imperial occupation directly to the best imperialist he knew. "Without the least levity of allusion, we may truly say, this is a transaction worth the school of Bonaparte." For emphasis he explained exactly what he meant by this.

> A country is partly bought, and partly conquered; for thousands of troops were in readiness to overpower any symptom of resistance which might appear, and which the order for the organization of those troops proves was expected. The American flag was hoisted under the protection of American arms. The purchasers of the country without the slightest reference to the opinions of its inhabitants, form a constitution for them, to which they must submit.

To the nineteenth-century American reader, this all sounded suspiciously like how Bonaparte treated his imperial conquests in Europe.[38]

However, it was not only the betrayal of republicanism that worried *The Repertory* editor. Just as concerning was what he saw as the expansion of despotic executive power made possible by imperialism à la Bonaparte. He saved his most biting remarks for Thomas Jefferson in an explicit comparison between the president and the First Consul. The act creating the new government in Louisiana gave the president virtually unlimited power, the editor fumed. "Have we got an angel in the shape of Thomas Jefferson," he asked sarcastically, "that a territory of this boasted extent, bordering on a country not the most friendly to us, and peopled by inhabitants who will be very difficult to govern, should be solely entrusted to him?" Or, he added ominously, is Jefferson, "as Bonaparte announced himself, the delegate of heaven, commissioned to regulate the destinies of men?" The editor of *The Repertory* was not alone in his assessment that the imperial administration of Louisiana represented a dangerous expansion of executive power, though he perhaps was the most vocal.[39]

Writing in the *Washington Federalist*, "A.B." made similar accusations about the dangers posed by imperial executive power. "When Bonaparte took possession by violence of the government of France," he wrote in February 1804, "the democrats, who till that event had been in the habit of extolling him as the purest and best of republicans, immediately denounced him, as a usurper, and a traitor because, forsooth, he had undertaken to rule a people without previously obtaining their consent." Was this any different than what Jefferson had just done in the Louisiana territory, he asked rhetorically. "He is surely as much of a usurper, as Bonaparte—for he has become their master, and is in the exercise of the most despotic and absolute authority without having consulted them on the subject." A.B. thought the president's supporters hypocritical for "instead of applying to Jefferson, the angry and harsh epithets with which, but a short time since, they loaded Buonaparte, they hail him as the best of men and patriots." They would probably continue to do so, A.B. sneered, even if Jefferson, like Bonaparte, "were to enslave, and by fraud or violence, reduce one half of Europe under his dominion." While Jefferson was certainly the first American president whose accumulation of political power would be likened to Bonaparte, he would not be the last. These two articles and others like them unleashed a new phase in American imperial discourse—instead of appealing to Napoleon as an actual political actor to be countered, they turned to Napoleon as an oppressive and illiberal symbol, not be emulated.[40]

The debate over the occupation of Louisiana shows that the use of Bonaparte had started to shift. Rhetoric that initially treated Bonaparte as a dangerous and unscrupulous political actor who had ceded Louisiana only to create a country of French allies turned to using Napoleon and his empire as negative imperial examples. With Bonaparte removed from the American continent, he and his methods became yardsticks—symbols—by which to measure the legitimacy of American expansion. The debate also shifted to how elastic the rhetoric of Bonaparte could be in the hands of Federalists by 1805. Where some Federalists expressed concern that the Purchase Treaty required the inhabitants of Louisiana to *become* members of the American nation, others voiced concern about the *lack* of popular participation in the Louisiana government. Both groups ultimately tied their arguments to Napoleon Bonaparte and his empire. This became even more evident in the pro-imperial arguments that developed over the next several months as Jeffersonians appropriated the language of their opponents to justify and even celebrate national expansion to the American public.

The Great American Empire

As they celebrated the addition of Louisiana to the United States, Jeffersonians and their allies found that they could not help but compare their new American empire to that of Bonaparte's France. By appropriating Napoleon's imperial image as an illiberal and violent example, they turned the anti-expansionist rhetoric of their opponents into a positive, pro-imperial argument and provided a new imperial identity for the United States as the anti-Bonaparte.

Even before the ink was dry on the treaty, the Jeffersonian senator from Kentucky, John Breckinridge, cheered the acquisition of Louisiana as the "most splendid [transaction] which the annals of any nation can produce." The old revolutionary emphasized that the American empire had been won "from the most powerful and warlike nation on earth, without bloodshed, without the oppression of a single individual . . . through the peaceful forms of negotiation." To Breckinridge, the Louisiana Purchase showed just how different the peaceful conquests of the United States were in comparison to the bloody wars of Bonaparte. Indeed, it showed that peaceful conquest could overpower even the mighty Napoleon. Ironically, it had been Breckinridge who had introduced the Jeffersonian bill that called on the president to prepare eighty thousand militia for use in Louisiana in response to the Ross resolutions. Even more ironically, within weeks of making this speech Breckinridge would introduce the legislation for the military occupation of the Louisiana territory.[41]

No one was more vocal in this comparison between the American and Napoleonic empires than David Ramsay. Though he had served as a doctor during the War for Independence and completed multiple terms as a member of the South Carolina legislature and in the Continental Congress, he was probably best known to Americans of the nineteenth century as a historian. His two-volume *History of the Revolution in South Carolina* was the first book to receive an American copyright. Among a host of other historical writings, he published several volumes on George Washington, as well as the first comprehensive history of the American Revolution. So, on May 12, 1804, when Ramsay gave a stirring speech to "a very large audience" at St. Michael's Church in Charleston, South Carolina, celebrating the Louisiana "cession," it was reprinted all over the nation. Within the month, anxious readers all over the nation could buy a printed copy for twenty-five cents at their local shop. One modern commentator has dismissed the speech as the simple aggressive rhetoric of an "adolescent" nation. What the speech actually represented, however, was a carefully planned attack on the opposition to American imperialism.[42]

Ramsay's message was similar to that of Breckinridge. He began with a geographer's introduction to the new territory, which painted a country of "prairies or natural meadows of inexhaustible fertility" and forests that abounded "with excellent timber." This was a none-too-subtle rebuke of Federalists who had based part of their early opposition to the treaty on the bareness and thus foreignness of the region. Indeed, Ramsay reversed the arguments of writers such as Calculator and Fabricius. For Ramsay, the greatness of the territory was a direct reflection on the greatness of the nation that inhabited it. If Louisiana was a vast land full of great wonders—even mammoths—this was a divine indication of the imperial destiny of the United States. "May we not, therefore" he asked, "indulge a hope that the inhabitants of such a country so eminently distinguished by the Author of Nature, are destined to form political associations of a large size?" Instead of the dangerous wilderness that anti-treaty writers had seen, Ramsay saw the land of Louisiana as a symbolic marker that justified American imperialism.[43]

It did not take long, however, for the historian in Ramsay to think about the Louisiana "cession" within a comparative geopolitical context. "In other countries, and under the direction of other governments," he pointed out, "the energies of nations have been called forth—thousands of lives have been sacrificed—seas have been crimsoned with human blood in the attack or defense of a few acres or of barren rocks." In 1804, no one would have had any doubt which "other government" Ramsay had in mind. In case his audience was not already thinking about any number of Bonaparte's bloody victories, Ramsay provided Malta as an example. For his audience, this would have immediately called to mind Napoleon's attack on the tiny island in 1798, and which a mere five years later had provided the catalyst for the resumption of war between Great Britain and France.[44]

Not so for American expansion, Ramsay claimed. "We have gained this invaluable territory," he continued, "without the imposition of any new taxes; and at the same time with the consent of the inhabitants, and without giving offense to any of the powers in Europe." With these words Ramsay simply brushed aside Federalist concerns about the lack of popular participation in the new territorial government or the lingering doubts about

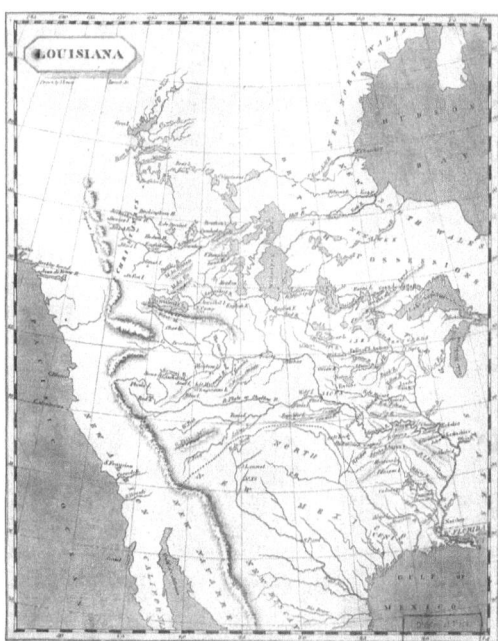

FIG. 2. As this 1805 map shows, Louisiana's western and southern boundaries were largely undefined—which was probably a deliberate ploy by Napoleon. (Library of Congress)

Spanish title to the territory. He also countered Federalist apprehension about paying $15 million to support Bonaparte's wars in Europe by insisting on calling the Purchase a "cession." This choice of words linguistically turned the tables on Federalists who had railed against Jefferson's naivety in dealing with Bonaparte by suggesting that it was actually Jefferson's hard-nosed negotiations that had gotten the best of the First Consul.[45]

With the minds of his audience already on Napoleon, Ramsay stayed on the theme. He asked the audience to consider what would have happened if Louisiana had stayed "in the hands of that wonderful man, who presides over France." He imagined that Bonaparte would have used New Orleans as the "fulcrum of an immense lever by which he would have elevated or depressed our western country in subserviency to his gigantic projects." He would have turned Kentucky and Tennessee into virtual colonies, and eventually this would have inevitably led to a rupture between east and west. "The union of our rising empire would soon have been severed," warned Ramsay, and, he continued, "our nearest neighbors would have become our enemies." Thus, for Ramsay, Bonaparte's imperialism generated civil war and bloodshed, but the exact same action taken by Americans produced peace.[46]

In many ways, this reflected a question over whether the United States was something new—a nation freed from the history of Europe. For the Federalists, the answer had been "no." They saw the United States as a nation that would have to play by Europe's rules, which is why they so strongly argued for seizing Louisiana by force before the transfer to Napoleon took place during the Mississippi Crisis. On the other hand, for Ramsay and his fellow Jeffersonians, the bloodless acquisition of Louisiana through negotiation seemed to prove that the United States was truly different than Bonaparte, Europe, and the rest of the world.

Other Jeffersonians picked up on this thread. In a newspaper retrospective of 1804, one proud expansionist explained the difference between the United States and France. "Looking on America," he began, "we see an extensive empire, enlarging her territory . . . at peace with the world and rising with happy celerity to that rank in the scale of nations, to which her character, her institutions, her privileges, her pursuits give a title." On the other hand, across the Atlantic, one saw Bonaparte, "actively employed in equipping numerous armaments to make a descent on England, and at the same time squabbling with all the rest of Europe." Like Ramsay and Jackson before him, this author highlighted American exceptionalism by seeing expansion by the United States as establishing peace in North America while simultaneously viewing French expansion as conquest. This final debate on the Louisiana Purchase showed the potency of Bonaparte as a negative symbol and showed that the Jeffersonians had adeptly turned the rhetorical weapons of the Federalists against them.[47]

The overwhelming passage of the Louisiana Purchase Treaty showed that Americans had largely accepted that their nation would embrace imperialism. The raucous debate surrounding the treaty and the terms of occupation, however, demonstrates that Americans still disagreed over how the nation ought to expand, how the empire ought to be administered, and what American expansion meant for the rest of the rest of the world. As they contested these important questions, Napoleon increasingly became the standard by which Americans measured their decisions over expansion and the administration of their new empire—but increasingly as a symbol rather than as a political actor. As a result of these comparisons, Americans began to claim a positive imperial identity that was no longer tied to national security. As many had foreseen, though, Louisiana would not be the last place Americans coveted for their own. In fact, even establishing the boundaries of Louisiana was a perplexing question that the Purchase Treaty had not settled. Over the next four decades Americans sought to work out exactly where their "empire of liberty" actually was and how they ought to approach it. As they did, the vocabulary of Napoleon as both a symbol and as political actor continued to occupy an important place in their debates.

3

Allies

Florida and the War of 1812

The Baltimore readers of the *Federal Republican* would have had little reason for cheer as they opened their papers on April 7, 1813. For almost a year, the United States had been at war with Great Britain, and the news was bad. The British navy was tightening its economic noose on the mid-Atlantic coast, and despite early promises of an easy campaign to annex Canada, American soldiers were encountering unexpectedly stiff resistance near York (modern-day Toronto). At the southern end of the nation, American forces were in the West Florida panhandle fighting to wrest control of Mobile from the decrepit Spanish empire. If they had looked past the front page, readers of the *Federal Republican* would have found an article titled "Short Answers to Short Questions," which attempted to made sense of the aggressive imperial expansion taking place at both poles of the American empire. The article probably would not have lifted their spirits, but it would have given voice to what Federalists had long believed about the foreign policy aims of the Madison administration.[1]

The article took the form of a series of questions and answers about the War of 1812 that read very much like a religious catechism. In one question, for example, the Federalist faithful read, "Q. Was it ambition which declared [the war]?" To which the answer was, "Yes. Low, sordid, despicable ambition. The ambition to be dignified by the title of Ally to Imperial France." Shortly thereafter the readers came to this question regarding the motives for war. "Q. Is it the thirst for dominion? A. Not content with Louisiana and West Florida, the declared object of the war was the conquest of Canada . . . and the occupation of her territories." Near the end of the article, the reader came across a similar question with a similar answer. "Q. Is [the war] for the unjust plunder of a poorer neighbor? A. Let the Indians, Canadians, and Floridians answer." This article shows the evolution of anti-expansionist rhetoric in the decade following the Louisiana Purchase. While the argument still relied on the use of Napoleon's image as a dangerous political actor, expansionists were portrayed, not as the naive blunderers who had bought a wilderness from Napoleon, but as willing allies of the French emperor with misguided and ambitious designs far beyond the Gulf Coast.[2]

The decade between the Louisiana Purchase and the beginning of the War of 1812 was characterized by increasingly acrimonious and hyper-partisan debates over the future of American imperialism. After the Louisiana Purchase, though clearly in the minority, Federalists and disgruntled Jeffersonians managed to hold the upper hand in the expansion debate until the end of Jefferson's time in office. They derailed administration plans to force a sale of Spanish Florida in 1806, then used the Burr conspiracy and Napoleon's usurpation of the Spanish throne to revitalize fears of French imperial designs on North America. Elected in 1808, the new Jeffersonian president, James Madison, turned the tables on the opposition. In 1811, he took advantage of a revolt in West Florida to seize that province from under the nose of the Spanish despite fierce opposition from Federalists who painted the new president as an ally of French despotism. In 1812, Madison was able to secure the necessary votes for America's first declared war despite vigorous opposition from his Federalist opponents, only to have them turn the tables back again with their coherent response to what they saw as an unjust war of imperial expansion inspired by Napoleon.

This chapter explores how Americans developed and refined their discourse of expansion using Napoleon between the Louisiana Purchase and the French emperor's exile on Elba. During this time, an American imperial identity based on national security fears regained traction as Bonaparte's own imperial appetites reemerged as a threat to American sovereignty. At the same time, Federalist anti-expansionists and their allies were able to craft a coherent critique of Jeffersonian expansionist policies in the Gulf regions and elsewhere using two mutually reinforcing motifs. First, they continued to compare the aggressive form of American imperialism to the violent and duplicitous example of the Napoleonic empire in Europe. Secondly, they increasingly portrayed American imperial actions as being in direct service of the Bonapartist empire.

Jefferson's West Florida Fiasco

After losing the debates over the Louisiana Purchase, anti-imperialist Federalists spent 1805 regrouping and waiting for an opening through which to launch a rhetorical counterattack. In 1806, they got their chance when expansionists made a colossal tactical blunder in their pursuit of Spanish Florida. The West Florida debacle allowed Federalists to reinsert Bonaparte into North America through the imagery of foreign tribute and the "sister republic." This gave revitalized potency and immediacy to their rhetoric that cast the French emperor as a grave threat to national security. Building on the rhetoric that they had developed during the Louisiana Purchase, Federalists argued that the real danger to American national security was involving the United States politically with Bonaparte.

Many Americans had long seen Florida as a natural part of their economic and physical security. Not a few militant expansionists had suggested seizing Florida along with New Orleans to protect American interests during the Mississippi Crisis of 1802–3. In particular, West Florida, which referred to that part of Florida that lay west of the Perdido River, captivated the imagination of many Americans. In the hand of the United States, the numerous rivers of the area would provide a rich commercial outlet for the burgeoning American settlements in what would become Mississippi and Alabama. The Spanish, however, saw this same strip of land as their last piece of leverage against the monstrous territorial ambitions of the United States.[3]

In their haste to snap up Louisiana from Bonaparte in 1803, American negotiators had failed to pin the French down on the exact limits of the territory. This was almost certainly a deliberate ploy of the First Consul. With the borders between the United States and Spain left open to interpretation, only he could act as ultimate arbiter of the Purchase Treaty—an extremely useful bargaining chip with war looming. As Bonaparte intended, the nebulous boundaries immediately led to friction between the United States and Spain, with both nations appealing to Napoleon for support. In the dreams of American expansionists (including the Jefferson administration) Louisiana included both East and West Florida, most of Texas, and even Oregon. Meanwhile, the Spanish insisted that neither Florida nor Texas had been part of the original retrocession to France and thus could not have been part of the French sale to the United States. In typical Bonaparte fashion, the newly crowned emperor played both sides of the issue for as long as he

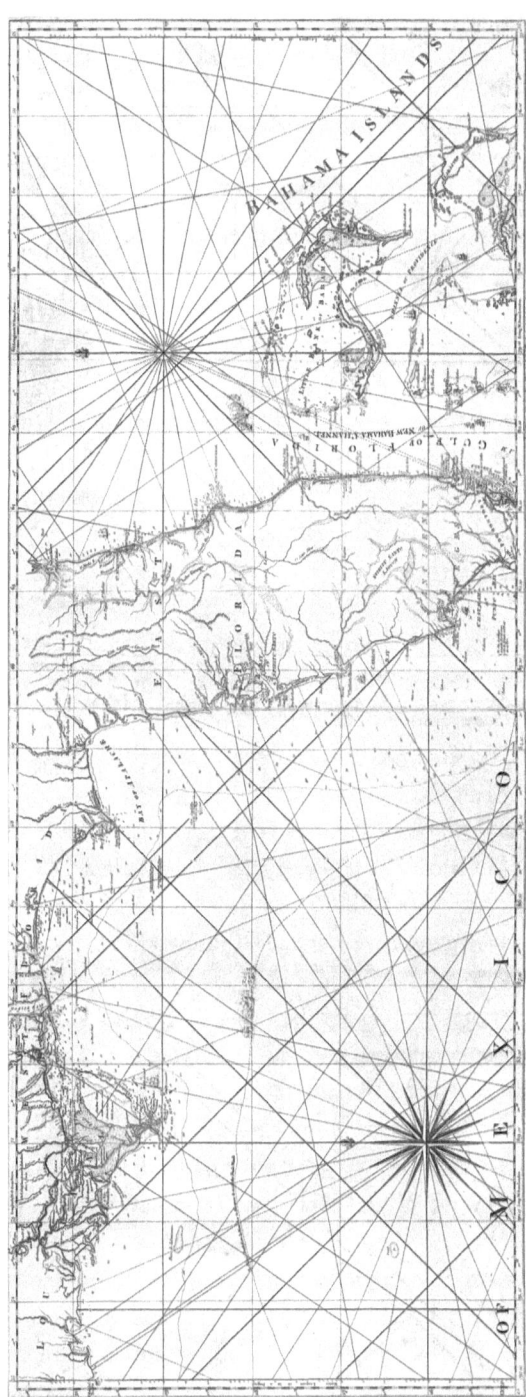

FIG. 3. As this 1775 map shows, the Gulf Coast of colonial Florida stretched from the Florida Keys to the Mississippi River. The region included valuable river outlets, as well as the coastal towns of Pensacola and Mobile. (Library of Congress)

could. Eventually, however, war forced him to publicly support the Spanish claims. Spain, after all, had proven itself to be one of Bonaparte's more reliable, if reluctant, wartime allies. Equally important, it possessed a large fleet with which Napoleon could challenge British naval supremacy.[4]

In West Florida, matters deteriorated. The failure of American diplomats to make good on their claims to the region encouraged anglophone settlers in the area to take matters into their own hands. A confusing series of unsuccessful rebellions by American immigrants in 1804 and 1805 led to increasing tensions between the United States and Spain. Understandably, the Spanish believed that the American government had something to do with the plots against colonial rule, and when the territorial governor of Louisiana refused to extradite conspirators who had fled into the United States, the wary Spanish began shifting troops into the disputed area. In response, the president dispatched a sizeable portion of the tiny American army to the region. In December 1805, Jefferson sent a State of the Union message to the new Congress that sounded a bellicose tone. Officers and soldiers of the government of Spain had committed depredations in an area claimed by the United States as part of Louisiana, he warned ominously. "Our citizens," he wrote, "have been seized, and their property plundered." A few days later, Congress went into a secret closed-door session. War seemed but a matter of time.[5]

When Congress emerged in early February, most Americans were stunned at the result. Instead of the expected vote for war, Congress had passed "An Act Making Provision for Defraying Any Extraordinary Expenses Attending the Intercourse between the United States and Foreign Nations." This vaguely worded act, popularly referred to as the "Two Million Dollar Act," authorized the president to spend up to $2 million to negotiate for Florida. To Americans who viewed West Florida as having been part of the original Louisiana Purchase, this seemed like paying for the same real estate twice. Others were uncomfortable with what looked suspiciously like bribe money. Horrified at what one prominent Jeffersonian—the Virginian John Randolph—saw as a "base prostration of national character," the congressional opposition began launching devastating rhetorical salvos at the administration almost as soon as the prohibition on releasing details of the secret proceedings was lifted at the end of March. As before with the Louisiana Purchase, the vast majority of the opposition focused their attack on the chosen method of expansion rather than on the idea of imperialism itself. As they went on the offensive, anti-imperialists reminded Americans of the dangers inherent in dealing politically with Bonaparte.[6]

Common to opposition thought was the image of the president prostrating American interests at the feet of Bonaparte. One typically bellicose Federalist, for example, was extremely disappointed to hear that Congress's secret session had not been called for the raising of, "ships, troops and taxes" for a war with Spain, but instead for voting "TRIBUTE to Bonaparte!" He found it unconscionable that the United States should pay for Louisiana a second time. This was, he fumed, nothing more than "servile condescension to the French tyrant" who demanded "*Tribute, Tribute, Tribute.*" Federalists had long seen Jefferson and his party as kowtowing to the French empire, but the emphasis on the United States becoming a full-fledged tributary to the French republic was a new device that owed its sting to what Americans saw as the ill-treatment of Napoleon's "sister republics" in Europe.[7]

The idea of tribute was a powerful one in early America because the word implied dependence on an international scale. To Americans, dependence on anyone or anything was dangerous because it robbed an actor of their freedom to act in the best interest of the community. Americans understood this freedom to act independently—liberty—as the characteristic that made republican government possible. Without it, an actor was little better than a slave. The actor might be an individual, but it could also be a community or even a nation. Napoleonic Europe furnished perfect models of this tribute-fueled dependence in the semi-autonomous "sister republics" of France. As the Napoleonic wars engulfed the European continent, Americans increasingly saw these dependent satellite states being milked for money and men to supply the ravenous needs of the French war machine. This tact of portraying the United States as in mortal danger of becoming a client state of Bonaparte was an innovation, but one that capitalized the national security fears that Federalists saw as inherent in dealing with the French emperor.[8]

Because the connection to the French empire's "sister republics" was so effective, other opposition writers quickly took up the refrain of "tribute" to Bonaparte in the wake of the Two Million Dollar Act. Many publicly questioned whether the United States was truly the master of its own foreign policy—the hallmark of national independence. One author, for example, cringed at "giving *Two Millions* of dollars to France, to have Bonaparte's permission to treat with Spain." The author had no faith in the Jeffersonian members of Congress to protect American interests or independence. "If Jefferson & Co. should pass a law to transfer the independence and liberties of this country to the Emperor Napoleon," he snarled, "a majority of these exclusive patriots would be found to justify the measure."[9]

Others adopted the same message. For example, take "Col. Cent," who wrote under a headline that cleverly reversed the famous rallying cry of the XYZ Affair from "Millions for Defense, not a Cent for Tribute" to "Millions for Tribute, not a Cent for Defense." Col. Cent sadly suggested that "the word Independence be stricken from our records and the declaration thereof sent off with the tribute money." Another (misinformed) opposition author sadly concluded that that since sixty tons of silver had set sail for France as a "peace offering to Bonaparte" even before the Congress had lifted the veil of secrecy from its disgraceful proceedings, "these states, once free, sovereign and independent, [have] become a humble tributary to France."[10]

Not every member of the opposition was quite so maudlin, however. The West Florida fiasco provided a marvelous opportunity for Federalists to sharpen their satiric wit. Several newspapers offered a reworked version of the old revolutionary song "Yankee Doodle" that they saw as more appropriate for the times. It featured the rousing chorus:

> Yankee Doodle keep it up!
>   Yankee Doodle dandy!
> A word or two from *Bonaparte*
>   goes down like sugar candy.

The ditty closed with the biting verse:

> Our State Machine is mov'd about,
>   Some say on slippery rollers;
> We've sent a *Hornet's* Nest to *France*
>   To sting the French with *dollars*
> To make them feel our desp'rate power,
>   So secret was the doing,
> That few e'er thought, at *Bona's* nod,
>   A *tribute* was a brewing.

The core message of the song was essentially the same as in the other pieces. However, by appropriating a popular song of the revolution, the opposition portrayed Jefferson's actions not only as fundamentally weak and laughable but also as betraying the ideals of the revolution itself. The song was also the opening salvo in opposition efforts to reach an audience beyond the Federalist elite of New England.[11]

Another similarly irreverent format that the opposition began to use was the satirical cartoon. In response to Jefferson's West Florida woes, cartoonist James Akin produced a popular cartoon titled "The Prairie Dog Sickened at the Sting of the Hornet." The cartoon was only produced as a stand-alone print, but it was reproduced widely enough to justify sardonic commentary in two of the most important Federalist newspapers of the period. In the cartoon, Jefferson is portrayed with the body of a prairie dog—undoubtedly a reference to the "wilderness" of Louisiana. He is in the act of vomiting up $2 million while a French diplomat teases him with maps of East and West Florida. Napoleon appears as a hornet that has just stung the prairie dog, thus, in the words of the *New York Gazette,* "acting as a violent emetic on the terror-struck spaniel." Though Bonaparte is the smallest figure in the drawing, the cartoon is clearly a commentary on his inordinate

FIG. 4. One response of Federalists to the "Two Million Dollar Act" was this 1806 Charles Akin cartoon. Napoleon (at far left) is depicted as a hornet stinging President Thomas Jefferson, who is portrayed as a prairie dog, causing him to vomit up a quantity of gold for the Floridas. (Library of Congress)

power over Jefferson. The title of the cartoon indicates the diplomatic connection between the prairie dog and the hornet and offers a clear indication of which man Akin thought was in control of the relationship.[12]

In case anyone missed the point of the cartoon, the Federalist newspapers quickly published a satirical explanation that highlighted the new role of Bonaparte in directing American foreign policy. The cartoon was, the article insisted, a "historical" piece of art and not a caricature—as suggested by some "ill-natured folks." Indeed, said the article, it was such a masterpiece that it now hung in the halls of the Bonaparte's palace, where it was greatly enjoyed by the emperor himself. With great attention to historical detail, the article continued, the painting depicted Bonaparte administering a new purgative to a unique species of North American dog that caused him to "disgorge *Two Millions of Dollars* at the feet of a certain little Marquis." The "dreadful operation" of this medicine was already well known in "Holland, Spain, Italy, and most parts of the Continent of Europe, by the name of the Napoleon physic." [13]

The parody of "Yankee Doodle" and Akins's humorous cartoon demonstrate a brief turn toward the satirical in the American discourse over expansion using Bonaparte's image. They show that the French emperor had become a political symbol with whom Americans regardless of class could identify and that Federalists were making rhetorical attempts to reach beyond the New England elites who made up the base of the party. The darkly sardonic commentary on the Akin's cartoon, with its emphasis on the word "historical" and the reminder of the fate of Bonaparte's "sister republics," however, demonstrates that Federalists based their tribute rhetoric on the image of Napoleon as a real and dangerous political agent, not simply as an abstract symbol against whom Americans could measure their own imperial policies.

For one of the rare times in American history, the opposition was so effective that it completely derailed plans for expansion. The shadow of a Napoleon at the height of his power loomed large over the United States, and Jefferson failed to comprehend how his actions would be perceived by the public. Stunned at the furor he had created and at the defection of many in his own party, Jefferson dropped all ideas of using the French emperor as a mediator for West Florida. After a fresh round of negotiations with Madrid failed miserably in 1806, he quietly let the matter drop. The damage had been done, however, and despite their fervent insistence otherwise,

Jefferson's allies could never quite shake the accusation that they were the toadies of Bonaparte. This charge became even stronger as the events of the next several years reinvigorated American fears of the French emperor's designs on North America.

The Burr Conspiracy and the American Emperor

After the decisive French victory at Austerlitz in 1806, the third coalition broke apart, leaving Britain to carry on the struggle against Bonaparte alone. A fourth coalition went to war again later in the year but was crushed by the end of 1807. Buoyed by his unbroken string of success, Bonaparte looked to reshape the map of Europe once again. In 1806, he abolished the ancient Holy Roman Empire and formed in its place the Confederation of Rhine—a political organization much more sympathetic to his foreign policy goals. Later that year, when he felt the Batavian Republic was becoming too independent, he replaced it with the Kingdom of Holland and placed one of his brothers on its throne. In 1807, he organized the Grand Duchy of Warsaw (modern Poland) as a counterbalance to Russia and, through the Decrees of Berlin and Milan, established the Continental System to put economic pressure on Great Britain. The Continental System proclaimed a blockade and closed all European ports to British ships—and to neutral ships that had traded with Great Britain. By the start of 1808, Napoleon was approaching the height of his power, and even his opponents marveled at his ability to remake political systems at will.[14]

Americans too watched Bonaparte with a mixture of wonder and alarm. To understand why Bonaparte's moves in Europe played perfectly into the fears of Americans who were already concerned about events on their southern border, we must leave Florida for the moment and take a digression into the murky world of the Burr conspiracy. Even after over two hundred years, historians have a difficult time explaining exactly what took place in 1806 and separating the fact from the newspaper frenzy that resulted. Many modern historians have accepted the traditional account of Burr as the national traitor. Put very briefly, this version runs as follows. After killing the Federalist darling, Alexander Hamilton, in the famous duel at Weehawken, New Jersey, the vice president emerged a marked man. Ostracized by his political friends and shunned by the president, he concocted a plot to recruit an army of secessionist westerners and, with help from

Britain and Spain, establish a new empire in the states and territories west of the Alleghenies. Once this task was complete, he expected to lead his victorious army into Mexico and Spanish Florida and, possibly, march to Washington to displace Jefferson.[15]

More recent research, however, suggests that Burr probably only planned to take advantage of the war scare on the Texas/Louisiana border and lead a filibustering expedition into Spanish Mexico with the assistance of the British navy. Filibustering was a privately backed military invasion intended to topple a government by encouraging residents to "liberate" themselves from alleged tyranny. It had also been an integral part of the Jeffersonian strategy of natural expansion for many years. Burr was so ambiguous as to his plans that even those he attempted to recruit were somewhat mystified as to his ultimate intentions. One he attempted to sway was Andrew Jackson, who was at that time a major general in the Tennessee militia. When Jackson reported on his odd meeting with Burr to his superior, he wondered if Burr's actions were occasioned by a desire to prevent Louisiana from being snatched up by "the rapacious hands of Bonapart," who, according to Jackson, "might be a troublesome neighbour to the united States." So ingrained in the American imperial consciousness was Bonaparte that Jackson could think of no other reason that Burr would be gathering an army.[16]

Burr's filibustering plans fell into disarray during the fall of 1806. His chief coconspirator, the slippery General James Wilkinson (who had been on the Spanish payroll for decades as a double agent) turned on his erstwhile confederate. Alleging that twenty thousand Burrite freebooters were traveling south to attack New Orleans, Wilkinson fired off letters to Washington warning of the grave danger. Meanwhile, he set about preparing a defense of the Crescent City and purging the town of Burr's associates. In actuality, no such invasion force existed, and Wilkinson was merely covering the tracks of his own long list of misdeeds. Once Burr realized Wilkinson's betrayal, he briefly attempted to flee. After only two weeks on the run, however, the former vice president, along with about one hundred cold and hungry supporters, surrendered to authorities in Mississippi on January 12, 1807.[17]

Such were the facts. What the nation's newspapers reported, however, was quite different. Burr had accumulated many political enemies in his life, and now all of them sensed blood in the water. Accusations of treachery were made even more sensational when the subject was portrayed as the American Napoleon. Burr's ambitious character had been associated with that of Bonaparte since at least his presidential run in 1800, but his treason trial breathed new life into this old accusation. Early Jeffersonian reports of Burr's activities noted the similarity between the ambitions of Burr and those of the French emperor at a symbolic level. For example, the *Richmond Enquirer* suggested that the object of Burr's mission appeared to be establishing a western empire and that such a territory could only be run by an emperor "bearing a resemblance to *Bonaparte.*" Many papers linked the two men through use of the word "emperor." Almost immediately, Burr was styled the "Emperor of the Quids"—the anti-Jefferson branch of the party—by the highly influential Jeffersonian paper, *The Aurora*, in an attempt to distance Burr (himself a Jeffersonian) from the presidential wing of the party. Other papers called him "the little emperor." In this way, Jeffersonians asked Americans of the Early Republic to make a symbolic link between the ambitions of the former vice president and Napoleon.[18]

Even well after Burr's acquittal, Jeffersonians continued to see him as the American Napoleon—and thus a powerful symbol of treacherous imperial ambition. In 1808, the *Universal Gazette* printed a letter originally from the *National Intelligencer.* "We have enemies within our walls, inexorable, vigilant and powerful," warned the anonymous author. "The same inordinate love of power which has raised Napoleon to his lofty eminence, impels them; and if they do not pursue the same means to attain their ends, it is because we are vigilant and powerful." It was worth remembering, concluded the author, that such treacherous enemies would have made Aaron Burr president, "and who doubts but that either he would have been another Napoleon or that our fields would have been crimsoned with blood." Ultimately it was this linking of Burr to Bonaparte in the Jeffersonian mind that turned a filibustering expedition into treason.[19]

For the Federalists, on the other hand, the Burr affair demonstrated everything that was wrong with uncontrolled Jeffersonian expansion beyond the Mississippi. For them, the Burr conspiracy was not simply a chance to highlight the dangers of ambitious men, but a chance to uncover a dangerous plot hatched by none other than Napoleon. For as long as Federalists could remember, the dark, foreboding western regions of the country had seemed to breed discontent and threats of disunion—a place ripe for Bonaparte's political intrigues. To them, Burr's actions demonstrated the weakness of the federal government in the west, and they focused on the threat to union highlighted by the imagined plot. The timing of the conspiracy also seemed suspicious to Federalists. For several years, Bonaparte's armies had been occupied in Europe, but with Napoleon's dramatic destruction of the Third and Fourth Coalitions, and Napoleon's dramatic reshaping of Europe, many thought they saw the ambitious and treacherous hand of the French emperor behind the machinations of Burr.

On January 1, 1807, the Federalist *New York Gazette* reported with certainty that muskets of "new and of *French* manufacture" had been seized from the conspirators. Also, it was reported, among Burr's associates there were two "foreign gentlemen . . . who spoke the *French* language." This could only indicate one thing, according to the editors of the *Gazette:* Burr's actions had been "conducted under the auspices of Napoleon." A week later the *Western World* warned its readers that if the rumored destruction of the Prussian army at Jena-Auerstedt were true (and they were), it would clear the way for Bonaparte's restless ambition to turn its gaze westward once again. The author warily concluded that "since the late operations of col. Burr," he suspected anyone who suggested that Bonaparte was not still interested in the conquest of North America of trying to "lull us into security, the more easily to conquer us." Even after his acquittal, the perceived treachery of Burr remained linked to Bonaparte for many years to come. In mid-1810, with West Florida descending into chaos, Baltimore's *Federal Republican* warned that Louisiana "contained a mass of excitable matter, every way fitted for the conjoint projects of Burr and Bonaparte."[20]

The fact that so many Federalists were willing to believe stories of Napoleonic intrigue in the Burr conspiracy is a testament to how intensely they believed that Bonaparte was a dangerous political agent who continued to harbor imperial designs in the Americas. Over the next few years, these fears were fueled by Napoleon's popular portrayal in American media and by Bonaparte's efforts to remake Europe as an extension of his ambitious will. These led to renewed calls for defensive American expansion to counter Napoleon's North American dreams.

The Wily Corsican

The threats of internal dissention and international intrigue to the young republic that undergirded the Federalist response to the Burr conspiracy took on a new urgency due to popular renderings of Bonaparte in the American press. The first best-selling Bonaparte book in the United States was *A Secret History of the Court and Cabinet of St. Cloud*, which was already on its fourth printing in the United States by 1807. This lengthy work purported to be a series of letters written in 1805 from a "gentleman" in Paris to his confident in London. Many of the anecdotes contained in the book found their way into the daily papers. The book portrayed the "wily Corsican" and his cronies as petty, cruel, conniving, self-serving, amateur aristocrats who did not play by the accepted rules of international diplomacy. Instead, the Bonapartist regime relied on subterfuge and illegitimate force to achieve their foreign policy ends. Interestingly, the American-printed 1807 version of the book included a series of miscellaneous sketches at the end, one of which—the sketch of Swiss folk heroine Martha Glar—undoubtedly interested American readers a great deal as it included a direct warning to the people of the United States.[21]

In the first sentence, the Martha Glar sketch emphasized to Americans that the conquest of the "virtuous, peaceful, and happy little Republic of Switzerland" had been accomplished by the "intrigues . . . more than by the arms of France." What followed was a dismal tale of "horrid outrages" perpetrated by the French and their treacherous collaborators on the poor people of Switzerland and the tragic death of Martha Glar. In 1797, the patriotic speech of this sixty-four-year-old grandmother had roused the peasants of her village to resist the French invasion of republican Switzerland. Stirred by her call to arms, men, women, and children marched out to defend their homes, but after fighting valiantly most were butchered by the French army at the battle of Frauenbrun. Among the dead numbered Glar herself, her husband, her father, two of her sons, both of her daughters, her brother, and three of her granddaughters. Such stories of desperate female martial valor in defense of freedom easily recalled to the American mind the Revolutionary War images of Molly Corbin and Jane McCrea, and Glar's story tapped into an already established trope of American popular culture.[22]

The author saved his most important point for last. The sketch ended with words of warning to his American audience. "May the sad fate of the simple, virtuous, and unoffending Swiss republics," the author wrote, "be a solemn warning to all other states and kingdoms." They must be ever on guard against the "perfidious machinations of the French." In case the point was not clear enough, however, the author continued. It was inevitable that "the free, happy, and prosperous republic of the United States of America, shall ... in the course of a very short time, be exposed to the threats of Gallic tyranny." The author feared it might already be too late for Americans to open their eyes to the dangers of French duplicity. "God grant," he prayed, "this sad prediction not be verified; God grant that we be guarded in time against French *intrigues* and *arms,* and that *at least* the present generation may not be witness to the ruin of their country."[23]

Americans heard similar words of warning against treacherous Bonapartist foreign policy from other sources. In 1807, Thomas Branagan published *Political and Theological Disquisitions on the Signs of the Times Relative to the Present Conquests of France.* Branagan's career was remarkable. Irish by birth, he worked on slave ships and as a foreman on a plantation in the British slave colony of Antigua before having a Methodist conversion experience and embracing abolitionism. With his newfound faith he moved to Philadelphia and began writing against slavery. In *Disquisitions* he found a way to yoke his favorite subject to the looming threat of Bonaparte.[24]

Branagan started his book by warning Americans that the dangers to the republic came in two interconnected forms. First were internal threats, which he defined as "domestic factions, foreign spies, and at least 900,000 mortal enemies who are continually gnawing the vitals of the body politic." By the last, he meant the enslaved portion of the United States who might very well rise in revolt if given the opportunity by a treacherous foreign power such as Bonaparte. After the chaos and violence of the successful slave revolt against the French in Saint-Domingue, American enslavers were already on edge about what might happen if their own slaves rose up against them. The idea that Napoleon might actually encourage such indiscriminate violence was carefully calculated to illustrate how treacherous and opportunistic the emperor could be. The second threat was the large number of French emigrants who, according to Branagan, secretly maintained their allegiance to Bonaparte—not unlike the "French" inhabitants of Louisiana. He expected that unless Americans realized these dangers quickly, it would only be a matter of time before Bonaparte's agents raised a fifth-column element in the United States made up of French immigrants, domestic "partizans" of Napoleon, and rebellious slaves. Once that was done, Bonaparte's crack troops could easily complete what the "secret artifice and intrigue" of his agents had started.[25]

Lest Americans think this an unrealistic scenario, Branagan reminded his countrymen of the fates of Europe. "What was it that ruined Switzerland?"

he asked, "I answer French diplomatic artifice." "What annihilated the Batavian Republic?" he continued, "I answer French fraternizing violence." Furthermore, he warned, there was no reason to think that Napoleon would be content with his European empire. "The quibbling policy of the court and cabinet of St. Cloud respecting the boundary of Louisiana," he pointed out, "should be sufficient evidence of the hostile intentions of France." "Be assured," said Branagan, it was ultimately Bonaparte who was "at the bottom" of the Spanish "insolence" on the West Florida issue as well as the Burr conspiracy. For Branagan, these events showed clearly that Bonaparte was preparing the North American continent for subjection into his empire. The trope of Bonaparte as the wily Corsican in the popular press gave increasing legitimacy to the Federalist charge that he continued to harbor ambitious designs in North America that could only be ignored at the peril of the United States.[26]

The Spanish Usurpation

American concerns about Napoleonic intrigue in foreign policy gained additional momentum after Bonaparte ousted the Bourbon monarchy of his ally Spain in mid-1808. This was of particular importance to Americans since it was an action that provided Napoleon the potential to reassert claims to a North American empire. Napoleon had been justifiably suspicious of his Spanish ally after Spanish officials considered joining Prussia against the French in the Fourth Coalition of 1806. The catastrophic Prussian defeat at Jena-Auerstaedt convinced the Spanish to reconsider their moves away from Bonaparte. The Spanish, however, continued to greatly resent their domination by France, especially after they were forced to acquiesce to the French Continental System, which was Bonaparte's answer to the British blockade of Europe and closed all European ports to British goods in 1807.[27]

With the Spanish monarchy unable to prevent British influence in neighboring Portugal, Napoleon sent almost one hundred thousand French troops into Spain to assist. This move proved extremely unpopular with the Spanish people and led to a military coup that forced the abdication of the ailing Charles IV in favor of his son. The older Bourbon monarch appealed to Bonaparte to act as an arbiter in the dynastic dispute. Always the opportunist, Napoleon forced both father and son to cede their throne to Bonaparte's brother Joseph in March 1808. Within months, however, a nationalist Spanish resistance movement developed in the rural areas and set up an opposition government loyal to the Bourbons. The country descended into a brutal guerilla war that hamstrung Napoleon for the remainder of his time in power.[28]

Americans watched events in Spain very closely, and it seemed to play directly into the notions of Bonaparte that the popular press had been fomenting since at least 1805. Many, especially Federalists, applied the events of Spain to their own nation. When they connected the usurpation of the Spanish throne to the popular perceptions of Bonaparte in the media, the result was something like what appeared in the *North American and Mercantile Advertiser* in September 1808. In this letter to the editor, "A Ploughman" wrote that he had fallen asleep while reading reports of the brutal French occupation of Spain and had a dream. In this dream, "a little Frenchman" stood before him and handed him a copy of the Jeffersonian newspaper *The Aurora*, which contained a series of eleven edicts that mirrored French policies in Spain. Among other draconian policies, the edicts named his imperial majesty Joseph Bonaparte "King of the Continent of North America," forbade prints of Washington and Hamilton, and threatened to shoot those who kept weapons in their homes or gathered in groups of more than eight. Children, at least, could gather in groups of up to twelve.[29]

Dreams were particularly important to Americans of the early republic. Often, they saw them as portents of things to come. This was true on an individual level, as when relatives would write to loved ones worrying about their health after seeing a coffin in a dream, but it was also true on the national level. So, it matters little if this or other dreams about Napoleonic disasters were actually dreamed. They had a cultural power that lent them legitimacy. The aspect of this dream that would have stood out the most to the nineteenth-century reader was the complicity of other Americans in these usurpations of their own liberties. After all, it was not by accident that these edicts were being issued through the Jeffersonian papers and that one of the edicts authorized William Duane, the firebrand editor of *The Aurora*, to "arrest all printers who have published aught disrespectful to the Emperor and see that their bodies are pierced and stung on a pole." Conspiratorial stories of Napoleon's imperial treachery in Switzerland, Holland, and Spain created a volatile environment of suspicion in American politics perhaps only rivaled by the Red Scares of the twentieth century and forced Americans to reconsider their own place and role in the world.[30]

The portrayal of Bonaparte's perfidious and violent means of expansion in Europe, especially in Spain, and the seemingly very real threat of his subterfuge undermining the American republic reinvigorated a belief that foreign empires—especially that of Bonaparte—on the North American continent were dangerous to American national security. How to react to these threats, though, provoked debate, even among political allies. These themes played an increasingly important role as Americans considered the ramifications of the overthrow of the Bourbon monarchy in Spain to the persistent problem of Florida.

Bonaparte and the West

Even before it was clear that Bonaparte would overthrow the Bourbons in Spain, rumors flew about how the decaying situation in the Iberian Peninsula would alter American territorial ambitions along the Gulf Coast. In what was almost a replay of the initial debates over New Orleans, some believed the national security situation was serious enough to warrant military intervention to head off Bonapartist intrigues. Others countered by arguing that taking preemptive military action would make the United States no better than Napoleon's authoritarian empire in Europe.

In late 1807 and early 1808, an extract of a letter from a well-placed source in Washington, D.C., appeared in many papers, emphasizing the seriousness of the situation facing the United States. The author reported that rumors in the "most respectable circles" claimed Bonaparte would soon issue a proclamation in which he would no longer acknowledge American shipping neutrality—a reasonably accurate explanation of Bonaparte's Milan Decree. Furthermore, and less accurately, it hinted that Napoleon would guarantee the United States Canada and Nova Scotia for American entry into a war against Great Britain. The timing of this warning seemed to fit since relations between the United States and Britain were rapidly deteriorating over issues related to the maritime rights of neutral nations. In the infamous Chesapeake incident of June 1807, a British warship had fired on and then boarded an American naval vessel in search of deserters from the Royal Navy.[31]

This article touched off a brief firestorm. Federalists worried that the Jefferson administration would take the bait and plunge the United States into a military conflict with Great Britain for the misguided purposes of territorial aggrandizement. On January 5, 1808, the *Boston Repertory* published another "Dream," which described the outcome of such a conflict. In this apocalyptic dream, the author traveled to New York, but instead of finding a prosperous port, he found ships laid up, soldiers patrolling the streets, and fortifications being built along the East River. "The Genius of Bonaparte prevailed," wailed the dreamer. "His imperial fiat: his imperious command, have been heard . . . and his voice was obeyed in terror on our shores." The author cursed his "deluded leaders" for their ambition and warned his fellow countrymen. "Think not . . . that the wily Corsican will better keep his word with you than with the exhausted Republic of Holland," he warned. "Think not that you will be left peaceably to occupy the provinces of Canada or Nova Scotia when conquered by your allied forces . . . think not the mighty Bonaparte will generously yield up the boon of the Floridas." Such were the miseries, he concluded, that flowed from "an ambition of territorial aggrandizement."[32]

Other articles also warned that a conflict with Great Britain based on the territorial promises of Bonaparte would backfire catastrophically. An author identifying himself only as "AB" wrote an article that ran in several newspapers, including page one of the *New York Spectator*. He asked the administration if they really believed that Bonaparte would allow any nation to rival his own empire. Did they truly think that Bonaparte would actually allow the United States to "remain as it is now, ONE VAST OR RATHER BOUNDLESS STATE?" This was an interesting line of attack. In effect, AB imagined a bipolar world dominated in the west by the United States, and in the east by Napoleon. Such a world might seem reasonable to the starry-eyed Jeffersonians, but not to Bonaparte. Would the emperor, asked AB rhetorically, allow the United States "to cross in any direction, his gigantic march toward universal dominion?" The answer, was, of course, a negative one.[33]

Another gloomy take was offered by an author writing under the pseudonym "Peace." In an article that circulated in the Federalist papers of the Northeast titled "War Unnecessary and Ruinous," he decried any war against Great Britain because it would do nothing but eventually draw the United States into an unwinnable war with Napoleon. Like AB, Peace could not imagine a world in which Bonaparte could allow the United States to remain the dominant power in the Americas. There were no limits to French ambition, he wrote, and it was useless to trust in patriotic American unity in case of war against the French. Almost quoting verbatim from *A Secret History of the Court and Cabinet of St. Cloud*, he wrote, "France has done more by her intrigues than her arms," and, he reminded his readers, "are there not Burrs and Wilkinsons in our country?" "My fears for the independence of my country," he stated flatly, "are founded on the character of Bonaparte." It was the height of foolishness, he wrote, to trust any territorial promises made by the emperor. In what was becoming standard Federalist rhetoric by 1808, he asked, "where are the nations who have negotiated with Bonaparte . . . and what has become of his guarantees?"[34]

Peace then questioned the entire idea of expansion from a national security standpoint. "As to possessing Canada and the Floridas—of what use would they be to us—of what use is Louisiana to us, unless to hatch treasons." Canada was a country of Frenchmen, he continued, echoing arguments made about the population of Louisiana five years earlier, "and Frenchmen are always Frenchmen." With the British defeated using American help, what then? With both Canada and Louisiana full of French sympathizers, the United States would be hemmed in territorially and fall easy prey to Bonaparte's treachery. "I tremble for the independence of my country," he concluded, "when it must rest on the faith or humanity of a conqueror." These authors questioned the entire notion of American imperial expansion that required trust in the good will of a treacherous Napoleon and inserted the United States into areas that were ultimately "French." This rhetoric provided the framework for Federalist opposition to the War of 1812.[35]

Federalists who breathed a sigh of relief when the Jefferson administration did not actually plunge the United States into an ill-conceived war for Napoleon in 1808 still could not escape two uncomfortable and interrelated facts. The first was that the decaying Spanish empire—nominally under the control of Joseph Bonaparte—still laid claim to large swaths of the Americas including both of the Floridas as well as Mexico and Cuba. Under the Bourbons, Spain had continued to dispute the validity of the entire Louisiana Purchase. No one in the United States was quite sure whether a Bonaparte on the throne would change that policy. Second, despite the United States spending $15 million and nearly going to war to prevent Napoleon from becoming its western neighbor in 1803, there was once again a Bonaparte on their borders. As one Federalist newspaper editor groaned forlornly, "Thus ends the miserable policy of attempting to attain security by purchasing the ground that a suspecting and meddlesome tenant might occupy." Another lamented, "Has not Bonaparte one foot in Spain, and another in South America? Are not East and West Florida his own? Let him but raise a standard there and we shall soon see, furnished from our own bowels, thirty thousand men glittering in arms."[36]

As they had in 1803, many Federalists called for an immediate military solution to the Florida problem posed by Bonaparte's designs in North America. "If Napoleon obtains a footing on this continent we are undone," stated one in an article in the *American Citizen*. The Floridas, the author believed, would probably fall "under the dominion of the grand despot," Bonaparte. Yet, the author wrote, almost petulantly, "They should *belong to us.*" "They must be purchased or conquered," he declared, for it seemed inconceivable that Napoleon would part with a colony with which he could exert such great influence on the United States. There was but one alternative, he concluded: "We must *take* them." Fortunately, the author reasoned, "very little fighting will be necessary." Without a navy, he argued, Napoleon was, for the present at least, unable to oppose the designs United States in the Americas. Thus, when the moment for action came, Americans had an excellent chance to defy Bonaparte if Americans remained "faithful to ourselves, faithful to our interest [and] faithful to our safety."[37]

Other Americans—mostly Jeffersonians—looked with cynical satisfaction on the Napoleonic usurpation of the Bourbon monarchy as finally marking an end to the political fiction that Spain was actually in control of its own foreign policy. For example, in July 1808, an editorial in *The Monitor* stated that the United States had little to fear from a Bonaparte on the throne of Spain. Indeed, the editorial argued that it had the potential to be an excellent real estate opportunity for the nation. Like Louisiana in 1803, reasoned the author, Florida was little more than a target for the Royal Navy, and thus Napoleon would likely be interested in divesting himself of the vulnerable property as soon as possible. The article ended with cynical optimism. At least there would now be no more "baffling responses from Madrid to Paris and Paris to Madrid, but the avowed and responsible authority will be found in the person of Bonaparte." This fact, the author concluded, "will certainly be an advantage to all nations." Enough Americans seemed to agree with this sentiment for a Federalist author in the *Newburyport Herald* to explode in rage over Jeffersonians who would rather see "every man woman and child in Spain, spitted on the bayonets of Bonaparte's war dogs, than lose their fifteen millions."[38]

Rusticus and the New World Order

Not all Federalists were such aggressive imperialists, however. With the Iberian Peninsula in chaos, nationalist rebellions against European rule began brewing in several parts of Latin America. At least a few saw the independence movements in the Spanish colonies as an opportunity to build an entirely new world order in the Americas—one that explicitly rejected the Napoleonic model of imperialism. The most eloquent and thoughtful example of this type of thinking occurred in a series of five articles first published in the Federalist-leaning *Virginia Patriot* but later printed throughout the East Coast under the pseudonym "Rusticus" during the fall of 1810, in response to a revolution that broke out in Mexico. The Rusticus articles are particularly instructive because they demonstrate an artful weaving together of the two strands of Napoleonic argument—the first that reacted to the real danger to national security posed by Bonaparte and the second that used Napoleon's violent and immoral example as America's imperial measuring stick.[39]

Rusticus began his series of articles by acknowledging that Bonaparte's ruthless imperialism had reshaped Europe in his favor. Yet, he continued, Napoleon's usurpation of the Spanish crown had also led to the rise of independence movements in Spain's American colonies. It thus appeared that vigorous new nations would rise from the ruins of the Spanish empire. This was, Rusticus wrote, of paramount interest to the United States as it would give the nation "formidable neighbors who will be able to manage their own affairs." "The Atlantic," he wrote, "will no longer roll between the U. States and the mighty potentates of the earth. They will border upon us to a great extent and touch us at points particularly vulnerable." Unlike most Americans, Rusticus believed that the Western Hemisphere would not be a monopolar world dominated by the United States.[40]

Rusticus tried to explain how he believed the United States ought to react to this new, multipolar geopolitical reality in the Americas. According to Rusticus, there were two outstanding issues that needed to be resolved to preserve the economic and political security of the United States in this new world order. First was American acquisition of the Floridas, which would provide settlers in Alabama and Mississippi the water routes they needed for the transportation of goods to Mobile and the Gulf of Mexico. Possessing Florida would also prevent these same settlers from being influenced by "powers"—obviously he had only one in mind—hostile to the United States. The second issue was the frustratingly vague boundary between the United States and Mexico, which would, he wrote, cause no end to enmity between the two nations once Mexico became a "distinct power." Resolving these disputes without "employing the sword" would undoubtedly be a difficult proposition that would "take a great deal of moderation and of mutual good will," according to Rusticus. Making things even more difficult was the dubious circumstances by which the United States had acquired Louisiana. As Rusticus pointed out, these borders had been deliberately calculated by Bonaparte to "make impressions unfavorable to that friendship which it is in the interest of neighbors to cultivate with each other."[41]

With the groundwork laid, Rusticus moved into the heart of his argument. In doing so, he compared American imperial conduct directly to the image of Bonaparte. French imperial methods, he wrote, were those of an "ambitious despot." According to Rusticus, Bonaparte's expansion came through "sinning against heaven and earth . . . violating the most sacred laws divine and human, [and] betraying friends who trusted implicitly in him." In his usurpation of the Spanish throne, Rusticus wrote, Bonaparte had "robbed an ancient and high minded people of their sovereignty, and on atrocious deeds founds his whole claim to dominions over their American brethren." Yet, Rusticus continued, "the right given by force and fraud can only be coextensive with the means which gave it." In other words, expansion done through deceit and unlawful force could only be maintained though the same means. Rusticus thus maintained that it would be near impossible for Bonaparte to maintain his grasp on the distant American colonies because his rule could only be enforced directly through coercion and deceit.[42]

So much for the cruel and treacherous expansion along the Napoleonic model. If Americans persisted in using those same methods to expand their own empire, warned Rusticus, it could only lead to endemic warfare and political instability in the Americas. "The Floridas may be seized," Rusticus admitted, "under various pretexts." But obtaining this critical piece of territory through "force or intrigue would make a deep and lasting impact on Spanish America"—a clear reference to Bonaparte's actions in Europe. "A generous mind," he went on, "cannot view without extreme disgust a nation boasting its justice and moderation and liberty lying in wait for the distress of its neighbors and seizing the moment when they are struggling for existence . . . to wrest or seduce from them an extremely valuable portion of their territory." Put simply, if the United States were to expand through Napoleonic means, it would set the stage for perpetual animosity and war in the Americas.[43]

On the other hand, said Rusticus, if the United States considered the "abstract right" and the "great, unalterable principles of justice" in their imperial policy, it would set the conditions for a permanent friendship with the newly formed governments of the Americas. In his final article, Rusticus explained explicitly how to apply these principles of just expansion to the situation facing the United States. First, the nation had to support these nascent colonial independence movements to prevent Bonaparte from making good his imperial claims on Florida and Mexico. Second, to ensure perpetual friendship among the new empires emerging in the Americas, the United States should give up the half of Louisiana west of the Mississippi to an independent Mexico in return for the Floridas. Mexico resented the loss of its northern territories, he explained, and these territories were full of strange peoples who could never be really assimilated into the United States, and the vague boundaries would invariably cause problems between the two nations. Florida, on the other hand, was a knife poised at the heart of the United States, but it was disconnected from and therefore useless to Mexico. Ultimately, claimed Rusticus, this territorial trade would have the happy benefit of divesting each nation of "a territory of no value to the owner, but of immediate importance to the opposite party." Just as important, it would set a tone of cooperation and peace in the Americas. For Rusticus, then, peace in North America could only come from a deliberate and rational retreat from the imperial methods of Bonaparte.[44]

Rusticus's radical new world vision demonstrated both continuity and change in the American discourse of imperialism. On the one hand, he built on long-standing assumptions about Bonaparte's political character. Rusticus took it as an article of faith that America's security and independence were predicated on keeping Napoleon's dangerous influence off the continent. Like Charles Brockden Brown during the Mississippi Crisis, Rusticus rejected earlier notations of natural borders based on self-evident geographic features and insisted that imperial boundaries were made by governments. Frontiers, then, could be irrational—such as those deceitfully and violently created by Napoleon. Irrational boundaries were dangerous and bred conflict by upsetting the balance of power between empires. Here he harkened back to the worldview held by Vattel. Where Rusticus deviated most radically from earlier American discourse on expansion was in his response to these irrational imperial boundaries. Rusticus argued that American national security was actually predicated on a rational retreat from empire and a rejection of defensive imperialism. He wanted the United States to be the anti-Bonaparte and establish a balance of power between states in the Americas. In this way, he artfully combined both Napoleon the negative imperial example with Napoleon the deceitful and dangerous political actor into a grand vision for the future of the Americas. Even as Rusticus was writing, however, events in Florida were spiraling out of control due to factors that neither Napoleon nor the Americans had considered.

The Acquisition of (Some of) Florida

In the flurry of ideas flying through the press about national security and expansion, few Americans apparently considered that the West Floridians might have something to say about their own future. After the failed rebellions of 1804 and 1805, three factions gradually developed in West Florida. At least initially, the largest faction comprised those settlers who were content with laissez-faire Spanish rule and those who owed their land grants and positions of authority to the imperial government. Another, smaller group made up of mostly immigrants from the United States supported American annexation of the territory as a separate state, and a third faction sought to set up an independent republic of West Florida. As in other places in the Spanish empire, Napoleon's overthrow of the monarchy in Spain and crumbling authority of the Spanish governor, however, led to the fatal weakening of the loyalist faction and caused the Floridian populations concentrated around Baton Rouge, Mobile, and Pensacola to reconsider their future.[45]

Taking advantage of the situation, pro-independence residents of the four parishes west of the Perdido River (the coastal "tails" of what are now Mississippi and Alabama) called for a convention in late July 1810. The convention delegates carefully avoided any overt talk of rebellion but drafted a document pledging nominal support for Bourbon Spain and offering to "assist" the governor by taking over most of his executive duties. This was a thinly veiled attempt at home rule, but with only twenty-eight Spanish soldiers at his disposal, the governor had little choice but to cooperate with the convention. Quietly, though, the governor attempted to send secret messages to Spanish officials in Pensacola requesting aid to reestablish his authority. Learning that messages had been sent and fearing harsh reprisals, the convention delegates deposed the governor as "unworthy of their confidence" and quickly mustered a force of pro-independence militia. This force easily overran the tiny Spanish garrison at Baton Rouge on September 23, 1810, and the convention declared the Republic of West Florida an independent nation shortly thereafter. On October 10, officials of the newly independent Republic of West Florida warned that their sovereignty was threatened by the "partizans" of Bonaparte and formally requested admittance to the United States.[46]

The request of West Florida to join the union created something of a foreign policy crisis in the Madison administration. Madison could not simply recognize the independent West Florida government, even to accept it into the union, without effectively renouncing the American claim that West Florida had been bought and paid for with the original Louisiana Purchase. This would also allow both Bourbon and Napoleonic Spain to legitimately claim West Florida as a rebellious province and view any American interference there as an act of war. The British might also view any American meddling with West Florida as an attack on their new Spanish ally. There were already reports that runaway slaves and Indigenous peoples were being stirred up by Spanish agents along the border with East Florida. It would be all too easy for the British navy to step in on behalf of their ally in the name of restoring order to the chaotic situation.[47]

With these factors in mind, Madison moved quickly and attempted to thread the needle of foreign diplomacy. Without waiting for Congress to reconvene in December, Madison decided to simply ignore the West Florida government altogether so as not to jeopardize American claims to the area. Instead, in a carefully worded proclamation on October 27, he announced that the United States would occupy the region pursuant to the title conferred by the Louisiana Purchase in order to preserve the "tranquility and security of our adjoining territories." In separate instructions, Madison ordered the governor of the Orleans Territory, William Claiborne, to immediately incorporate West Florida into his own jurisdiction and authorized him to use the army, navy gunboats, and militia from Louisiana and Mississippi to quell any resistance from the government of West Florida. Even though most inhabitants of the area did hope to become part of the United States, they wanted to do it as an independent state, and many resented the heavy-handed methods of the American government. Despite some initial protests and threats to resist an American invasion, however, it was abundantly clear that Claiborne had overwhelming military force at his disposal. After seventy-four days as an independent republic, the nation of West Florida quietly fell under the jurisdiction of the United States at the point of a bayonet. Even this occupation did not entirely solve the Florida issue, however. The key population centers of Mobile and Pensacola remained under Spanish control, as did the rest of the Florida Peninsula.[48]

Allies of Napoleon?

Federalist newspapers were apoplectic at Madison's handling of the West Florida affair and vented their rage through the Napoleonic rhetoric that was already second nature to them. As they had learned in the 1806 crisis over Florida with Jefferson, the most effective attacks were those that made out the expansionists as willing accomplices of a dangerous Napoleonic regime. However, Madison and his allies proved cleverer than Jefferson in responding to such attacks and managed to paint the opposition as hypocritical and petty by turning Napoleonic rhetoric against them.

Most Federalists were probably surprised when they read about Madison's military annexation plan for West Florida, but they quickly adapted their lines of attack to correspond to the new reality. Of course, Bonaparte was still central to their rhetoric. On December 18, the *Boston Repertory* published a long discussion of the president's proclamation. *The Repertory* acknowledged that the United States had a "clear and unquestionable" title to West Florida. The means of asserting this claim, however, were very important. Perhaps with the writings of Rusticus in mind, the author asked, "Is it consistent with sound policy and the pacific professions of the United States to oust the Spaniards at the point of the bayonet?" This tact appealed to Americans who sought to claim a positive, republican imperial identity, in contrast to the authoritarian empire of Bonaparte.[49]

The author also found the timing of the territory's "forcible seizure" extremely questionable. Even though Americans had argued that Florida was part of the Louisiana Purchase for a decade, the paper pointed out, "while Spain was the ally of France, we did not dare assert our rights in arms." In 1810, however, the situation was reversed, *The Repertory* continued. Bourbon Spain was the ally of Britain, struggling for its independence against the Bonaparte regime, and it was precisely at this point that Madison chose to forcefully assert American claims in West Florida at the risk of starting a war with Great Britain. Small wonder the *Repertory* believed there was more to the policy than met the eye. Why, asked the author, had Madison suddenly become a "military man" so interested in "offending Great Britain and patriotic Spain?" For the editor of *The Repertory*, the bottom line was simple: "he serves Bonaparte." "We think it a just speculation," concluded *The Repertory* article, "that West Florida has been seized, not only with the consent of France, but with her special insistence, and is probably to be held in *secret trust* for Napoleon until the fate of Spain is decided." This interpretation of Madison's expansionist policies highlights the shift to a much darker rhetoric on the part of Federalists. In the eyes of *The Repertory*, by committing military forces to Florida, Madison was not simply acting out of foolish naivety, or reacting in fear of Bonaparte, but was actively working as an agent of French foreign policy in the Americas.[50]

Accusations of the administration's complicity with Bonaparte in foreign affairs quickly gathered steam. There had been occasional suggestions of this in earlier times, but before the West Florida revolt the debate had been in the abstract. The actual use of the army to enforce the American claims in West Florida by military fiat was so distasteful to many Federalists that it led to an unmistakable ratcheting up of this rhetoric. For example, a typical article making the rounds of the Federalist presses in early 1811 wondered if the United States was "actually and openly" taking part in Bonaparte's "unnatural war against commerce and civilization." The author warned his readers that the nation's military was now arrayed against the interests of the American people and ready "to carry the projects of the Emperor into execution." Another characteristic article in the *Federal Republican* accused the United States of being "an instrument of Bonaparte's aggrandizement."[51]

As the articles quoted above show, Federalists believed that the most damaging attack on Madison's expansionist policies in West Florida was the accusation that the United States had finally become an active participant in Napoleonic expansion—a true, servile "sister republic" to France. To understand this attack, an understanding of the early American idea of "alliances" is necessary. In the eyes of Federalists, Bonaparte's regime threatened to upend the whole Vattelian balance of power, which was held in place by a complex system of alliances designed to ensure that no single state became too powerful. Since the Treaty of Westphalia in 1648, alliances were understood by Europeans as necessary to maintain a proper international balance of power—if one state became too powerful, an alliance of others could hold it in check. Napoleon's alliances, however, perverted this system because they only reinforced his dreams of "universal monarchy." This is why *The Enquirer* of Richmond was so struck by the remaking of Europe after the French victories of 1806. *The Enquirer* marveled at the ability of Bonaparte to create new kingdoms with a snap of his fingers and then weave them into the fabric of his empire through a complex system of alliances to suit his ambitious needs. "If his success should warrant an exorbitant extension of his power," the article explained, he could then "reduce Holland, Italy, and even Wittenburg and Bavaria, into humble provinces of his empire." On the other hand, "if the situation of Europe did not favor his ambition," he could simply "consider them like the Swiss Cantons, as simply connected by alliance to his kingdom, but not subjected to his control." In this way, he did not have to actually govern another state directly; he could obtain just as satisfactory result by entangling his neighbors in webs of deceitful alliances.[52]

Thus, when Federalists accused their political opponents of making a military alliance with Bonaparte, they were no longer simply suggesting that the Jeffersonians were naively making a bad deal for a worthless piece of real estate in the west. Instead, the Federalists suggested that the Madison administration and its followers were actively scheming to pervert the basis of the entire world order. Not only were they allying with a power that sought to establish a boundless monarchy through a system of complex alliances, but they were also putting the nation's very sovereignty at risk since an alliance with the emperor would only be good so long as it suited the needs of Bonaparte. When it was within his power, the United States would be reduced to a "humble province" of the French empire, just like Holland and Switzerland.

In the wake of the furor over the annexation of West Florida, Jeffersonians fought back harder than they had done in years against Federalist attacks on their expansionists policies. Recognizing the power of Napoleonic language in mobilizing public support, they too framed their arguments using Bonaparte. On December 14, 1810, while the rest of Boston was reading biting commentaries on the administration's military occupation of Florida, the Jeffersonian readers of the *Old Colony Gazette* were treated to a front-page, seven-year retrospective on the benefits of the Louisiana Purchase. "The cession of Louisiana to the United States was an event," the article began, "the importance of which does not appear to have been duly appreciated." The article singled out one group in particular that did not seem to understand the value of Louisiana: "those whose distempered imaginations discover in every passing cloud a squadron of French balloons, with an invading army of exterminating jacobins." This, of course, was a jab at the Federalists, who always seemed too ready to believe the incredible stories they read about the duplicity of the emperor.[53]

It ought not be forgotten, the article continued, that there was, at one time, a very real threat to the United States from Bonaparte. At the very moment the Louisiana Purchase was worked out, "the terrible Napoleon was on the point of sending out a formidable expedition of French troops, for the very purpose of colonizing the country under consideration." According to the article, it was only through the shrewd diplomacy of Jefferson that the horrors of a Napoleonic colony as a neighbor had not come to pass. In case the audience had forgotten, the article was happy to remind them what the terrible consequences might have been. For this, the author reached back to America's favorite historian, David Ramsay, and quoted at length from his Charleston speech celebrating the Purchase. In particular, he highlighted the point where Ramsay argued that a French military colony would have checked the expansion of the United States or led to its dismemberment through to French economic pressure.[54]

"I think," the article concluded, "we cannot too highly applaud the wisdom of that policy . . . which so happily exempted the nation from the inconvenience and danger of a formidable and restless neighbor." Though it was cleverly disguised, the underlying message of this article was not hard to discern, given the context. The Jefferson administration had done whatever it took—including overlooking some its most cherished constitutional principles—to prevent Bonaparte from gaining an American colony. In doing so, Jefferson had saved the nation from great danger. At the end of 1810, with the prospect of Bonaparte gaining control of the Floridas, it had been vital for the Madison administration to do the same. This article neatly turned the Federalist argument on its head by using America's own historical experience with Bonaparte to justify aggressive expansion to contain Napoleonic influence in the present.[55]

Another way Jeffersonians defended Madison's actions in Florida was by attacking Federalist hypocrisy on the subject of Napoleon. On the first day of 1811, an article in the *New Hampshire Patriot* went on the offensive against what it called the "uncandid and inconsistent conduct of the Federalist faction in regard to taking possession of this territory." The editor asked his readers to recall that only five years ago, the same Federalists who now claimed Madison's actions as an act of war against a foreign power had recoiled at the prospect of paying $2 million for territory that the United States had already bought in the original Louisiana Purchase. Quoting from prominent Federalist papers, the article continued. In 1805, the Federalists had called Jefferson "cowardly" and "under fear of Napoleon," for not daring to "take possession of what was indisputably our own." These same men now claimed that Madison was acting out of "fear or love of Napoleon" for doing exactly what they had counseled before. No, the article continued, Madison's policy actually demonstrated that the imperial course of the United States would be charted in spite of Napoleon's bluster and not because of it. In the end, though, the author doubted his logic would change any minds. "Each and every thing is condemned," he complained. "The President and Congress is stigmatized and abused—one is called a 'French President,' and the other declared to be guided by the 'secret hand of Napoleon.'"[56]

In January 1811, the Jeffersonian-dominated Congress attempted to clarify the situation in Florida by passing a resolution that provided for the "temporary occupation" of West Florida, and warned Spain that it would not tolerate the transfer of the territory to any "other foreign power." It also gave the president power to "take possession of, and occupy" any parts of Spanish Florida east of the Perdido River that the "local authorities" in the area might be willing to "deliver up" to the United States or that might be threatened by a third power. When Spain still refused to give up Mobile and Pensacola, Madison attempted a more aggressive solution to the issue. Seeking to duplicate the success of the West Florida revolution, American officials quietly armed and organized a clandestine group of American-born Floridians along the Georgia border with the understanding that these "local authorities" would be more amenable to American annexation than the Spanish officials. Backed by US gunboats anchored menacingly offshore, and American soldiers never far away, the rebels—calling themselves "patriots"—quickly took Amelia Island and the town of Fernandina in March 1812. As planned, the "patriots" immediately offered to "cede" the territory to the United States. The surprised Spanish were forced south to St. Augustine. This was a new, much more aggressive form of the "natural expansion" ideology championed by the Jeffersonians.[57]

At St. Augustine, however, the rebels ran into stiff resistance, and the fighting devolved first into a stalemate and then into a nasty guerilla war. Surprisingly, a bill that would have authorized the administration to officially take possession of the land already offered to the United States by the rebels failed to pass the Jeffersonian-controlled Congress in June 1812 when northern Jeffersonians sided with Federalists. This forced Madison to reconsider his policies on the southern border. Realizing that such aggressive expansion in Florida would further exacerbate a deeply divided nation already at war with Great Britain, and stung by sectional defections within his own party, Madison officially withdrew US military support for the East Florida rebellion but insisted the withdrawal of American forces take place as "tardily" as possible to allow the rebels time to consolidate their gains. Georgia militiamen were still in Florida when, in January 1813, the Senate defeated another bill that would have authorized the use of American military force in the region. The game was up. Devoid of American support, the "patriot" rebellion collapsed. Almost as an afterthought, however, Congress authorized the administration to seize Mobile as a part of West Florida in February 1813. This was easily completed in April by forces under the command of none other than the slippery erstwhile Spanish secret agent General James Wilkinson.[58]

From Florida to Canada

Federalist anti-imperialist rhetoric extended its geographic range beyond the Gulf Coast during 1811 and the first half of 1812. Even as Federalists responded to Madison's secretive East Florida incursion, public pressure mounted for the administration to respond forcefully to the Royal Navy's impressment of American sailors on the high seas and to the covert British support for Native peoples resisting American encroachment in the west. Many Jeffersonians concluded that the only solution to this intransigence was the complete expulsion of the British from the North American continent. So, just as Bonaparte—still at war with Great Britain—laid plans to invade the Russian empire as punishment for Alexander I's noncooperation with the continental system, Americans began to debate the invasion of British Canada—a territory that had, like Louisiana, been part of the French empire until 1764. Aggressive imperial schemes on both ends of the United States led to a common language of opposition among Federalists. Combining opposition to "offensive" wars in both East Florida and Canada through the political image and moral symbolism of Bonaparte led to a coherent anti-imperial rhetoric that harshly critiqued American conduct during the War of 1812.

The best example of opposition to Madison's East Florida fiasco was an article initially published in the *Charleston Courier* and later reprinted in several other Federalist papers. It pointed out the uncomfortable moral connections between Madison's actions in Florida and Bonaparte's actions in Europe. "Madison did not pretend to have any claim of right to this territory, but urged its conquest upon the plea of mere *expediency*, to prevent it from falling into the hands of the British," the author pointed out. "This was," he continued, "precisely the reason given by Bonaparte for the conquest of Switzerland, of Holland, of Italy and the neighboring republics and his present efforts to subdue Spain and Portugal; to prevent the influence of the British in the affairs on the continent." Like Federalists commenting on the West Florida occupation the year before, the *Courier* author also found timing of American involvement suspicious. "During the time that Bonaparte was a friend and ally of Spain, and England her enemy, *expedience* never suggested to our administration that East Florida might be conquered by Great Britain." This article shows that as time went on Federalists became increasingly adept at weaving together the deep-rooted American desire to keep Bonaparte's influence out of North America, with his underhanded and immoral imperial example.[59]

As the United States drifted toward war with Great Britain in the spring of 1812, Federalists throughout the United States proved adept at retooling their Bonapartist rhetoric for the coming conflict. Given American assumptions about Bonaparte's territorial ambitions and the recent examples of American expansion in Florida, it proved relatively simple to broaden the geographic scope of their arguments. As in Florida, much early Federalist opposition to the impending war was based on the perceived danger to American sovereignty that came with entangling the United States with a treacherous military despot. Many Federalists based their arguments on a widely reprinted article from the Bonapartist mouthpiece, *Le Montieur*. According to this article, the emperor had announced, "In India, in America, in the Mediterranean, *everything that is and has been French shall always be so. Conquered by the enemy, by the vicissitudes of war, they shall return into the empire by the other events of the war, or by the stipulations of the peace.*" This supposed proclamation sent alarm bells off in the heads of Federalists for whom it recalled Napoleon's insistence on the fuzzy and irrational "ancient limits" of France during the Mississippi Crisis a decade before.[60]

One article that used this declaration began its life in the *Connecticut Current* and was printed as far south as the *Alexandria Daily Gazette*. In the first part of the article, the author tied American territorial ambitions in Florida to the new proclamation from the emperor. "West Florida as far as the Perdido River, was owned and occupied by the French," he reminded his readers. To make matters worse, he pointed out, the American government had "employed some very extraordinary measures" to conquer it. This, of course, recalled the warnings of Rusticus about immoral territorial expansion. Ultimately, however, whether Americans had "got it by purchase, or by the sword," he wrote, "Bonaparte declares that it will be his at last." Therefore, the author concluded, tying American imperial policy to the character of Napoleon was a highly dangerous prospect.[61]

From there, the author connected his concerns over American intervention in Florida into his opposition to a war with Great Britain—demonstrating the expanding geographic range of American anti-imperialism. "Nova Scotia and Canada were owned by the French," he explained, and "now . . . there is a plan afoot for conquering Canada." This was too much for the author. "Is not," he asked, "'the hand of Bonaparte' in this thing?" Knowing the difficulty of a cross-ocean invasion, the author surmised, Napoleon intended to make the United States a tool of his own imperial aggrandizement. Yet, it went even deeper than that. "Over and above all this," the author reminded his readers, "a very large part of the United States has been heretofore claimed by France." Ultimately, he wrote, Bonaparte's imperial dream included the entire western half of the North American continent as well as Florida and Canada, and an ill-advised war with Great Britain would only help the treacherous Bonaparte realize his immoral dream of "universal monarchy."[62]

While the author of the *Connecticut Current* article tactfully refrained from describing American imperial policy as an alliance with Bonaparte, a prolific writer calling himself "Nestor" was perfectly willing to draw that connection for his readers. In one article, he reported that he had been accused of using imprecise language by suggesting that the relationship between the United States and France was one of alliance. He shrugged off such concerns. "I presume that I was correct in using the term alliance, for though we may, in pure finesse, abstain from signing a formal treaty offensive and defense, our conduct will include all the necessary parts of the treaty." "I presume," he continued with thinly veiled snark, "that no instance will be produced of two nations aiding one another by making war on a third nation without being called allies."[63]

Nestor was a prolific writer, and all together he penned five articles castigating the Madison administration's foreign policy. In one article, he combined a decade's worth of Federalist arguments against imperialism and turned them into a case against a war with Great Britain. He built on already existing Federalist fears about Bonaparte's usurpation of the Spanish monarchy by warning that the Iberian Peninsula was only the emperor's means to a sprawling overseas empire. Nestor accused the United States of playing an "auxiliary" to Bonaparte's imperial dream since war with Great Britain would force that country to divert troops from Spain to Canada and Nova Scotia. Britain would soon be brought to the bargaining table. Yet, Nestor continued, the Spanish empire was only the start of Bonaparte's overseas ambitions. He would claim "Maurilius, Bourbon, the Cape of Good Hope, Martinique, Guadalupe, Demerara, and Suriname" as having once been part of the French empire—a direct reference back to Napoleon's promise to restore France's "ancient limits."[64]

Nestor continued by explaining what this would mean for the United States. Bonaparte, he went on, "will then tend to his American provinces that were given him by Spain." Nestor then showed the expanding geography of American anti-imperialism by noting that both East and West Florida would soon have "French settlers and French garrisons." With the perfidious French in Pensacola, Nestor went on, he did not need to remind his readers "what a submissive and tractable set of people our new French citizens in New Orleans are likely to prove"—a recalling of persistent Federalist fears about the Napoleonic loyalty of the "French" inhabitants of Louisiana that had been voiced in debates over the Louisiana Purchase Treaty. "Their revolt," Nestor growled, "is absolutely certain for they know that we should not venture to reduce them by force." Nestor left his audience with a final question. Having helped Napoleon "conquer peace" through a war with

Great Britain, how long did they think it would be before he "picked a quarrel with the United States?"[65]

In this article, Nestor did not so much innovate as connect the various anti-expansionist arguments that had emerged over the previous decade to the new context of Florida and the impending war with Britain. He did this by using American fears over Bonaparte's deposition of the Spanish monarchy and turning them into a clear concern for American national security. He deftly blended concerns about Napoleon's loose interpretation of "ancient limits," now that he held the reins of Spain, with the demographic concerns about natural boundaries that Federalists had raised a decade earlier when discussing how to assimilate the peoples of Louisiana into the American union. With Bonaparte kept out of North America, Nestor hoped that the peoples of Louisiana would eventually assimilate to American political and social norms, but with the treacherous Napoleon reintroduced to North America through his Spanish colonies or restored French colonies, it would only be a matter of time before the west devolved into chaos and bloodshed.

In only one place did Nestor innovate: his depiction of the United States as an "auxiliary" to Bonaparte. This was a deliberate choice of words, perhaps even a tweak at his detractors since Nestor had used and explained the use of the word "ally" in earlier articles. Nestor chose "auxiliary" as a classical term, which Bonaparte himself used, to denote a military force that was working with another nation's military but that was clearly subordinate to the other nation in terms of strategy and foreign policy. This was an obvious downgrade from an "ally"—a nation that at least retained its free will in foreign policy. Even this, however, was not terribly innovative. Nestor might very well have chosen the Napoleonic term with which Americans were equally familiar: "sister republic." Nestor's work was reprinted widely throughout the nation during the first half of 1812. His work was so effective because it successfully combined nearly a decade of fears about Napoleon's imperial designs and applied them to the new context of war with Great Britain.

Napoleon and the Rhetoric of 1812

By June 1812, the calls for action from the western-aligned "war hawk" wing of the Jeffersonian party had become too loud to ignore any longer, and

Madison reluctantly asked Congress for a declaration of war against Great Britain. After eighteen days of debate, Congress acceded to the president's request by the slimmest margin in American history. In a surprising twist of fate, the vote for war occurred during the same week that Napoleon launched his invasion of Russia. Though he had been able to scrape up enough votes for war, Madison was unable to unite the nation behind his foreign policy. Federalists vigorously opposed the War of 1812, using the anti-expansionist rhetoric inherited from the Florida fiasco. The inconclusive nature of the conflict during its first two years only emboldened the Federalists in their efforts to oppose what they saw as an immoral war of aggressive expansion waged on behalf of Napoleon.[66]

The war went badly from the start. Despite confident Jeffersonian assurances that with the British occupied by Napoleon, conquering Canada would be a "mere matter of marching," American invasions in 1812–13 were stymied by a surprisingly tenacious Canadian defense, American military incompetence, and the refusal of many American militiamen from Federalist regions to cross an international border and engage in an "offensive war" on behalf of a French despot. Farther west at Fort Detroit, an ill-prepared American force surrendered to a smaller British army partly because the American forces had not yet received news that war had been declared. At sea, the Royal Navy easily outmatched its undersized American foe and established a crippling blockade. About the only good news for Americans was that the British were unable to capitalize on their advantages since Napoleon still occupied their attention in Europe.[67]

Almost as soon as the war began, a familiar trope took form when Federalists questioned the very legitimacy of American military conquest through unflattering comparisons with Napoleonic imperialism. Just before the commencement of hostilities, an article in the *Poulson's American Daily Advertiser* reminded Jeffersonians that in 1802 their own papers had warned that Bonaparte's elevation to First Consul had demonstrated the importance of avoiding wars that were not "purely defensive." Yet in 1812, the article pointed out, all the Jeffersonians talked of was "foreign conquests—invading Canada, [and] taking possession of Florida." In reporting the declaration of war, the New York *Commercial Advertiser* wrote that the bill for war included a provision that allowed the president to issue a proclamation, "in the Bonapartian style, inviting the Canadians to revolt," while also providing the executive with the power to "march troops into Canada and to conquer it."⁶⁸

Heated debates over the expansion of the regular army in 1812 dripped in Bonapartist rhetoric since a professional army, unlike state militias, would undertake military campaigns beyond the national borders. One of the most powerful arguments was made by Elijah Bringham, a long-time congressman from Massachusetts. To his congressional colleagues he depicted the new army as one raised solely for aggressive imperial purposes outside the United States. What right, he asked pointedly, did the United States have to Halifax, Nova Scotia, the Canadas or East Florida? What right did the United States have to "invade and break into a foreign territory, and there establish a slaughter house for the sons of America . . . destroy cities, demolish houses and plunder the inhabitants?" He answered his own question, "There is no right but a Napoleon right, and that is power." A year later, Massachusetts governor Caleb Strong announced in a speech to the legislature that American imperial expansion in Canada and East Florida "annulled the distinction between power and right and authorizes a government and its subjects, whenever they are able, to subdue and destroy the neighboring state." "It seems," he continued, "impossible not to see the hand and realize the morals of Bonaparte marking our destinies." Strong's phrasing, "see the hand" of Bonaparte as a dangerous political actor, and "realize the morals" of Bonaparte as a treacherous imperial example, is an elegant demonstration of how, by 1812, the two strands of anti-imperial rhetoric based on Napoleon were woven together.⁶⁹

The Bonapartist rhetoric had an impact on at least the Federalist population of the United States. In New England, public denunciations of the war reverted back to the same arguments they had heard from their political leaders for over a decade. In the "Providence Resolves," published in the *Newport Mercury* in April 1811, Federalists of Rhode Island asked their fellow countrymen if they were willing to see their sons drafted "like French conscripts" and engage in a war on behalf of "Bonaparte, who has destroyed the liberties and subjected every Republic on the Continent of Europe; witness Holland, Switzerland, Venice, Lucca, Genoa, whose citizens like Slaves, are exercised under the iron rod of Bonaparte." The resolves warned that support for the war would end with American citizens "reduced to the same state." The men of Essex County in Massachusetts also publicly tied the war to Bonaparte. They ascribed all the boundary disputes of the United States to the "intrigues of France" and accused the administration of conducting an ill-conceived war at the behest of a French regime that would immediately demand the cession of Canada, Louisiana, and Florida at the conclusion of hostilies.[70]

In 1814, the already dim American fortunes took a further turn for the worse when the British were finally able concentrate their forces in North America and take the offensive in the American theater. The British raided the Chesapeake, easily brushed aside American resistance, and burned the national capital. Only a stubborn defense of Baltimore forced the British to withdraw from the region. Farther south, the British assembled a large invasion force in the Caribbean for the purpose of conquering New Orleans and the Gulf Coast. Opposing them was a handful of regular army troops, western militiamen, free men of color, American Indians, and even a motley crew of bayou pirates, all under the command of Major General Andrew Jackson. Few Americans were confident that such a force could repel the impending British invasion. An American defeat would have important imperial implications. If the British took and held in New Orleans, it seemed unlikely that the United States would be able to justify holding on to their western empire at ongoing peace negations in Ghent. Americans watched and waited for news of Bonaparte, and for news of Jackson.[71]

Federalists at Floodtide

As the fate of the western American empire hung in the balance around New Orleans, Federalists displayed remarkable unity as they opposed imperial expansion. Their fight against aggressive Jeffersonian imperialism in Florida provided them a common language and a common yardstick with which to oppose expansion. Napoleon's duplicitous treatment of his "sister republics" and his usurpation of the Spanish monarchy in the years following the Louisiana Purchase led to a reshaping of the American imperial identity. Expansionists, both Federalists and Jeffersonians, justified aggressive American imperialism along the Gulf Coast by portraying Bonaparte's own imperial aspirations as an imminent threat to the national security of the United States. Simultaneously, however, anti-expansionists were able to use Napoleon's violent and rapacious imperial image to question the entire nature of American expansion. Both of these factors came together for

Federalists during the War of 1812. They opposed American imperialism both for its Bonaparte-like qualities and for fear of what a de facto alliance with Bonaparte would mean for American national security in the future. What Americans did not, and could not know, however, was that Bonaparte's days on the throne of France were drawing to a close. Their imperial identity would take on a dramatically new shape once the French emperor was no longer a threat to their own imperial ambitions.

4

Democracy

Waterloo to Andrew Jackson

The people of Austerlitz—a tiny hamlet in Columbia County, New York, have an intriguing origin story. According to a local legend, which was later recorded in the official county history, when the town was first incorporated in 1819, Martin Van Buren was a state senator and "an ardent admirer of the great Napoleon." Apparently, Senator Van Buren was rather incensed when one of his political opponents succeeded in having a town in Seneca County, which Van Buren represented, christened "Waterloo"—after Napoleon's greatest defeat. In response to this perceived insult, Van Buren successfully moved to have the new town in his rival's district named "Austerlitz"—after Napoleon's greatest victory. Having carried his motion, the future president supposedly returned to his seat muttering pointedly to his opponent, "There's an Austerlitz for your Waterloo." Like many local stories, this one is difficult to corroborate. Martin Van Buren was indeed a state senator in 1819, and he apparently was known as a Napoleon aficionado, since, in 1820, a political rival ridiculed Van Buren for allegedly dropping a letter from the Dutch spelling of his first name, in "ridiculous imitation of Bonaparte." Sadly, the records of the New York State Assembly do not record such sidebar conversations, and most of the records prior to 1910 were lost in an archives fire in 1911. Nevertheless, the competing ideas of Napoleon that are at the heart of this story do have a basis in reality.[1]

The quarter century between the Battle of Waterloo in 1815 and the end of Andrew Jackson's presidency in 1837 witnessed a remarkable shift in the American understanding of Bonaparte and, with it, the American imperial identity. With Bonaparte no longer a threat to national security or to expansion after the Battle of Waterloo, the American discourse of empire returned to debating the moral character of the imperial republic and, increasingly, the moral character of those who created it. However, after Bonaparte's death in 1821, a flood of Napoleon-themed printed material found its way into American bookshops and libraries, where it was lapped up by an eager reading public. These biographies, memoirs, and anecdote books tended to be written by authors who found much to admire about Napoleon, and they refashioned Bonaparte into an iron-willed yet egalitarian and democratic hero whose empire had spread the blessings of liberal democracy through a Europe held in bondage by the *ancien régime*. As this reimaging occurred, the United States was undergoing its own process of democratization and a mass reorientation of civic values. The results were stunning. For most Americans by the end of the 1830s, Napoleon had come to embody positive, democratic character traits and habits of empire that the United States ought to emulate rather than to eschew. This reorientation of imperial values set into motion a rhetorical battle over the meaning of Bonaparte and the American empire that would not be resolved until the end of the Mexican-American War in 1848.

Shifting Images of Napoleon

Between 1803 and 1814, the strongest arguments in the American discourse of expansion had centered either on the unacceptable national security risk posed by the French emperor or on his violent and rapacious imperial image. Imperialists had justified aggressive expansion in Louisiana and Florida to prevent Napoleon's influence in North America, while others opposed such moves because they might draw the United States into a dangerous diplomatic relationship with the wily Corsican. Anti-imperialists argued against expansion by linking American imperial methods to those used by Bonaparte, and imperialists countered by pointing out how the American empire was the antithesis of Bonaparte's. This rhetoric was possible due to a common American understanding of Napoleon's imperial image. Whether they supported imperial expansion or not, Americans agreed that Napoleon's empire was that of a treacherous, rapacious despot and that his imperial ambitions represented a real danger to the United States.

As discussed, while initial reaction to Bonaparte was mixed when Americans first became aware of the republican general in the 1790s, once

Bonaparte showed an interest in re-creating France's North American empire and then crowned himself emperor in 1804, most of his overt support in the United States evaporated. The threat of the ambitious, treacherous, military despot replaced the image of the courageous, republican, military genius. A few public supporters of Bonaparte could still be found within the United States, of course. In the August 14, 1809, edition of Boston's *Independent Chronicle*, for example, one writer cautiously suggested that Bonaparte's breaking of the European monarchies had been beneficial for oppressed peoples in Hungry and Poland, and that he had always retained a "pacific disposition" toward the United States. Such opinions, however, were quickly targeted by vicious counter articles. One response directed at the *Chronicle* author quoted above decried those American "jacobins" who excused Napoleon for the innocent "blood which he has poured in torrents over the continent of Europe." In such a climate, wise Americans kept any pro-Bonaparte thoughts to themselves.[2]

This common American understanding of Bonaparte, however, began to fall apart during the second decade of the nineteenth century. The biggest reason for this was that Bonaparte could no longer be portrayed as a legitimate national security threat to the United States. In June 1812—on the same week that the United States declared war on Great Britain—Napoleon launched a massive invasion of the Russian empire spearheaded by his Grande Armée and augmented by allies drawn from all over Europe. Despite initial French successes during the ensuing months and the capture of Moscow in September, the Russians refused to come to the bargaining table. In October, the first snows arrived. Running short of provisions and unable to secure a strategic victory, the French army began a long, dismal retreat. As James Madison won reelection in the United States, French and allied soldiers straggled west harried by hunger, cold, disease, and ruthless Russian Cossacks. Only about 110,000 of the original 685,000 men who began the campaign made it back to central Europe. Capitalizing on the disastrous loss of French men and prestige in Russia, a sixth anti-Bonaparte coalition formed in the spring of 1813. After a year of hard fighting, it eventually drove Bonaparte from the throne of France and into exile on the Mediterranean island of Elba. This seismic geopolitical shift set into motion a chain of events that allowed increasing numbers of Americans to genuinely sympathize with Napoleon instead of seeing him as a dangerous and deceitful imperialist who threatened the United States and its imperial future.[3]

At least a few Americans had begun to moderate their views of Bonaparte even before he was forced from power. In 1808, Hume Robertson, who billed himself as a former American military officer living in Paris, published a self-styled "American" account of Bonaparte's rise to power. Within the first pages of the book, Robertson warned his readers that "it must be remembered that Bonaparte assumes different characters as policy dictates." He explained what he meant: "when a General many of his actions were distinguished as being mild and humane," but, he went on, "when a Consul, he began to exercise that overbearing tyranny that power so often engenders." Finally, Robertson concluded, "when we behold him on the imperial throne and arrived at the summit of his conquering ambition we see him degenerated into a bloody tyrant." In this passage, Robertson was encouraging his readers to take an approach to Bonaparte that allowed them to admire some parts of Napoleon's career, especially those associated with his military exploits, while still seeing his political policies as violent and despotic. This separation of the civil from the military was probably a convenient one for those younger Americans who found it difficult to hide their fascination with the undeniable military skill of Bonaparte. It probably also appealed to those of the founding generation who preferred to see the career Napoleon as a morality tale that confirmed their deep-rooted suspicion that political power corrupted even the best of men.[4]

Within weeks of learning of Napoleon's exile to Elba, articles began to appear in American newspapers that marveled at Napoleon's military prowess while quietly skirting around political aspects of his reign. Examples of good American generalship were rare enough during the first few years of the War of 1812, so newspaper editors looked to France for useful comparisons. Reporting on Andrew Jackson's odd little army gathering at New Orleans, the *Baltimore Patriot and Evening Advertiser* opined that they expected to hear good news from that locale soon, since "General Jackson appears to possess that wonderful talent which rendered Bonaparte so successful, that of making good soldiers of the most incongruous material." While this was the first time that Jackson was compared to Bonaparte, it would be far from the last. In any case, Americans did not have long to wait. By the time the article appeared in late January 1815, Jackson had, in fact, already won a major victory over the British at New Orleans earlier that month.[5]

The Events of 1815

As might be expected for a war-weary public, Americans made a great deal out of this last-minute victory. Historians have often dismissed the importance of the battle, but in reality, it was the Battle of New Orleans that finally cemented American claims to Louisiana, both politically and in their minds. It is important to remember that the Spanish—a key British ally during the late Napoleonic Wars—still viewed Louisiana as having been cheated from them by Bonaparte and considered West Florida as a province in revolt. Without Jackson's victory, it was likely that the British would have successfully backed Spanish claims to Louisiana and West Florida at the bargaining table in Ghent. Ultimately, it had to be a decisive military victory that established indisputable US claims in the Spanish borderlands. The American public, however, added an additional component to the significance of the battle: they used it as an opportunity to claim a military victory over Napoleon by proxy.[6]

Despite French provocations in Louisiana and on the high seas during the first fifteen years of the nineteenth century, the United States never embroiled itself in a war with Napoleon. Americans, however, turned the victory at New Orleans into next best thing. As they commemorated their victory over the British, many transformed it into a virtual victory over Napoleon. One widely reprinted article informed its readers, "It ought also to be remembered that Jackson's troops were 'backwoods militia,' who had never before smelt gunpowder, and Packenham's were the 'choicest veterans of the Peninsula,' the conquerors of the legions of Bonaparte." A popular ditty held a similar theme,

> Ten thousand men they landed
>   as Packenham demanded!
> The hero who commanded New Orleans to destroy
>   all men of valiant heart who had *beaten Bonaparte*
> But what was that to Jackson?

Jackson's later biographers carried this theme forward into the next few decades. One set of sentences that was repeated with little variation in numerous biographies described Jackson surveying the scene from the American lines at New Orleans: "Before him was an army proud of its name and distinguished for its deeds of valor—an army, the finest that ever appeared on our shores,—one that had driven the warriors of France, the conquerors of continental Europe, from the pillars of Hercules to the Pyrenees." The article, the song, and the later biographies emphasized the British as the soldiers who had beaten the unconquerable Napoleon, and thus linked Jackson's military prowess to that of Bonaparte. The logic, then, ran as follows: if the British forces at New Orleans had bested Napoleon, and Americans had bested the British forces, then the Americans must have been more than a match for Napoleon himself.[7]

Even in exile, then, Bonaparte remained ingrained in the minds of Americans when they looked to their southern borders. Americans had almost gone to war in 1803 to prevent him from controlling New Orleans and then had seized West Florida from Spain in 1811 to prevent his influence there. It was his questionable title to Louisiana and deliberately murky boundaries that had caused over a decade of frustrating political conflict with the Spanish empire. This military victory over Bonaparte by proxy probably helped Americans accept their questionable claims to both Louisiana and West Florida. It also was the first in a series of events that year that "defanged" the dangerous Napoleon for Americans.

The European events of 1815 also allowed many Americans to make peace with some of the political aspects of Napoleon's rule when it was compared to the alternative. Following hard on the heels of the victory at New Orleans and the Treaty of Ghent, which finally ended the War of 1812, Americans learned that Napoleon had slipped off of Elba and returned to France. Americans waited breathlessly for news from Europe—no doubt cursing the slowness of the mail ships. Soon they learned that the royal French military units sent to prevent Napoleon's approach had defected and returned him to the throne in Paris. They then learned that yet another anti-Bonaparte coalition had formed and finally faced down the French at the Belgian village of Waterloo in June.[8]

Napoleon lost the battle at Waterloo, but it was not entirely clear what would happen next. Rumors abounded in the United States. Some said that Bonaparte had been arrested by his own troops and beheaded. Others reported that he had been taken prisoner by the British. Still others said that Bonaparte was attempting to flee to the United States and seek asylum. In actuality, both of the last rumors were true. Bonaparte had indeed seriously considered going into exile in the United States, as had many of his officers and family members. In the end though, Bonaparte surrendered himself to the British. The British, unsure what to do with their arch-antagonist, sent him into exile again. This time under guard and to the remote South Atlantic rock of St. Helena. Napoleon's handler was none other than Admiral Sir George Cockburn, the man whom Americans held directly responsible for the burning of Washington, DC, in 1814—a fact that elicited some sympathy for the deposed emperor from many quarters of the United States. With Napoleon gone, the victors convened the Congress of Vienna, which reestablished the balance of power in Europe and restored the Bourbons to the throne of France in the uninspiring person of Louis XVIII.[9]

Americans read about all these events with fascination, and they began to democratize and romanticize Napoleon's image. When compared to Louis XVIII, even Napoleon appeared to have democratic legitimacy. Most Americans learned of Bonaparte's return by reading the official French versions of the event that their local papers simply translated and printed. These accounts, of course, painted Napoleon's return in strikingly sympathetic and even democratic tones. For example, in the account that most Americans read, when Napoleon first encounters the royalist troops who were sent to arrest him, Bonaparte dismounts, announces himself, and tells them, "The first soldier who chooses to kill your emperor may do so." According to the article, the unanimous reaction from the soldiers was to tear the white Bourbon cockade from their caps and replace it with the Napoleonic tricolor as they cry, "Long Live the Emperor!" A few paragraphs later, the emperor returns to Paris to the wild shouts of "Down with the Bourbons! Down with the enemies of the people! Long live the Emperor and a government of our choice!"[10]

Americans could not help but notice the contrasts in democratic legitimacy between Napoleon and Louis XVIII illustrated in the Paris articles. In a letter to a friend, Andrew Jackson wrote, "The *wonderfull revolution* in France fills everybody and *nation* with astonishment." Jackson noted one part of the article in particular: "The tricoloured cockade being found in the bottom of each soldiers knapsack," he wrote, "tells to all europe that Naepoleon reigns in the affections of the soldiers that were to oppose him, and their dislike to the Bourbons." For Jackson, as well as many other Americans, the French soldiers' unanimous choice to restore Napoleon over Louis XVIII demonstrated the democratic legitimacy of Bonaparte's reign. Louis, after all, had been installed by the foreign machinations of the

FIG. 5. This 1875 engraving shows how most Americans imagined Napoleon's return from exile on Elba in 1815: a triumphant and democratic coup against the aristocratic Bourbon monarchy. (Library of Congress)

Congress of Vienna, while Napoleon at least had been elected to the post of emperor through a national plebiscite and then confirmed in this position by the army and the cheering crowds of Paris. His return to power allowed Americans to see Bonaparte not simply a king-breaker but also a man who truly reflected the democratic wishes of the French people.[11]

The second exile of Napoleon allowed Americans to juxtapose the bloody, forced restoration of the Bourbons with Bonaparte's seemingly democratic return from Elba. One example of this was an article originally published in the *Boston Gazette* titled "The 'Usurper' and the 'Legitimate.'" In the article, the author reminded his readers, "When the *sanguinary* Napoleon returned to Paris from Elba, not a single drop of blood sullied the glory of his career." Yet, the article went on, dripping with sarcasm, when the "*Legitimate* Louis" returned, supporters of the Napoleonic regime were "barbarously arraigned and most inhumanly executed." After describing one of the executions in heartrending detail, the author left his readers with little doubt which of the two—Napoleon or Louis—was the usurper, and which was the legitimate, democratic sovereign.[12]

Even Americans less inclined to read received the same message about Napoleon's democratic politics. A print originally from Britain but copied and distributed by the Philadelphia firm of William Charles in 1815 provided a humorous commentary on the chaotic nature of French politics after the Bourbon restoration. In it, a portly Louis XVIII struggles up a greased pole toward a crown symbolizing imperial legitimacy. "Support me or I shall fall" he cries. To help his endeavors, Louis stands on the backs of squabbling figures representing various foreign powers. Noticeably absent from his support are the people of France. In the background, but still prominent, is Napoleon on the rock of St. Helena carefully guarded by British cannon. Watching with a hint of amusement, the Napoleon figure comments, "I climbed up twice without any help." Whether they read the original reports of Napoleon's return from Elba or saw the commentary that followed, many Americans drew the similar conclusions: even if Napoleon was an emperor, he was at least a popular and a democratic one.[13]

Even though American attitudes about Napoleon grew increasingly sympathetic as a result of the events of 1815, his image as a treacherous imperial despot continued to hold significant rhetorical power for at least some Americans. Reeling from accusations of disloyalty stemming from their nonsupport for the War of 1812, the tattered remnants of the Federalist Party attempted to regroup partly by using the anti-Napoleon rhetoric that they had used for over a decade. A great many Americans were genuinely glad when Bonaparte was forced from power. Public gatherings, especially in the last Federalist strongholds of New England, were full of orations praising his downfall and the return of peace.

One example of this type of rhetoric took place during Napoleon's first exile in 1814, when the respected physician Charles Caldwell addressed the Washington Benevolent Society of Pennsylvania at their annual Independence Day gathering. Caldwell began with a brief account of the rise and fall of Napoleon using the trope of the bloody, treacherous tyrant. Then he discussed what he saw as the unfortunate American dealings with the emperor. During America's own revolutionary struggles, he pointed out, Spain and Holland were "sincerely attached to our interests." Yet, in the last few years, the United States had shamefully yoked itself to "him who carried carnage and mourning into both Holland and Spain." This was, of course, disgraceful, said Caldwell, but the actions that had followed were even worse. In reference to Florida, he thundered, Americans had acted "in an equal violation of magnanimity and right" to Bonaparte when they "invaded a defenseless province." This speech demonstrates an attempt at continuity in the weaving together of both strands of the Napoleonic argument that were the hallmark of the final phase of Federalist rhetoric during the War of 1812. Not only was Napoleon a dangerous political actor, but his methods of imperialism were gross violations of international and moral law.[14]

With Napoleon no longer a threat to North America, however, rhetoric portraying him as a nefarious political actor was increasingly ineffective. As desperate as they were, most Federalists were politically astute enough to realize this and made more use of Napoleon as a negative symbol of empire. They continued to point out the painful similarities between the imperial methods used by both Bonaparte and the Madison administration. A scathingly sarcastic commentary on the British-American peace talks in Ghent from the New York's *Courier, and Mercantile Directory*, shows this quite clearly. Written during the period of Bonaparte's first exile, this passage directly compared American territorial ambitions to Napoleon's imperial policies:

> The commissioners in the name of the United States, indeed, disavow all projects of aggrandizement whatsoever; and acts of theirs having a contrary appearance, are all accounted for by particular circumstances; and so were all aggrandizements of Bonaparte; it was his enemies that forced him to extend the power of France from the Rhine to the Elbe, from the Elbe to the Vistula. It was mere friendship for the royal family of Spain, that made him place his brother on the throne of that kingdom; so it was Spain that made it necessary for the United States to acquire Louisiana; it was Spain that compelled them to seize the Floridas, and Great Britain that prompted them, at an unlucky hour, to seize the Canadas.

Messages like this one condemned opportunistic, territorial expansion by comparing it to the duplicitous example of Napoleon. Even as the wars of Napoleon and the War of 1812 came to a close, Federalists in their death throes were still able to rely on a generally shared American understanding of Napoleonic imperialism as rapacious, violent, and deceitful.[15]

Surprisingly, even after the Treaty of Ghent was signed, some Federalists continued to argue stubbornly that the War of 1812 had been waged in support of French imperial dreams. For example, when one Federalist editor was told that Napoleon intended to seek asylum in the United States following his loss to the Duke of Wellington, he hoped it was true. If it was, he snidely opined, the emperor ought to be held by the government and exhibited for money until all the debts incurred by the War of 1812 had been paid off. After all, the editor reasoned, reverting to the rhetoric that had served his party so well, the Madison administration had waged the war on Napoleon's behalf. The sheer number of these arguments show that they were still judged to be useful by the Federalists—at least on the local level. Bonaparte, after all, was still living, even if in exile, and his designs on North America had not yet been forgotten, even if they no longer were a threat to the United States. This type of anti-Bonaparte diatribe probably served more as a rallying cry for the few remaining Federalists than as a true form of discourse. For the American public as a whole, such rhetoric probably looked increasingly like what it was—the dying gasp of a once great political party.[16]

Florida, Again

Between 1811 and 1813, bands of desperate Indigenous peoples on the western fringes of the United States rose up to defend their lands from encroaching American settlers. The southern theater of this conflict is known as the Creek War, and it was in this conflict that Andrew Jackson first came to the attention of the American public. Jackson's ruthless pursuit of the Creeks and their allies came to a climax at the Battle of Horseshoe Bend—a catastrophic defeat for the Indigenous resistance. The harsh Treaty of Fort Jackson, which ended the Creek War in 1814, left the Creek people divided and dispossessed of their Georgian and Alabamian homelands. Despite clauses in the Treaty of Ghent that promised to restore their territory, the defeat at New Orleans forced the British to renege on their promises to support their erstwhile Indian allies. Desperate and abandoned, many Creeks moved south into Florida, where they joined bands of Seminole Indians and formerly enslaved people who had liberated themselves by crossing into Spanish territory. Over the next few years, land pressures in the Florida borderlands led to increasingly violent tit-for-tat raids between American settlers and Seminole war bands, who used the ill-defined international border between East and West Florida as a sanctuary.[17]

In March 1818 tensions boiled over. With vague orders to protect American interests and citizens in Florida, the senior army commander in the region, Major General Andrew Jackson, launched a full-scale invasion of Spanish East Florida with nearly four thousand soldiers, militia, and friendly Creek allies, claiming that he was pursuing enemy Seminole war parties. Through a combination of bluster, ruthlessness, good fortune, skill, and Spanish unpreparedness, Jackson's army quickly overran not only most of the Seminole villages in the territory but also all of the major Spanish garrisons. So rapid and complete was the victory that the French ambassador described Jackson as the "Napoléon des bois"—Napoleon of the backwoods. During the campaign, Jackson's army captured two British nationals: Alexander George Arbuthnot, a Scottish trader, and Robert Ambrister, a former Royal Marine. Jackson accused the men of providing firearms to the Seminoles (which they probably did) and of inciting them to make war on American settlers (which they probably did not). Like Bonaparte, Jackson was never one to bother much with the international implications of his actions. He convened a military court that quickly found both men guilty and ordered them hanged.[18]

Foreign reaction to Jackson's invasion was decidedly negative. Britain vigorously protested the summary execution of its citizens. The men were unfortunate noncombatants in the wrong place at the wrong time, they said. Spain, of course, vehemently objected to the invasion and occupation of its territory. Neither country, however, was in a place to make good on its complaints. Britain did not wish to damage relations with its best trading partner and eventually let the matter drop after a suitable period of righteous indignation. Spain was more difficult. Jackson's invasion endangered ongoing negotiations between Spain and the United States over the fate of Florida. In the end, Secretary of State John Quincy Adams took advantage of the situation and issued a letter blaming the whole conflict on the British, the Seminoles, and the Spanish. The episode actually strengthened Adams's diplomatic hand in the long run. Once negotiations resumed, he demanded that Spain either control its Indian subjects in Florida or cede the territory to someone who could. With Jackson's army firmly ensconced in Florida, the Spanish reluctantly came back to the bargaining table. In the resulting Adams-Onís Treaty, the Spanish ceded East Florida to the United States in return for the United States renouncing its claims on Texas—another offshoot of the murky borders of Louisiana that would have profound consequences a few decades later. Finally, nearly two decades after the Louisiana Purchase had given the nation a tenuous claim to Florida, the United States finally had possession of the territory. Unlike Louisiana, however, which had been secured by diplomatic purchase, expansion into Florida had undeniably been the result of aggressive military expansion.[19]

Just because Jackson had avoided the international consequences of his actions did not mean that he had completely escaped punishment. He had some powerful enemies in Congress, and they refused to let an opportunity like this go to waste. In early 1819, the House Military Affairs Committee issued a report condemning Jackson's actions in Florida. Based on their recommendations, the House of Representatives readied itself to debate a series of bills that would have disavowed the aggressive expansionism of Jackson. There was no guarantee that such bills would fail. After all, on at least three previous separate occasions Congress had derailed aggressive expansion in Florida. The ensuing debate took almost a month, which, at that time, was the longest ever spent debating one issue, and was carefully followed in the papers by the American public.[20]

Despite the obvious similarities, surprisingly few of those in the anti-expansion camp took the opportunity to draw parallels between Jackson's actions and those of Bonaparte. Even the most eloquent orator in the House of Representatives, Kentucky's Henry Clay, shied away from bringing too many references to Bonaparte into his anti-Jackson speech. Born in 1777 and a lawyer and hemp plantation owner by trade, Clay spent virtually his entire adult life representing Kentucky in Congress. He rose to prominence as a leader of the so-called War Hawks during the War of 1812 who pushed for American entry into the conflict. He had built a reputation, however, for moderation in expansion and fostering good relations with the Latin American republics. When, as Speaker of the House of Representatives, he stood to address the House and a packed gallery on January 12, 1819, he knew that he was speaking to the American people and not just to his congressional colleagues. If they expected a long harangue tying Jackson's treatment of the Creeks and Seminoles to Bonaparte's treatment of Italy, Holland, Spain, Prussia, or half a dozen other places in Europe, however, they would have been greatly disappointed.[21]

While Clay did denounce the Treaty of Fort Jackson as unreasonable and found nothing in international law that could sanction Jackson's invasion of a foreign colony, he tied neither of these episodes to Bonaparte. Instead of linking Jackson to illegal national expansion through Napoleon, Clay saved his Bonaparte references for what he saw as Jackson's overly aggressive and ambitious character. Clay's strongest attack came in his condemnation of Jackson's execution of Arbuthnot and Ambrister. Jackson's best biographer, Robert Remini, characterized Clay's allusion to Bonaparte here as "subtle." It was not. Considering the executions, Clay claimed he could think of only one analogous incident, that of the arrest and execution of the Duc D'Enghein. Here, Clay referred to, and described in considerable detail, an infamous incident in which Bonaparte had an exiled French royalist seized by his military from the neutral German state of Baden, arrayed on trumped-up charges, and quickly executed. It was this incident, and, thus by implication, not Bonaparte's expansionism, that, according to Clay, "had brought more odium than almost any other incident on the unhappy Emperor of France."[22]

Napoleon appeared one other time in Clay's remarks. In this case also he was used less to contest expansion directly, and more as a warning against the character of military heroes—which, Clay pointed out, must be the result of imperial conquest. Near his conclusion, Clay warned that aggressive imperialism had the tendency to erode the liberties of free societies. Wars resulted in glory-covered heroes, and such men had a habit of swaying the democratic crowds to do their will, no matter how injurious to liberty. Of course, Clay cited Bonaparte as the obvious example of this. Nevertheless, Clay was quick to point out that he did not think Jackson to be another Napoleon. Lest anyone doubt that such things could happen in the United States, however, Clay warned that Bonaparte had proven the dangers of "military chieftains" to unwitting societies. Quoting from a popular biography of Napoleon by the indomitable Madam De Staël, Clay pointed out that well-regarded Frenchmen had insisted that they would never again see monarchy in the very month that "Bonaparte with his grenadiers had entered the palace at St. Cloud ... and laid the foundations for that vast fabric of despotism which overshadowed all Europe."[23]

Why was the usually confident Clay so cautious in his attacks on Jackson? One plausible explanation might be that the Speaker was reluctant to attack the character of a man who was notoriously quick to take offense at any perceived personal insult. After all, Jackson had already killed a man in a duel in 1806. Or it may have been the opposite. Clay may have recognized that any comparison to Napoleon might be seen by the American public as more of a personal résumé enhancement rather than a condemnation. As the imperial image of Bonaparte began to soften, Americans became increasingly comfortable with their own expansion, even when it could not be cloaked in claims of national security. The very vagueness of Clay's remarks is evidence that the rhetorical ground Bonaparte occupied was shifting. Clay felt comfortable using Napoleon as a negative political example but shied away from the next step of linking the political to the imperial except in the most ambiguous terms. In doing so, Clay laid a groundwork for a new critique of empire that was centered less on the fact of empire than on its character and on the character of those who made it.

Surprisingly, in at least a few cases, Napoleon was used by Jackson's allies in Congress. Representative Ballard Smith of Virginia spoke after Clay and used much of his lengthy speech to refute the Speaker. In the middle of his remarks, he spent what must have been several minutes discussing the ultimate justification of American expansion. "The gentleman," he began, referring to Clay, "asks what would be said to our unreasonable demands were the Treaty of Fort Jackson to be seen by the powers of Europe. And I ask who would presume to find fault with them." It certainly could not be France, he sneered, "who so recently demanded Spain, Portugal, Italy, Holland and Germany." In essence, Ballard was suggesting that Napoleon's imperialism had overturned the old Vattelian world of rationality and balances of power and replaced it with a realpolitik system in which nations could expand as far as their means and ambition could take them. This was a rather bold move by Ballard in a country where so much of the rhetoric of expansion had been built on not being like Napoleon, but it seems not to have hurt the final result. Indeed, the final result probably had more to do with pro-expansionists carefully not using Napoleon rather than through their use of him. Not only was Jackson completely exonerated by Congress, but by a vote of 42 to 112 the House refused to pass a more general bill that would have prohibited the invasion of a foreign country without the express authorization of Congress.[24]

The Great American Empire?

The shakeup of American imperial discourse after 1815 led to some older rhetorical points being put forward to justify expansion. The first of these emerged as Americans surveyed their acquisition of Florida. Even though Florida had been gained through questionable imperial methods, expansionists gloried in the aftermath of the Adams-Onís treaty. With the great geographic extent of Napoleon's empire still fresh in the minds of Americans, some expansionists revitalized rhetoric similar to that advanced in David Ramsay's 1804 valedictory on the Louisiana Purchase. As previously discussed, Ramsay had favorably compared the emerging American empire to Bonaparte's vast European one. Such rhetoric went out of fashion when Napoleon's grand imperial vision reemerged as a threat to the American vision of empire. But with Napoleon a prisoner on St. Helena, Americans saw little harm in recognizing the true scope of his imperial project. The geopolitical situation of 1819 dictated one obvious change to the basic calculus of comparison, however. Americans no longer needed to compare their own imperial growth to a growing French empire at the height of its power, but to a collapsed empire that had already run its course.

One example of this type of argument came almost as soon as news of the Florida Treaty became known. Perusing the reaction to the treaty from Europe, a triumphant editor of the *Providence Patriot* was hard pressed to contain his glee. "The gigantic schemes and comet-like progress of Bonaparte dazzled and confounded the vision [of Europe]," he wrote, "but the steady inevitable march of Columbia to unparalleled greatness arrests the attention and commands the admiration of every intelligent observer." Europe, he continued, had contrived to halt the progress of Bonaparte, but "it is in vain that the governments of the old world would strive to check the rising glory of the new." The words the editor chose were significant. Napoleon's empire was built on the fleeting "gigantic schemes" of one man, while the American empire was an inevitable march of the nation that demanded admiration. In other words, though Napoleon's empire might have been great, the rising American empire would be even greater both geographically and morally.[25]

The best example of an argument that favorably compared the American empire to the Napoleonic one was printed in 1826. In a charming article titled "Napoleon and Franklin," one author imagined a postmortem dialogue between the French emperor and that quintessential American, Benjamin Franklin. Bonaparte starts the conversation by pointing out the weakness of the American grasp on North America. "Why do you not take Mexico and Cuba?" Bonaparte asks, "And why do you let the Russians keep a foot on your continent?" Franklin patiently explains that Americans have no need to conquer such places and points out that "the peaceful possession of all the really valuable part of [Europe]" would have been more effective in fulfilling Napoleon's own ambitions. To this, Napoleon scoffs and explains that Franklin underestimates how global his ambitions truly were. He explains that, given the chance, he would have conquered all of Asia and the Americas. Considering this new information, the ever-wise Franklin doubts that such a far-flung empire built solely on one man's talents and ambition could possibly have survived his death, even if Bonaparte had not been forced from his throne prematurely.[26]

The system of expansion practiced in the United States, Franklin explains, is of a more lasting kind than that practiced by Napoleon. The Americans, Franklin says, "have founded an empire destined to be wider than the Roman," and through the "plain race" of Americans, the language of liberty has already been spread "through vast regions." Furthermore, Franklin continues, Americans have no need to impose their empire on conquered people as Bonaparte did with his "iron legions on Europe." Theirs is an empire that requires no bloody imperial conquest, says Franklin, merely "peaceful colonization and expansion." In this American empire of "peaceful, fertile and free land," concludes Franklin, there is no need for "the glory of conquerors." Even the brilliant Napoleon struggles for words to contradict the wisdom of the American sage and finally grumbles, "Enough, Doctor, this philosophizing is worse than Moscow."[27]

The heart of the Franklin piece was in the difference between imperial conquest and imperial expansion. Napoleon's empire represented the first. According to the author, Bonaparte's empire was artificially created around the will of a single individual. An empire created by conquest had to be imposed by armies and violence and, without these elements, was fleeting. Because of this fact, even an empire as great as Napoleon's could not long endure and brought only suffering to those who fell within its influence. On the other hand, the expansion of the American empire was portrayed as a natural and beneficial historical force. The American empire expanded and colonized fertile and empty western lands but never resorted to bloody conquest. Because it was not held together by violence and the glory of military heroes, it represented an enduring empire of liberty—one that that would last for generations and benefit the entire world rather than conquer it.

With Bonaparte no longer a threat to American national security or expansion, many Americans quickly began to claim a positive imperial identity that saw the United States as a benevolent republican empire. As they did, expansionists became increasingly willing to acknowledge the great scope of the Napoleonic empire, while still viewing it as an empire built on bloody conquest. Comparing their own empire to that of Bonaparte's was comforting. Their own expansion in Florida, after all, American imperialists reasoned, paled in comparison to Bonaparte's bloody, world-spanning ambitions. Bonaparte's great, but doomed, empire allowed Americans to view their own aggressive imperialism in a far better light and see themselves as architects of an empire of liberty that would soon overshadow even the most impressive empire of the age.

Democracy in America

Franklin's "meeting" with Bonaparte in the article above was made possible by the latter's death on St. Helena in 1821. Death humanized and rendered Bonaparte even more harmless in the minds of second-generation Americans, which accelerated the democratization and liberalization of his image that had begun with his exile. In one telling example of this process, the editor of the *Easton Gazette* discussed the elaborate funeral observances for Bonaparte taking place in New Orleans. For almost two decades, many Americans had suspected Louisianans as representing a dangerous fifth-column element in the United States who secretly maintained their allegiance to the French emperor. Yet, after the death of Napoleon, even such overt support for Bonaparte seemed benign, and even banal. According to the author in the *Easton Gazette*, it ought not surprise Americans that the "old French feelings still exist" in the hearts of Louisianans. Yet, he continued with a rhetorical shrug, there was as "little danger to us now in paying honors to Napoleon as there is to Nero or Caligula."[28]

Even more than his death, it was the tidal wave of Napoleon-themed printed material that appeared in the United States in the two decades after his exile that reimagined the image of Bonaparte for a new generation of Americans in a heroic and liberal mode. Newspapers were full of advertisements by booksellers for the latest biography of the French emperor. According to literary historian Scott Casper, by 1830 most American households owned a Bible, a hymnal, and a biography of Washington and

Bonaparte. Other Americans borrowed biographies of Napoleon through their burgeoning library systems. The overwhelming majority of this material painted Napoleon as a democratic emperor, full of heroic valor rather than as an ambitious, bloody tyrant. Instead of comparing the greatness of American imperialism to the underhanded methods of its Napoleonic counterpart, as had been done in earlier arguments, this new material asked readers to sympathize with and even to emulate the character of Napoleon as an empire builder.[29]

It is important to notice that this printed material did not emerge in an American vacuum. The single most important change to sweep over the United States between 1815 and 1850 was the expansion of American democracy. The social and economic changes wrought by the early industrial and market revolutions emphasized the ability, indeed the expectation, of the individual to work their way up the socioeconomic ladder through an ideology of capitalism and free labor. This system championed the choice of the individual, and choices were determined by an individual's character. Individual economic failures were thus also moral failures. At the same time, Americans were no longer producing for their neighbors in systems of local production and distribution. Instead, more and more Americans were producing crops and goods for distant markets that were prey to economic forces they usually did not fully understand. Thus, the economic gains of the industrial revolution proved to be uneven and often fleeting. The reoccurring boom-and-bust cycles of the nineteenth century led to prolonged economic uncertainty and fear of moral failure. This economic anxiety led to demands by the middling and working classes for the rapid expansion of the voting franchise, which, by 1850, had been extended to virtually all white men.[30]

The democratization of American politics led to a new two-party system that eventually replaced the old Jeffersonian-Federalist divide. Painted by Jeffersonians as treasonous for their vocal (and effective) opposition to the War of 1812, the Federalist Party had ceased to be a viable political force by 1816. For two presidential cycles, in which James Madison's successor, James Monroe, ran virtually unopposed, American political differences reflected local and sectional divisions rather than national partisan ones. However, the election of 1824 ushered in a new era of mass American party politics. This election saw four presidential contenders including John Quincy Adams and political heavyweight rivals Henry Clay and Andrew

Jackson—neither of whom had forgotten Clay's censure of Jackson in the congressional hearing on the Florida invasion. Clay finished last in the electoral vote but used his enormous clout in the House of Representatives to elevate Adams to the presidency and was duly offered the coveted post of secretary of state. Jackson's supporters called the whole affair an undemocratic "corrupt bargain," noting that the Tennessee general had garnered the most popular votes. They vowed to elect their man in 1828 and immediately began organizing. For the next quarter century, the competition between Jackson's Democratic Party and its opposition—first called National Republicans and later Whigs—defined American politics.[31]

Despite the political changes, it is vital to recall that the process of democratization in the United States was far more than simply expanding the voting rolls or the emergence of new political parties. As Andrew Burstein has noted in his work on the emotional dimensions of this era, "Over time, democratization in America became a temperament, a moral quality, a vision of progress." For most Americans, the democratization of the early nineteenth century was a vision of national improvement through the improvement of individual citizens. This new attitude of democratic progress celebrated and elevated the free economic, political, and moral choices of the individual rather than the common national good of classical republicanism. It was within this democratic vision of society that Americans read and internalized their printed materials about Bonaparte. As discussed, it was difficult, though not impossible, to paint Napoleon as a true model of political democracy; it was far easier to paint him as a model of democratic character.[32]

The Character of Bonaparte

American consumers of Napoleonic printed material during the nineteenth century could not have helped but notice the democratic character of the French emperor. The overwhelming majority of Bonaparte biographies portrayed his career as an incredible "rags-to-riches" story that highlighted his personal determination and self-construction. Almost every biography had some comment like the following one from the introduction to the popular book *Memoirs of the Military and Political Life of Napoleon Bonaparte*: "In his rise and in his career of prosperity and glory, [Bonaparte] greatly surpassed . . . the heroes of antiquity." The author went on to explain that while Alexander the Great and Julius Caesar had come from elite families and had powerful friends to assist them, "the early advancement of Bonaparte was without any such powerful aids, and at the same time more rapid." Even young American children imbibed this characterization of Bonaparte. One grammar school reader noted, "Napoleon Bonaparte was one of the greatest warriors who ever lived. He won many battles and rose, by his skill and courage from a poor Corsican boy to be an emperor, and the most powerful sovereign in Europe." Stories of this sort held a germ of truth. In reality, Bonaparte came from a minor family of provincial Corsican aristocrats who painfully felt the condescending gaze of their French social betters. These stories resonated deeply in an American society steeped in messages of self-construction. The message was clear enough for readers of all ages and conditions: Napoleon's rise was worthy of careful study in a democratic world where character and merit mattered more than birth or wealth.[33]

If Napoleon's rise was incredible, however, it was not simply a matter of chance; rather, it was a matter of his industrious character. Biographies regularly described his calm, calculating demeanor, seemingly inexhaustible energy, and attention to the tiniest of details. A passage from the very popular, five-volume set titled *The Napoleon Anecdotes* reported a well-liked story from Bonaparte's early military career that illustrates the general idea. Not long before daybreak, a friend of Bonaparte's cautiously opens his apartment door and is surprised to find the young officer fully dressed and surrounded by reports and maps. "What!" the friend exclaims, "Not yet in bed?" Napoleon scoffs and replies, "In bed? I have already risen. Two or three hours are enough for any man to sleep." Another anecdote described Bonaparte as the consummate planner. "No human precaution, which it was possible to adopt, was ever . . . neglected or forgotten by Napoleon." Napoleonic biographies were full of this type of character analysis. In the uncertain world of the market revolution, it was understood that this was the type of advice that would serve an ambitious young American clerk just as well as the future emperor of France.[34]

Perhaps more important than his own democratic rise was the perception that Napoleon had presided over the creation of a true meritocracy in France and had supported the democratic rise of others. The two ideas were certainly linked in the eyes of many Americans. In the most popular of all the Napoleon biographies, Sir Walter Scott's mammoth, nine-volume *Life of Napoleon Bonaparte*, the author of *Ivanhoe* wrote that the emperor "lay the foundation of his throne on the democratic principle which had opened his own career." Thus, because of his own democratic rise, Napoleon threw "open to merit . . . the road to success in every department of the state." Scott's egalitarian Napoleon evidently affected the thinking of young Americans such as feminist Margret Fuller. In 1847, she mimicked Scott's words almost verbatim when she wrote a dispatch to the *New York Daily Tribune*. A recent visit to Napoleon's tomb in Paris led her to contrast the monarchy of Louis Phillipe—another supposedly democratic emperor—to the era of Bonaparte. "Through Napoleon," she mused wistfully, "career had really been open to talent."[35]

Napoleon's Democratic Imperialism

It is important to recognize, however, just how men got ahead in the world of the democratic emperor. The vast majority of anecdotes in the literature of the Jacksonian era that featured advancement under Napoleon were tales of meritorious military promotion. "I made my generals out of mud," Napoleon was reputed to have said. There were a few stories that highlighted elevation of intelligent youths to civil offices, but these, however, were the exception. In one popular story, Napoleon is refused passage on a certain road by a watchful French sentinel who has orders to not let anyone pass by. The terrified soldier is later called to headquarters and made an officer for his strict attention to orders. In another case, a young lieutenant bravely steps out of ranks at a review to calm the emperor's horse and is promoted on the spot to a captain's position in the elite imperial guards. In perhaps the most well-known tale, the young general Napoleon promotes a brave sergeant at the siege of Toulon for coolness under fire. At the end of the anecdote, the reader discovers that this valiant soldier was none other than General Jean-Andoche Junot, who would eventually take a leading role in many of Napoleon's future campaigns. These tales of rapid military advancement based on merit seem to have convinced many American youths that gallant military service during wartime was an excellent avenue for their own rapid social advancement. This was an attitude that the French commentator Alexis de Tocqueville noted with some alarm during his famous trip to the United States in the 1830s. "In democratic armies," Tocqueville warned, "all soldiers can become officers, which generalizes the desire for advancement and extends the military ambition almost to infinity." This was particularly true during wartime, he continued, because "war empties places and finally permits violation of that right of seniority that is the sole privilege natural to democracy."[36]

As Tocqueville noted, the military advancement of so many young men was contingent on nearly constant warfare in the Napoleonic empire. Traditionally, war—especially aggressive, imperial warfare—was seen by Americans as a dangerous proposition and the bane of republics. Yet, this view rapidly lost ground in the two decades after Napoleon's death. The challenge came most strongly from the memoirs of Barry O'Meara, the Irish physician who attended Bonaparte on St. Helena. His sympathetic *Napoleon in Exile* captivated millions. Even in the midst of his first presidential campaign, Andrew Jackson found time to converse with a friend about the book. "I am happy you have read O'Meara's works," he wrote. "The world generally has taken up false ideas of Napoleon—much prejudice had been raised against him [but] I never had a doubt but he was a great & good man." Since O'Meara's work purported to record the conversations the doctor had with Bonaparte during the last years of his life, the statements within the book were regarded as the closest thing available to Napoleon's memoirs and treated as a truthful account of the great man's opinions.[37]

In O'Meara's hands, Bonaparte's wars became honorable, brilliant campaigns that had first defended the natural boundaries of France against the chains of European monarchs and that, later, had spread liberal values throughout Europe. O'Meara even managed to work a democratic trope into the idea of Napoleonic imperialism. According to him, even as emperor, Napoleon saw his empire as a "kind of republic," whose maxim was "the career open to talents without distinction to birth or fortune." With surprising speed, this became the dominant American understanding of Bonaparte's imperial identity. American histories of Bonaparte continued to use this trope of positive imperial expansion for decades. For example, John Abbott's wildly successful *History of Napoleon Bonaparte* compared Napoleon's expansion favorably to that of the United States in a passage that deserves to be quoted in its entirety:

> It was the plea of Napoleon that he was not going to make an unjust war on the unoffending nations of the East, but that he was the ally of the oppressed people, drawing the sword against their common enemy, and that he was striving to emancipate them from their

powerful usurpers, and to confer upon them the most precious privileges of freedom. He marched to Egypt, not to desolate, but to ennoble; not to enslave, but to enfranchise; not to enrich himself with the treasures of the East, but to transfer to those shores the opulence and the high civilization of the West. Never was an ambitious conqueror furnished with a more plausible plea. England, as she looks at India and China, must be silent. America, as she listens to the dying wail of the Red Man, driven from the forests of his childhood and the graves of his fathers, can throw no stone. Napoleon surely was not exempt from the infirmities of humanity. But it is not becoming in an English or an American historian to breathe the prayer, "We thank Thee, oh God, that we are not like this Bonaparte!"

Abbot, in other words, inverted the decades-old comparison of American and Napoleonic imperialism for his readers. For Abbot, it was the Americans who ought to follow the democratic imperial example of Bonaparte. O'Meara's book and the ones that followed gave Americans permission to begin seeing imperial warfare as a positive, even noble method of spreading democracy and freedom rather than simply a way to protect their national security.[38]

Printed material on Napoleon not only helped reshape American thinking on the legitimate ends of warfare but also shaped how many Americans thought about the physical nature of combat and military service in general. Americans had many biographical options from which to choose. In addition to O'Meara's work, they read volumes by British historians William Hazlitt and J. G. Lockhart with great avidity. Neither author came close to surpassing the influence of great British historical novelist Sir Walter Scott, however. His *Life of Napoleon Bonaparte* was a runaway American bestseller. A check of library holdings from the 1830s to 1850s shows that every library for which the American Antiquarian Society has records had at least one edition of Scott's work. Scott's take on Napoleon was actually mildly negative. While he admired Napoleon's military and administrative skill, he found fault with Napoleon's habit of hubristically confusing his individual will with that of the French people. Even this mild criticism was too much for many Americans for whom the will of the individual had become sacrosanct. In fact, Scott's work spawned a cottage industry of American biographies defending Napoleon from the British author. One

FIG. 6. Walter Scott's generally sympathetic treatment of Napoleon in his 1832 biography helped create a softer image of Napoleon among Americans during the 1830s and 1840s. (New York Public Library)

American newspaper reviewer noted, "The people of this country have ever looked upon Sir Walter Scott with suspicion since the production of this biography." Despite being castigated by Americans as an unfair, negative, portrayal of the great man, Scott actually painted a Napoleon who was ambitious, yet egalitarian. This fit nicely into the democratic American imagination.[39]

Napoleon's character, as illustrated by Scott, was far more important to Americans than his political career. For Scott, Napoleon's self-essence was marked by a single-minded determination to overcome any obstacle placed in his path. This was clearly illustrated in one of the most famous passages from Scott's work: the story of Bonaparte's crossing of the Alps during the Italian campaign of 1800. Even those Americans who did not have access to Scott's biography were familiar with his version of the story since it was presented for American students in the McGuffey readers. The readers were compendiums of short samples of exemplary prose that were widely used as textbooks in American classrooms from the late 1830s to the early twentieth century. From the start, William McGuffey, a protestant clergyman, intended the selections in his readers not only to teach reading and grammar but also to shape the character of American pupils. Unsurprisingly, Napoleon was a popular feature in the readers. Indeed, one later scholar of the McGuffey readers and their impact on the American mind grumbled that an "inappropriate" amount of attention was paid to Bonaparte in the series. In 1911, a longtime educator remembered that when he had begun his career in the mid-nineteenth century, the third-level reader had been particularly notable for its dramatic image of Napoleon on his "rearing charger" on the cover. Scott's passage describing Bonaparte's crossing the Alps was included in the original 1836 edition and remained a central part of the reader for a generation.[40]

In the reader, Scott's story of the Alpine crossing begins with Bonaparte asking his military engineers, "is the route practicable?" When they reply nervously that the route is "barely possible to pass," Napoleon simply orders, "let us set forward then." The prose then describes the French assent into "an immense and apparently inaccessible mountain, [which] reared its head among general desolation and eternal frost; while precipices, glaciers, ravines, and a boundless extent of faithless snows . . . appeared to forbid access to all living things." For Scott, it is Napoleon's will alone that brings his soldiers through the treacherous passes. "Foot by foot, and man by man, did the French soldiers proceed to ascend this formidable barrier, which Nature had erected in vain to limit human ambition . . . in places of unusual difficulty, the drums beat a charge, as if to encourage the soldiers to encounter the opposition of Nature itself." In this story, American students would have noted that even the boundaries set by nature could not constrain Bonaparte's will. It is well worth remembering that Bonaparte's callous disregard for natural boundaries had made him a threat to Americans in 1803. In 1836, as Americans faced their own western mountains and deserts, however, it had become a character trait worthy of emulation. By using this particular passage, McGuffey delicately avoided the issue of Napoleon's militarism. After all, McGuffey left out the fact that Bonaparte was crossing the Alps to wage a war of aggression against the Austrians. Instead, he made the story about Napoleon's character. In case this was not clear enough, at the end of the passage, McGuffey prompted American students with several questions, such as, "What traits of character did Bonaparte exhibit in attempting and carrying through this difficult enterprise?" The expected answer, of course, was a single-minded determination to carry his plans to their successful conclusion. Given the tone of the story and the

FIG. 7. One of the best-known Napoleon anecdotes was his crossing of the Alps during the Italian campaign of 1800. The event was immortalized in the McGuffey readers as well as lithographs such as this mid-nineteenth-century one from Currier and Ives. (Library of Congress)

intent of the text, it was clear that this was a trait that McGuffey believed American schoolchildren should admire.[41]

Scott's views on Napoleon's political life and character were certainly not the only thing that young Americans took from his work. Scott, was, above all, a romantic novelist, and he wrote his history using the literary devices that had served him so well in *Ivanhoe* and *Waverly*. Of the battle of Austerlitz, Scott reported: "Such were the preparations for this decisive battle, where three Emperors, each at the head of his own army strove to decide the destiny of Europe." The idea that a single titanic battle could decide the fate of three great empires was heady stuff by itself, but Scott went even further. On that fateful morning, "The sun rose with unclouded brilliancy," he wrote. "As its first beams rose across the horizon, Bonaparte appeared in front of his army surrounded by his marshals, to whom he issued his last directions, and they departed at full gallop to their different posts." Imagining such a magnificent sight could hardly have failed to stir the hearts of young American men. American commenters marveled at Scott's ability to evoke martial emotion in his work on Napoleon. The *Barre Gazette*, for example, printed the part of the biography in which Scott described Napoleon's crossing the Alps, and gushed that it was "one of the most graphic accounts of the feat which has ever been written." The *Salem Gazette* concurred with this assessment. In an editorial on Scott, the author wrote admirably of Scott's work on Napoleon: "The depictions of the battles are clear and graphic. All other men's descriptions are confused compared to his. They have fine words—he has fine images. They have plenty of smoke—he is all fire."[42]

Ultimately, that was the rub. Whatever their concerns were with Scott's analysis of Napoleon as a political animal, a large majority of Americans—especially young men—were enthralled by Scott's description of Bonaparte's indomitable will and his democratic tendencies. When that was yoked to the brilliant martial prose that made military service seem like a grand, memorable adventure and O'Meara's positive conception of Napoleon's liberal imperialism, the result was an American public that was ready to use military means to create their own empire on a Napoleonic model.

The Man of the World

In 1849, the New England Transcendentalist Ralph Waldo Emerson took up his pen to explain the nature of the Napoleonic character and its draw for Americans. The essay, titled "Napoleon; or the Man of the World" was published in Emerson's book *Representative Men* and neatly summarizes what Napoleon had come to mean for Americans by the midpoint of the century. "Every one of the million readers of anecdotes or memoirs or lives of Napoleon," wrote Emerson, "delights in the page, because he studies in it his own history." Emerson himself must have been one of these readers since he sprinkled his essay with a great number of short stories and quotations drawn from several Napoleonic biographies and anecdote books including, of course, Scott's biography and O'Meara's memoirs. In his essay, Emerson divided American society into two antagonistic classes: conservatives, who had made their fortunes, and the far more numerous democrats, who were seeking to make their fortunes. Napoleon, he argued, was the model of the latter. Democrats everywhere, Emerson noted, pointed to Napoleon as the "incarnate Democrat." Emerson concurred with such a view. Napoleon, he wrote, "had their virtues, and their vices; above all he had their spirit or aim." What he meant by this was that when the masses of the American middling classes read about Napoleon, they encountered a man with whom they could identify. Napoleon had relied on his talents and character to fashion himself into a democratic icon who could break the monarchies of Europe, just as they sought to rise above their social strata to challenge the conservative elites who had benefited the most from the economic changes of the market revolution.[43]

For Emerson, the character of Bonaparte was notable in two ways that would have stood out to his democratic readers in the United States. First was Napoleon's clearsighted will. It was through sheer, single-minded determination that Bonaparte had overcome all obstacles to challenge the monarchies of Europe. Bonaparte "had a directness of action never before combined with so much comprehension," wrote Emerson. Bonaparte "sees where the matter hinges, throws himself on the precise point of resistance, and slights all other considerations." Bonaparte's will was held within a physical body of seemingly boundless energy. He was, said Emerson, a "man of stone and iron, capable of sitting on horseback sixteen or seventeen hours, of going many days together without rest or food except by snatches." Like Scott's characterization a decade before, Emerson's Bonaparte was undeterred by natural boundaries, whether they be sleep or mountains. "In the plenitude of his resources, every obstacle seemed to vanish. 'There shall be no Alps,' he said; and he built his perfect roads, climbing by graded galleries their steepest precipices, until Italy was as open to Paris as any town in France."[44]

Napoleon's second notable character attribute was his democratic self-construction. Bonaparte, after all, was a still a man—and one who had come from humble origins. This was what made him accessible to American readers. "With him is no miracle and no magic," Emerson wrote. Indeed, Napoleon's genius was in realizing the possibilities of the ordinary and bending them to his will. "He is a worker in brass, in iron, in wood, in earth, in roads, in buildings, in money and in troops." As befitted a true model democrat, Bonaparte was a man who could rely thoroughly on himself. He was a man, according to Emerson, who "in each moment and emergency knew what to do next." Emerson echoed countless other literature when he painted a Napoleon who was entirely self-reliant and self-made. "His principal means are himself," wrote Emerson. "He asks counsel of no other." When Americans read of Napoleon, they encountered a man whose will and self-construction they recognized as entirely applicable to the fashioning of their own lives.[45]

According to Emerson, Napoleon was also a democratic hero for Americans because of what he did with his power when he obtained it. Throughout his career he "made no secret of his contempt for born kings" and smashed systems of hereditary privilege wherever he found them. With the advent of Bonaparte, "the day of sleepy, selfish policy, ever narrowing the means and opportunities of young men, was ended," wrote Emerson, "and a day of expansion and demand was come." Like Scott before him, Emerson credited Napoleon for creating avenues of upward mobility for others. "A market for all the powers and productions of man was opened; brilliant prizes glittered in the eyes of youth and talent," he wrote, "The old, iron-bound, feudal France was changed into a young Ohio or New York." Like Fuller, Emerson boldly claimed that "every species of merit was sought and advanced under his government," yet in that same paragraph, the reader is struck by the fact that Emerson supports this assertion by listing the seventeen men who had been elevated from common soldiers to high military ranks and by noting that the "crosses of his Legion of Honor were awarded for personal valor and not family connections." If every species of merit was truly rewarded by Bonaparte, it certainly seemed that military merit received the lion's share those rewards.[46]

Who was Bonaparte, asked Emerson in his conclusion. "I call Napoleon the agent or attorney of the middle class of modern society; of the throng who fill the markets, shops, counting-houses, manufactories, ships, of the modern world, aiming to be rich," he answered. What was it that drew the American democratic masses to Bonaparte? According to Emerson, it was that in Napoleon American democrats could see themselves. They saw a self-fashioned man who bent his iron will toward the destruction of established privilege. Of course, concluded Emerson laconically, "the rich and aristocratic did not like him." After all, Napoleon "was the agitator, the destroyer of prescription." However, Napoleon was also the great creator. He was "the internal improver, the liberal, the radical, the inventor of means, the opener of doors and markets, the subverter of monopoly and abuse." He was everything that democrats in the United States imagined themselves to be. Through Bonaparte they could aspire to a better world where they could advance above their stations; a world in which they could confront the conservative classes of the United States with the same vigor that Bonaparte had used to crush the monarchies of Europe.[47]

Democrats and the "Napoléon des bois"

This new image of a democratic, self-constructed Bonaparte appealed strongly to members of the new Democratic Party, which emerged after the election of 1824 as the supporters of Andrew Jackson organized themselves to elevate the general to the White House in 1828. The Democrats of this new Jacksonian era saw themselves as the defenders of the American common man who felt besieged by the economic and social changes occurring around him. This city laborer or poor farmer was buffeted by the mysterious economic cycles of the early industrial revolution, which he did not understand but which, he was sure, were deliberately orchestrated by conservative elites who sought their own enrichment at the expense of his economic liberty. To protect the common man from such powerful foes, the Democrats championed the political equality of all (white) men, conservative self-government at the state and local levels, and found a champion in the person, or perhaps the image, of Andrew Jackson. As discussed, Jackson had long been compared to Napoleon in terms of his military abilities. In the 1820s, however, Jackson's supporters pointed to the similarities of character between the two men. Like Bonaparte, Jackson was portrayed as a self-made, iron-willed breaker of entrenched economic elites, and Democrats reveled in their rough-hewn "Napoléon des bois."

While Democrats of the mid-nineteenth century generally championed individual autonomy and state governments at the expense of national power, in the case of imperialism they were willing to make an exception. Like the Jeffersonians before them, Democrats envisioned a sprawling continental empire that provided white men access to land and economic independence from the textile factories and cities dominated by eastern capitalists. Unlike the Jeffersonians however, the Democrats largely rejected the idea of "natural expansion" and instead sought aggressive national support for their imperial dreams. They were perfectly comfortable using national power and military force to expel Indigenous peoples from their lands to make room for white settlement. In this, Andrew Jackson proved to be their champion. As discussed, Jackson, as a general of the Tennessee militia, soundly defeated the Creeks in a conflict in 1813–14 and confiscated most of their homelands in Alabama and Georgia in the Treaty of Fort Jackson. The next chapter describes how, as president, Jackson would ignore the Supreme Court and numerous Indigenous treaties to lay the groundwork for the forced removal of the remaining Indigenous nations from east of the Mississippi. These executive decisions eventually resulted in tragedy. In Florida, the Seminole nation resisted removal and drew the United States into a bloody, destructive guerrilla conflict that lasted from 1835 to 1842. Other peoples, such as the Cherokee, were forced from their homes at bayonet point and endured a brutal forced march to new lands in Oklahoma—the Trail of Tears.

Americans regularly associated Andrew Jackson with Napoleon, but whether they liked the result depended on their political leanings. As discussed earlier in the chapter, many Americans made connections between the military prowess of Jackson and Napoleon in the aftermath of Jackson's victory over the British at New Orleans. In fact, the foremost historian of Jackson's image in the American public, John William Ward, has gone so far as to claim that American artists both consciously and unconsciously incorporated aspects of Napoleon's physical features and style into their own images of the general. It is difficult to assess the validity of this claim, but Jackson's supporters went beyond the physical and attempted to focus public attention on the connections between Jackson's attributes of character and those of Bonaparte. These drew heavily on the avalanche of sympathetic Napoleonic literature that Americans consumed in 1820s and 1830s. In particular, Jackson's partisans focused on his self-creation and his indomitable will.[48]

Like Napoleon, Jackson's resolute will was legendary in the eyes of his supporters. Through sheer, single-minded determination, Jackson's military and political aims were seemingly unaffected by the physical necessities of sleep or hunger. Like Napoleon, Jackson was, according to his biographers, possessed of boundless energy. Before the Battle of New Orleans, the magnitude of the task ahead of him was such that Jackson, like Bonaparte, "overcame the demands of nature and was for five days and four nights without sleep." If, according to Walter Scott, a morsel of food and a flask of wine were sufficient to support Napoleon for days, Jackson, according to his biographers, earned his nickname, "Old Hickory," by surviving on little more than acorns and pushing his soldiers to the absolute limit during the Creek War. Both men's ability to command men was awe-inspiring. One incident in particular had Napoleonic resonances. In 1813, a starving and injured Jackson quelled a mutiny in his army by riding out alone ahead of the rebels with a musket and threatening to shoot any man who did not return to his duty. Some versions of the story added the detail that Jackson announced to the rebels that they could either return to their camps "or take the life of your General; you have your choice." This language was very similar to the reports of Napoleon's return to France after his exile in Elba, when Bonaparte announced to the troops sent to arrest him, "the first soldier who chooses to kill your emperor may do so." In both cases, of course, the soldiers rallied around their iron-willed commanders.[49]

When Jackson's many detractors, such as Henry Clay, accused the general of being a "military chieftain" who threatened the liberties of Americans, it was an indirect reference to Bonaparte. Jackson's supporters fired back in a like manner, relying on the increasing sympathy of Americans toward the French emperor. In his 1828 pamphlet titled *A Vindication of the Character and Public Services of Andrew Jackson,* Henry Lee of Virginia snorted that "any school-boy in Richmond" knew full well that Bonaparte had not "destroyed the liberties of his country." Indeed, he continued, "who can say that France was free, when Bonaparte effected the revolution of the eighteenth of Brumaire? . . . Were not the *corruption and imbecility of their Directory,* the proximate causes of Bonaparte's success?—causes which made his iron rule relief to the French people?" In this remarkable passage, Lee connected the administration of John Quincy Adams to the corrupt French Directory and asserted that Jackson's assumption of the presidency would come as a relief to the American public, just as Napoleon's usurpation of the Directory had been a relief to the French nation. The positive portrayal of Napoleon's "iron rule" would have been laughable a decade previous, but such was the power of Napoleonic literature. In the person of Andrew Jackson, Democrats found a man of iron-will and self-construction who could Americanize the traits they admired in Napoleon. These were the traits of men who had the will to overcome the natural, legal, and human obstacles of the American continent to oversee the construction of a great American empire that would rival and eventually exceed Bonaparte's own.[50]

Military Chieftains

Andrew Jackson's supporters looked to him as an American embodiment of the traits they had come to admire in Napoleon through the tidal wave of Napoleonic literature that flooded American shores in the 1820s and 1830s. Jackson's opposition also made much of the apparent connections between the president and the emperor. Where Democrats found much to admire in Jackson's unquenchable iron will and military talent, however, Jackson's opponents found a "military chieftain" who embodied the worst traits of an ambitious and treacherous despot. As they attacked Jackson using the imagery of Napoleon, they sought to recall Americans to an earlier understanding of Bonaparte as a bloody imperial tyrant who rejected international norms and law.

As Jackson came more into the public eye, Jackson's detractors became more direct in their criticisms. Indeed, in some ways, Jackson made it easy for his opposition since, like many other Americans, he did really admire Napoleon. Jackson personally owned at least five biographies of Bonaparte—including Scott's *Life of Napoleon,* and, as noted earlier, his personal favorite, Barry O'Meara's *Napoleon in Exile.* Even more galling was a widely told story that first seems to have appeared in 1832. It involved Napoleon's brother Joseph, the former king of Spain, whose imperial claim to the Floridas had, in 1810, resulted in the American military annexation of the short-lived West Florida republic. Joseph had fled into exile in the United States in 1815 immediately following his brother's defeat at the Battle of Waterloo. He quietly established himself in comfortable retirement as the comte de Survilliers first in New York and later in Pennsylvania and New Jersey. According to the story, which Jackson never denied, when Joseph was reluctantly introduced to Jackson at the White House, the president remarked, "I have always, sir, taken your illustrious brother for my model in war."[51]

This last story proved to be too much for Jackson's detractors, who pounced on the president's claim to model himself after Napoleon. After repeating the story, which had run wild in the opposition papers, Richard Bayard, a senator from Delaware, snidely remarked, that Jackson's remark was to be sure "very modest." Lest anyone point out that there was some difference between "the campaigns of Italy and those of a Creek or Seminole war, between the invasion of Russia and that of Florida," he continued, "it should be observed that the remark does not import equality but merely imitation and we all know that a copy may be more or less humble, according to the means and abilities of the artist." In other words, Andrew Jackson could say what he liked, but he was, in the end, a poor copy of the original great imperialist. Nevertheless, Bayard concluded, after reading the same biography by Madam De Staël that Clay had read from a decade earlier, he had indeed noticed some troubling "points of resemblance in the character and policy of the two men." Jackson might be a poor copy—a backwoods, hayseed Napoleon—but his character and actions were dangerous to the republic.[52]

Other members of the opposition took the same tact with Jackson's ill-advised remark but through different mediums. One famous example was the widely disseminated lithograph titled "The Model of a Republican President." The image—probably from 1834—was completed by the French-born lithographer Anthony Imbert. In the cartoon, Andrew Jackson stands in full military uniform before a mirror. He is donning the long gray great coat and unmistakable bicorn associated with Napoleon. To Jackson's right stands an elegant statue of Napoleon, serene but with a hint of amusement on his face and his left hand placed in his vest—obviously Jackson's model. To his left, Jackson's cabinet flits around the president admiringly. Roger B. Taney, the secretary of the Treasury, and Martin Van Buren, the vice president, assure the general that he truly does resemble the great Napoleon—even if he is a little too thin for the role. Jackson himself stands with a wild grin on his face, saying, "I begin to see it myself, I feel like Napoleon, I thirst for glory!! Down with the Monster. Down with the Senate! Glory!!" In case anyone missed the point, below the cartoon was printed, "'I have taken your brother for my model'—General Jackson to Joseph Bonaparte."[53]

The message in both the speech and the cartoon were the same since in many ways they responded to the same issue. Democrats celebrated the similarities between Andrew Jackson and Napoleon, and the opposition both mocked and worried about such comparisons. On the one hand, they saw Jackson as a pale imitation of the emperor. In the cartoon, Jackson has to be assured by his toadies that he does indeed resemble the great man. Yet, the statue next to Jackson shows the utter nonsense of such statements. The Napoleonic garb that elegantly graces the statue hangs ridiculously when placed on the cadaverously thin Jackson. The serene look on Napoleon's face is a jarring contrast to Jackson's almost maniacal countenance. And yet, there is danger. Just as Senator Bayard noted a troubling resemblance between the character of the two men, so too the cartoon pointed to a worrisome love of glory that connected the two imperialists. However, as the opposition soon came to understand, Jackson was only the most visible symptom of a growing militaristic cancer that lay at the very core of Democratic imperialism.

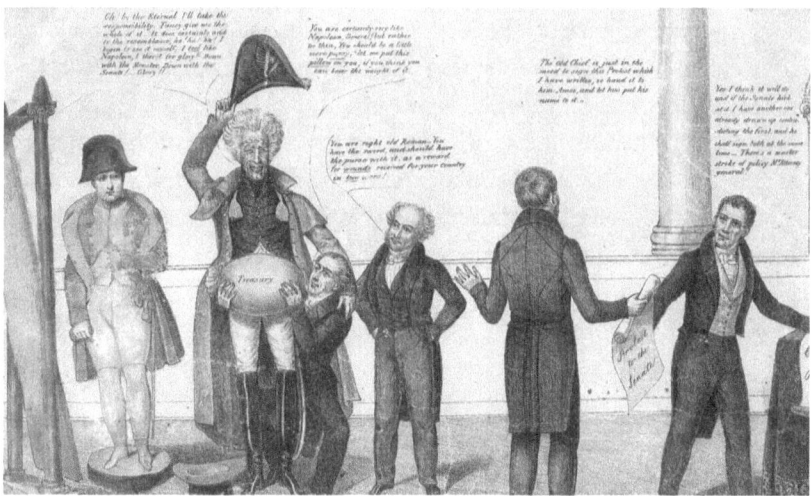

FIG. 8. This Anthony Imbert political cartoon from around 1834 depicts Andrew Jackson as a crude copy of Napoleon. Imbert was playing on a widely reported exchange between the seventh president and Napoleon's brother Joseph. (National Museum of American History)

The Bifurcation of Bonaparte

After serving two terms, Andrew Jackson left the presidency in 1837. His hand-picked successor was none other than Martin Van Buren—the man who had fought to get a town named Austerlitz as a state senator in 1819. The change in administrations caught the attention of the *New York Herald*. "Like Napoleon," the editor commented with admiration, "Andrew Jackson broke to pieces all the factions throughout the country.... General Jackson's iron will has mastered everything." The *Herald* was not as sure about his successor, noting, "We have parted with the bold, dashing hero, and got the smooth, bowing, diplomatist. We have exchanged Napoleon for Talleyrand." It was not a comparison that Van Buren would have appreciated. By the time Van Buren entered the White House, the legacy of Napoleon had undergone a momentous shift in the American mind. Napoleon's exile and death and, most importantly, the sympathetic work of authors such as Barry O'Meara and Sir Walter Scott had created an alternative narrative of the French emperor. Instead of a bloody and rapacious military despot, more and more Americans began to see Bonaparte as an iron-willed, egalitarian, military genius whose campaigns had spread the seeds of liberalism through the conservative monarchies of Europe. Such a recasting of Napoleon found fertile soil in a United States undergoing its own process of democratization and expansion. Nevertheless, this new image remained strongly contested. Over the next decade, imperial expansion into the lands of the American Indians and later into Texas and Mexico would force Americans to confront and ultimately resolve this bifurcation of Napoleon's image and, in so doing, resolve their own imperial identity. [54]

5

Glory

The Mexican-American War

In the dusty chaparral just north of what is now Brownsville, Texas, two small armies stood ready for battle at a site called Palo Alto on May 8, 1846. The day's engagement would be the first major fight of the American imperial foray into Mexico. As was typical, the fight began with an artillery duel between the two sides. The well-trained and better-equipped American gunners quickly gained the upper hand in the contest, and the Mexican bombardment of the enemy lines was largely ineffective. Nevertheless, some of the Mexican rounds found their targets. One of the few casualties suffered by the Americans during the artillery exchange was widely reported across the nation. The name of the unfortunate soldier was lost to history, for it was his background that was of far more interest to American readers: the soldier was one of Napoleon's veterans. According to the newspaper reports, this "noble-hearted fellow" had valiantly served the emperor at the Battles of Austerlitz and Wagram and then survived the disastrous Russian campaign and the Battle of Waterloo. As the veteran lay dying, his fellow Americans gathered around him. With the last of his strength, he waved disdainfully toward the enemy saying, "Go on comrades! I have only got what a soldier enlists for!"[1]

There is likely very little truth in this story. Even a young veteran of Napoleon's very last campaigns would have been over forty years old by the time of the battle at Palo Alto, and a veteran of Austerlitz would have been in his mid-fifties. The tale may have been concocted by a Francophone immigrant seeking to reinvent himself in his new home through a connection to the French emperor. Or, more likely, the story may have been invented wholesale by an overeager war correspondent. Ultimately, it does not really matter if the story was factually true. What matters is that Americans believed that it was true and that they clearly wanted it to be true. Why did this story resonate with Americans in 1846? It mattered to them because it symbolically melded together the Bonapartist and the American imperial projects as two empires seeking the same liberal goals. In a very real sense, Americans took the command "go on comrades" as a passing of the imperial torch from Napoleon to themselves.[2]

To make sense of the story, we must back up a decade to 1835. As discussed in the last chapter, in the years following Napoleon's final exile in 1815 and his death in 1821, Americans were inundated by Napoleon-themed paintings, prints, busts, sculptures, and other baubles, but especially printed material. The fact that the story of Napoleon's veteran at Palo Alto was widely recorded in both newspapers and war memoirs testifies to the successful packaging of Napoleon as a popular culture consumable for a generation of Americans that had been born after his death. It would not be a stretch to state that Bonaparte became a cultural meme for the second generation of Americans. Yet, even as familiar as they were with the stories

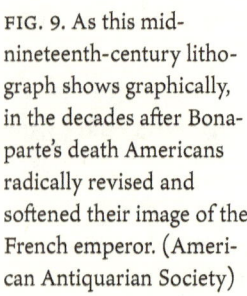

FIG. 9. As this mid-nineteenth-century lithograph shows graphically, in the decades after Bonaparte's death Americans radically revised and softened their image of the French emperor. (American Antiquarian Society)

and likeness of the French emperor, the men and women who came of age after Napoleon's deposition found that they could not agree on what his image or legacy represented. In short, the image of Napoleon had ceased to be a univalent signifier for Americans. This contest over Bonaparte's image played out in the American discourse over imperial expansion during the period between 1835 and 1850. For some Americans, Bonaparte continued to symbolize an ambitious, bloody despot—a warning against the political and human costs of aggressive and irrational imperial conquest. For others, however, Napoleon's imperial identity took on a character that was liberal, democratic, and infused with martial valor. Despite efforts from anti-expansionists to remind their countrymen of Bonaparte's violent and immoral imperial image, by the end of the Mexican-American War in 1848, Americans had largely embraced an aggressive, martial imperial identity that saw itself as the worthy liberal successor to that of Napoleon.

Whigs and the American Self

By 1832, the various factions in American politics opposed to Andrew Jackson had finally coalesced into a new national party called the Whigs. They took their name from the British anti-court party of the eighteenth century in symbolic reference to their stand against the president they referred to as "King Andrew the First." Where the Jacksonian Democrats emphasized the importance of the individual and their choices, Whigs championed what they identified as the public good of American society. For them, this usually meant a stronger national government that could knit the states together into a union through public infrastructure projects such as canals, roads, and harbors—which they called internal improvements—and sound economic policy through tariffs and a national bank that could regulate the money supply. If the Democrats saw themselves as the party of the laborer and the poor farmer left behind by the Market Revolution, the Whigs saw themselves the party of economic modernity and the growing American middle class.[3]

In terms of expansion and empire building, the Whigs, like the Federalists before them, were far more cautious than their rivals. They sought a rational American empire that would not upset the national union, which, by the end of the 1820s, was increasingly threatened by the question of slavery in newly acquired territories. One way the Whigs sought to do this was to unite the periphery of the American empire to its core through public infrastructure. In 1828, for example, a congressman from Pennsylvania articulated this principle to his Democratic colleagues. Charles Miner tapped into a familiar trope when he reminded his fellow representatives, "Napoleon gained his battles . . . by the rapid concentration of force upon a particular point." This, he continued, required nationally funded public roads, which Democrats were reluctant to support. He drew his conclusion using a familiar story. "The road of Napoleon over the Alps," Miner noted, "must be familiar to the recollection of every gentleman who hears me. And yet, can it be conceived, sir, that this government had the power to add an Empire to the Republic, and that it has not the right to make a road to that Empire?" Miner's argument hinged on not only his colleagues' collective knowledge of Bonaparte—a safe bet given the number of Napoleonic biographies and anecdote books that had crowded American bookshelves for nearly a decade by 1828—but also their acceptance of Napoleon's imperial project as one worthy of emulation.[4]

The Jacksonian reluctance to pay for infrastructure improvements for the benefit of the growing American empire was irritating enough to the Whigs, but what was even more concerning to them was the very character of Jacksonian empire building. As the 1830s wore on, Whigs grew increasingly worried that the American imperial character was personified in the legacy of Napoleon Bonaparte. To understand why this caused such concern, it is important to understand how Americans understood character and selfhood in the mid-nineteenth century.

The dominant model of selfhood was the "balanced character" of faculty psychology. Selfhood was composed of a number of hierarchical elements. There were divine components such as morality and rationality at the top, followed by animal elements such as instinct and emotion, and the vegetable component of simple mechanical reflexes at the bottom. Each of these components had its uses in a human self, but they had to be carefully balanced. As historian Daniel Walker Howe has noted, Americans believed that, "left to themselves, some of the lower powers could cause havoc." Ambition, for example, was not in itself a bad thing: it drove men to succeed and to improve themselves. However, ambition had to be checked by the higher components of moral conscience and reason lest it degenerate into amoral Machiavellian ruthlessness. For Americans, self-improvement was the process of cultivating a truly balanced character that regulated the passions. In addition, unbalanced character was not simply a danger to the individual. In democratic societies such as the United States, individuals driven by their unregulated passions could drive whole nations into a collective madness. Self-government for Americans, then, was understood as not simply the regulation of the individual self, but also of the entire political community. Aggressive war for the sake of empire was thus a failure of collective restraint and could quickly lead to national ruin.[5]

This is why the works of writers sympathetic to Napoleon that are examined in the last chapter greatly worried American Whigs. Works such as Scott's *Life of Napoleon* or Barry O'Meara's *Napoleon in Exile* celebrated Napoleon as a man whose ambitious self-construction and iron will overcame all obstacles, and whose democratic imperial project demolished the long-standing political constraints of the Old World. Yet, according to the Whigs, moral and rational constraints were precisely what ambitious men and their imperial projects needed. This discourse was even more concerning for anti-expansionists because it occurred in the midst of a redefinition of American manhood. As historian Amy Greenberg has shown, two rival conceptions of masculinity that had a bearing on American expansion emerged during the middle of the nineteenth century. The first was "martial manhood," which was characterized by the rejection of Christian moralism in favor of military glory and domination of others. This, she argues, was the gendered hallmark of aggressive expansionism. "Restrained manhood," on the other hand, was characterized by restraint in the form of Christian virtue, temperance, and family. To the horror of anti-expansionists, the romanticized historical image of Bonaparte could provide even young men who rejected the depravity of martial manhood a means to justify imperialism and military glory in service of a liberal empire. Between 1825 and 1848, these Americans—mostly concentrated in the old Federalist strongholds of the Northeast—were increasingly put on the defensive, but they managed to mount a respectable rear-guard action that called the sympathetic image of Bonaparte into question.[6]

Countering the Democratic Napoleon

These ideas about character and manhood wove themselves into the fabric of American discourse in surprising places. In April 1827, for example, Nicholas Biddle was asked to give a eulogy for the late President Jefferson by the American Philosophical Society in Philadelphia. The society thought so highly of Biddle's remarks that they published the eulogy for public consumption a few months later. Biddle was a lawyer and banker who had been in Paris during the crowning of Napoleon in 1804 and edited the first edition of the journals kept by Lewis and Clark on their expedition through Louisiana to the Pacific Ocean. When he gave the eulogy in 1827, he was also the president of the Second Bank of the United States—a position that would soon earn him the ire of President Andrew Jackson.[7]

As everyone expected, Biddle spent the first three quarters of the speech reviewing the highlights of Jefferson's career, including, of course, the Louisiana Purchase. Here Biddle praised Jefferson's actions in terms of their character. They were, he said, "a single act of honest policy, too distinguished for its rarity and destitute of all the common attractions of successful artifice or violence." The result of this careful restraint and honesty by Jefferson was to "double the extent and to secure the tranquility of his country." In choosing to describe the Louisiana Purchase this way, Biddle highlighted Jefferson's public character and its importance to national greatness. In Biddle's mind, Jefferson's restraint and honesty had led to a form of imperial expansion that had brought peace to the continent. To demonstrate how truly unique Jefferson's character was, in the last quarter of the speech Biddle chose to compare Jefferson's disinterested character to that displayed by "that extraordinary being," Napoleon Bonaparte.[8]

Biddle readily admitted that there was much to admire in Napoleon. Biddle listed out Napoleon's "great talents, varied acquirements, and many high qualities" as contributing to his unique genius. In fact, said Biddle (and this was a sop to those many Americans who now saw Napoleon as a liberal imperialist), Napoleon's own empire had certainly some lasting positive characteristics. "The very tide of his conquests over less civilized nations deposited in receding, some benefits even to the vanquished," Biddle noted, "and all that glory can contribute to public happiness was profusely lavished on his country." And yet, warned Biddle, there was something dangerous in all this imperial triumph. "Such are the delusions," he continued "which military ambition sheds in turn on its possessor and on the world." Ultimately, Biddle concluded, "the brilliant qualities" of Napoleon were ultimately subsumed into an "intense selfishness," and his "splendid genius" was perverted into a "poor love of swaying the destinies of other men—not to benefit, not to bless—but simply to command them." This selfishness lay at the root of all his imperial conquests. It was for this towering, unchecked ambition that Bonaparte "disturbed the earth with his insane conquests." In choosing words such as "insane" and "feverish restlessness" Biddle was highlighting that Napoleon's imperial ambition was unconstrained by the rationality that might have made it a benefit to mankind. Biddle asked his audience to contrast "this feverish restlessness which is called ambition" and an "expanded love for violence which makes heroes" with the peaceful, public disinterestedness of Jefferson's actions during the Louisiana Purchase. For Biddle, the true tragedy of Napoleonic imperialism was not the empire itself, but in Napoleon's selfish inability to see imperial power's noblest attribute, "the capacity to make man freer or happier."[9]

A similar theme appeared in comparisons between Napoleon and other American founders. Perhaps the best example is one that was found in the final chapter of a children's book titled *Pictorial History of George Washington* published in 1846, just before the start of the Mexican-American War. Though the work was published anonymously, the author was likely the New York editor and printer, and later Episcopal minister, Horatio Hastings Weld. The remainder of Weld's lengthy title promised to illustrate the character of Washington through a series of anecdotes and engravings for the young people of the United States. With this goal in mind, in the second sentence of the preface Weld felt compelled to remind his young readers in an anecdote from the siege of Toulon that even the "illustrious" Napoleon Bonaparte had referred to Washington as "great." Such was the power of two decades worth of Napoleonic literature that American children had to be reminded that Bonaparte had recognized Washington as his superior.[10]

The penultimate chapter in the *Pictorial History of George Washington* was devoted to a direct character comparison between the first president and Napoleon, since, according to the author, young readers were presumed to be familiar with the histories of both men. The difference, according to Weld, was "the superiority of virtue over mere genius." Napoleon, he admitted, was undoubtably the superior to Washington in the genius of action; one needed to look no further than his unapparelled military victories to see that. And yet, Napoleon was the "the absolute leader of an infuriated multitude." Napoleon's genius was in harnessing that unchecked fury of millions to his own ambition. He placed himself at the head of this "irresistible impulse, which was sufficient in itself to carry him to the summit of glory." But this was not enough for Napoleon, Weld continued. "He loved glory better than France, and sacrificed his adopted country on the altar of ambition." Weld tried to be scrupulously fair to Napoleon and acknowledged that what might appear to be "the frenzy of unchastised ambition, may have been nothing more than self-defense, which is sometimes, nay often, compelled to assume an offensive attitude of prevention." After all, he admitted, "it is not always that the invader is the aggressor; and it is at all times perfectly justifiable to anticipate a blow we see coming, by striking the adversary beforehand." Nevertheless, when Napoleon led his nation into "defensive" wars, they tended to be for the defense of his own right to rule and not to defend the liberties of his countrymen, and nothing could explain Napoleon's imperial aggression in Spain and Russia other than his own unchecked ambition.[11]

Weld then asked his readers to consider the contrast between Napoleon and Washington. Washington led his own countrymen in defensive wars but, as a servant of the Congress, not as the absolute monarch of an infuriated mob. Washington had struggled "for the rights of his countrymen," while Napoleon had "aimed at prostrating the rights of nations." Most importantly, Washington had ultimately surrendered his power: first as a military commander and then as president rather than allow his ambition to overrule his character. "The ambition of Washington was a virtue, that of Napoleon was a vice," Weld concluded. The key point that he wanted his readers to take away was that Washington, unlike Napoleon, had understood the importance of tempering his ambition with virtue. "The limits of the one was the freedom and independence of his country," Weld wrote, while "that of the other the subjugation of the world." Like Biddle's eulogy for Jefferson, the author of the *Pictorial History* took great pains not to condemn empire and war, but rather to emphasize the need to check baser emotions such as ambition, for not only the good of the individual but also the good of the entire nation.[12]

William Channing versus Walter Scott

By far the most popular anti-Bonapartist tract in the United States was William Ellery Channing's *Remarks on the Character of Napoleon Bonaparte Occasioned by the Publication of Scott's "Life of Napoleon."* Channing was one of Unitarianism's leading lights by the time he published his work in the Boston-based *Christian Examiner* in 1827. The essay was so popular, however, that it was printed as a separate pamphlet almost immediately after its initial publication. It proved most influential among the New England elite. For example, the son of President John Quincy Adams, Charles Francis Adams, wrote highly of the essay in his diary and noted discussing it over dinner with friends and arguing its merits in debating society. The young lawyer and future Supreme Court chief justice, Salmon P. Chase also wrote favorably of Channing's work in his diary: "Undazzled by the blaze of military and civil glory which has surrounded the Hero, he has deeply penetrated and faithfully exposed his real character."[13]

After reading Scott's work, Channing had grave concerns, but they were not those of the many Americans who thought the author had been too hard on the emperor. Instead, Channing worried that Scott's sympathetic view of his subject would affect the moral character of the young Americans who internalized it. "We war not with the dead," he insisted. "We would only resist what we deem the pernicious influence of the dead." Channing admitted that, like Scott, he could not deny Napoleon's military greatness. Born in 1780, he was old enough to remember with what "rapturous admiration" he first read of Bonaparte's Italian campaigns in the newspapers, and he wrote that even three decades later he could not read Scott's brilliant rendition of

FIG. 10. William Ellery Channing was a unitarian minister and one of several Americans who attempted to counter the new, softer imperial image of Napoleon that emerged in the decades after the emperor's death. (National Portrait Gallery)

Bonaparte's military exploits "without a quickened movement in the veins." Yet, with the wisdom of age, Channing had come to understand Napoleon's military successes quite differently.[14]

There was no question, Channing admitted, that Napoleon had been a true military genius. "He seized in an instant on the great points of his own and his enemy's positions," explained Channing, "and combined at once the movements, by which an overpowering force might be thrown with unexpected fury on a vulnerable part of the hostile line." Bonaparte was eminently, though perhaps not uniquely, able to direct physical force onto strategic and tactical problems and to break the old rules of warfare. Nevertheless, said Channing, this genius of action was marred by a distinct lack of intellectual and moral greatness that were both far superior to and necessary checks on ambition. The result was dangerous not only to Napoleon's character but also to the French nation and to the world. Napoleon's early military victories allowed him to indulge a "lawless, imperious spirit" unchecked by either Christian morality or the law of nations. Indeed, according to Channing, it was the very presence of Napoleon's martial prowess without the restraint of Christian morality that was responsible for the "unprincipled and open aggressions" that characterized Bonaparte's later imperial projects.[15]

Channing also had little good to say about Napoleon's administration of empire. Napoleon lived at a time, he wrote, when he might have done great good for the people of Europe. Channing had a long list of projects that Bonaparte might have pursued to "contrast himself strikingly and most advantageously with former governments." But Napoleon had not done so. Indeed, he merely tried to ape the old monarchies of Europe with his own court of sycophants. To Channing, Bonaparte seemed constitutionally incapable of thinking of such a project at odds with "that egotistical, self-relying, self-aggrandizing principle which was the most striking feature of his mind." Like Nicholas Biddle, Channing saw that as the great tragedy of Napoleon. "We will not quarrel with ambition," Channing wrote, "when it is wise enough to devote itself to the happiness of mankind." Instead, Napoleon's ambition had selfishly been directed toward raw imperial power.[16]

Channing argued that unparalleled military success had bred the dangerous notion in Napoleon's mind that an "empire of the world" was the "fulfillment of his destiny." Channing's choice of the word "destiny" was a deliberate swipe at Scott's writing. In Scott's saga, Destiny (always capitalized) was a nearly physical character. "She" was literally at Bonaparte's side "leading him by the hand, and at the same time protecting him with her shield." Napoleon was, according to Scott, "the man of Destiny." For Channing, this was dangerous, self-aggrandizing nonsense that would corrupt the minds of impressionable young Americans. Ultimately, Channing argued, it was Bonaparte's misguided and unrestrained sense of "destiny" that had led to the corruption of the entire French nation, which "in her madness and folly had placed her happiness in conquest [and] felt that the glory of her arms was only safe in the hands of the First Consul." For Channing's readers, it was a somber warning to Americans that their own republican imperial identity could be usurped and corrupted by unguarded militarism.[17]

According to Channing, Napoleon's military success and his sense of imperial destiny led to the most dangerous impulse of all: "an almost insane conviction of superhuman greatness." Napoleon, said Channing, quickly came to believe that he was not to be constrained by mere human conventions. "In his own view," according to Channing, Napoleon "stood apart from other men. He was not to be measured by the standard of humanity. He was not to be retarded by difficulties to which all others yielded. He was not to be subjected to laws and obligations which all others were expected to obey. Nature and the human will were to bend to his power." This freedom from constraints was exactly what Jacksonians celebrated about Napoleon, but for Channing, this was the ultimate warning of Napoleon's life. Ambition and military genius unchecked by moral or physical constraints led to catastrophic results not only for the individual self but for all humanity.[18]

All this led Channing to his final paragraphs in which he commented on the nature of war itself. As a rule, Channing was far more interested in the conduct of individuals than of nations. His chief concern with Scott's sympathetic portrayal of Napoleon's character was in its ability to convince the minds of impressionable young men that military genius and a sense of destiny were the chief ends in life. Yet, he felt obligated to lodge a brief commentary on warfare in general. Imperial warfare was, in his opinion, a very great evil—especially when it was conducted for the fulfillment of some misguided sense of personal or national destiny unconstrained by reason and morality. "Wearied with violence and blood," Americans, he wrote, should pray that God "subvert oppressive governments by the gentle, yet awful power of truth and virtue." Yet, if this was impossible, war could be necessary. Its most harmful effects, he continued, could be muted if those who engaged in it "took to the sword with awe," and remembered that they served a Christ whose "dearest attribute was mercy." In practice this meant that individual soldiers should "not stain their sacred cause by one cruel deed, by the infliction of one needless pang, [or] by shedding without cause one drop of human blood."[19]

For Channing, the lesson of Bonaparte was ultimately that imperialism was a reflection of individual human character. Bonaparte's empire was undeniably great, but as it was built on the corrupted character of a single ambitious man divorced from moral restraint, it could not be good. For Channing, imperial warfare and martial manhood were evils since they appealed directly to the animal faculties of self—passion and ambition. Only through the constraint of the higher faculties of reason and Christian morality could it be justified. Channing challenged Americans to recall Bonaparte's earlier, negative imperial identity as rapacious and dangerous—the one that Channing had grown up with. Like others of his generation, Channing did not disavow all imperialism, but he called on his listeners to consider carefully the modes of imperialism. Only through rejecting an imperial identity based on the methods of Bonaparte could the United States truly become an empire of liberty.

William Ladd and Anti-Militarism

A decade after the publication of Channing's *Remarks*, another book was published that addressed similar concerns in a slightly different way while still keeping Napoleon central to the message. Its author was one of the most remarkable, and yet unknown, men in the history of the early republic. William Ladd was born into a wealthy New Hampshire merchant family only two years after the United States declared its independence from Great Britain. After graduating from Harvard and serving for a time as a sailor on one of his father's merchant vessels, Ladd decided to change the world. Luckily for him, he was able to ride a growing tide of Christian humanitarian reform that swept through the United States during the first half of the nineteenth century. After a brief attempt to undermine African slavery by setting up a cotton plantation in Florida using paid immigrant labor failed miserably, Ladd listlessly moved from humanitarian cause to humanitarian cause before finally discovering the international peace movement in the early 1820s.[20]

Ladd began his crusade for peace in 1823 by starting a local peace society in his home of Minot, Maine. Over the remaining seventeen years of his life, Ladd worked diligently for his new cause. He successfully unified the disparate peace organizations across the United States into the American Peace Society and had some success in enlisting support for his cause from other humanitarian organizations. He had considerably less success, however, in realizing his dream of creating an international Congress of Nations to hear and arbitrate transnational disputes—a plan that presaged the modern United Nations. Ladd also devoted a considerable amount of time and energy to combating the growing tide of militarism that he saw emerging in the youth of America. He vocally opposed the creation of the Bunker Hill memorial, calling it a "monument to barbarism and anti-Christian spirit," and wrote numerous books advocating Christian pacifism that were aimed at American youths. One of the last books that Ladd wrote was published in 1838 and explicitly tied Napoleonic literature to the militarism that he believed was corrupting the youth of America.[21]

Written under the pseudonym "Philanthropos," which means literally "lover of humanity," *Howard and Napoleon Compared in Eight Dialogues* was aimed at older children and featured eight chapters, or dialogues, between two schoolboys named William and Henry. William is an idealized model of Christian virtue who represents restrained masculinity, while Henry is a representation of martial masculinity. Henry is a truly remarkable character. He has read all the latest Napoleon biographies and gripes about the pro-British bias in Scott's *Life of Napoleon* and de Staël's *Secret History of St. Cloud*. He has grown up surrounded by heroic pictures of Napoleon and his marshals. To make matters worse, the cadre of adults in his life—including his father, his school master, and his minister—have taught him that the chief end of life is making a great name for oneself in this world. Unsurprisingly, Henry virtually worships at the altar of military glory and its chief saint—Napoleon Bonaparte. He loves the martial spectacle of the local militia musters and longs to finish his education at a military academy and then become a military officer of great renown.[22]

Surrounded as he is by the new American martial culture undergirded by the new image of Napoleon, Henry is quite shocked—even outraged—when his best friend, William, questions his life's goals. William, however, is undeterred and attempts to reason with his friend along two parallel lines of attack. The first line of attack is reminiscent of Channing, though certainly more accessible to children. William asks Henry to compare the actions and objectives of his idol with those of a nondescript Christian merchant. Though Henry finds the biographies of such middling men "flat and uninteresting," William patiently coaches him to a new understanding of humanity. When pressed by William's keen logic, Henry finds to his surprise that there is a vast difference between greatness and goodness, and that Napoleon had the former without the moderating hand of the latter, which made him cruel and unjust. Even the French nationalism that Scott held up as Bonaparte's chief virtue William reduces to simple selfishness, for it demands that he love only a small portion of humanity at the expense of all others.

William's other line of attack is one to which Channing briefly alluded but never fully engaged. This is the dangerous "War Spirit" fostered by the celebration of Napoleon. Henry loves the spectacle of the local militia musters. "Oh how I love a sham fight!" he sighs while perusing Scott's *Life of Napoleon,* "and to hear the cannons roar, and the muskets rattle, and the drums beat, and the horses neigh, and feel the ground tremble." In words directly reminiscent of Scott, Henry comments on how he loves to see the bright glint of the sunlight off the bayonets and swords of the militia. "Oh! It is the most glorious sight in the world," he says to William. "If a sham fight is so glorious, what must a real fight be like?" With such magnificent spectacles, it is no wonder that Henry finds the biographies of Christian men so boring. In this passage Ladd was making a damning comment on how Napoleonic literature had ultimately developed into a new American culture that celebrated martial glory at the expense of Christian charity. Luckily for Henry, his friend has no illusions about the real nature of war.[23]

William makes his case in an innovative style. Instead of relying on the Bible as he did in his initial arguments, he goes to one of the most famous of Bonaparte military histories, the General Philipe-Paul, comte de Ségur's *History of the Expedition to Russia.* First published in English in 1825, this French history of the disastrous 1812 campaign remains in print. An 1841 introduction to an American edition noted, "Nothing can more effectively dissipate every illusion of military glory than the perusal of this dreadful narrative." So hoped William. Ségur's history in hand, he quotes lengthy, graphic descriptions of hungry and half-frozen French soldiers hacked to death by marauding Cossacks, blown to bits by Russian shells, or even committing suicide in despair. Ultimately, William concludes that "the life of the modern soldier is ill-reported by heroic fiction," and that if Henry persists in his dream of becoming an officer, it is likely that he will perish in "hopeless misery" as he languishes in a disease-riddled camp or a prison ship far from loved ones.[24]

William's stark description of the soldier life finally has the desired effect, and Henry resolves to give up his dreams of earthly glory—his martial masculinity—and focus his life on Christ rather than on Napoleon, thus embracing his restrained masculinity. Paradoxically, Ladd had to fight Bonaparte with Bonaparte, and though he probably did not intend it, the reader gets the distinct impression that it was actually the comte de Ségur and not the Bible that managed to sway Henry away from the dangerous influence of Scott's Napoleon.

The work of Channing and Ladd asked Americans to reject the new, sympathetic imperial image of Napoleon that had emerged in the wave of biographies that flooded the American market in the decade after his death. They recalled the minds of their readers to the earlier image of Napoleon as the ambitious, violent symbol of imperialism that had been virtually unchallenged during the first decade of the nineteenth century. Their work, however, was not enough to stem the tide. Americans, especially those of the younger generation who did not remember Bonaparte as a threat to American expansion, overwhelmingly adopted the image of Bonaparte as a liberal imperialist and adopted his martial imperial identity as their own. Like William, anti-imperialists increasingly found that if they wanted to make an effective argument, they had to work within the image of Bonaparte as the standard of imperial greatness.

Indian Removal

Following the Creek War in 1815, the United States dramatically accelerated a form of settler colonialism that had originated during the Jefferson administration. The problem was land. Southern and western states sought to open territory occupied by Indigenous peoples to white settlement and demanded the federal government protect their assertions of state sovereignty over tribal claims. What emerged over the ensuing decade were a series of federally sponsored plans to dispossess the remaining Indigenous peoples east of the Mississippi River of their lands in exchange for lands farther west. In this process of "Indian Removal" American officials chose to willfully ignore both the complex, decentralized reality of most Indigenous political societies as well as already existing treaties that, in many cases, had been signed decades before. It was easier for government agents to simply find a few compliant Indigenous leaders who could sign a new treaty favorable to the United States that was then claimed to be binding on the entire nation. While some Indigenous societies chose to migrate willingly, others did not. When Indigenous people resisted forced resettlement, the government called in the army to enforce the new treaties with bayonets and bullets. In this imperial conquest, only a few Americans drew connections to Napoleon. Nevertheless, those who did began to develop a new vocabulary that would reach its full form in the Mexican-American War.[25]

The Indian Removal Act of 1830, cheered on by Andrew Jackson, set the stage for the most dramatic phase of removal by authorizing the government to begin the process of negotiating new treaties with the most powerful Indigenous nations east of the Mississippi River. Those opposed to removal proposed a number of amendments to the bill that would have bound the United States to adhere to its already existing treaties with Indigenous nations. In the debates, Maine senator Peleg Sprague reminded his colleagues of the prior treaties that the Indian Removal Act threatened to overturn. He spoke his objections by first calling attention to what he saw as the unchecked imperial ambition that it embodied. "To give to conquest—to mere force—the name of right, is to sanction all the enormities of avarice and ambition," he argued. Passing the bill, he continued, justified even the lawless, imperial ambition of Bonaparte. Nevertheless, he continued, even the most strident imperial ambitions had to be checked by the force of treaties. "When Bonaparte dictated treaties of peace in the capitals of the nations which he had overrun," Sprague asked his pro-expansionist fellow senators pointedly, "was he not morally bound to observe them?" The congressional Democrats were not persuaded by this analogy and easily rejected all amendments to the act.[26]

Americans not in Congress also targeted the Indian Removal Act by holding Napoleon up as a negative example. One article that began its life in the *New York Observer* noted, "Bonaparte might be expected to break two or three treaties with Spain or Holland for the sake of bringing millions of men and hundreds of millions of money under his control," but the United States had no such explanation for its own imperial actions. "We have broken scores of treaties with dependent Indians, and descended to the most pitiful subterfuges and evasions," the author continued, "not to augment our national power and resources—not to avoid any danger—but to simply appease a groundless clamor and to make an insignificant acquisition of new lands." The author, writing under the pseudonym "Veritatis Amans" (lover of truth), was not rejecting empire itself, but he did call into question its rationality. Even in Bonaparte's lawless imperial actions the author could perceive rationality if not justification. When Bonaparte broke his treaties, it was ultimately in the service of a reasonable imperial end. Essentially, Veritatis saw Bonaparte acting as an amoral—not immoral—agent. On the other hand, Veritatis could see no such justifications in the actions that the United States was taking in creating its own empire. Not only was the government acting immorally with regard to the Indigenous nations, but it also was acting on behalf of an entirely "groundless" and irrational demand for new land.[27]

Some Indigenous societies resisted the forced migration westward. In 1831, the Sauk war leader Black Hawk led his band of some two thousand followers back onto lands in Illinois that he argued had been illegally transferred to the US government by a rival Sauk leader. In April 1832, hostilities broke out between Black Hawk's warriors and Illinois militia. Despite some initial victories that caused consternation through the region and led to the dispatching of federal troops, Black Hawk was defeated at the Battle of Bad Axe in early August 1832 and turned himself in to US authorities a few weeks later. Black Hawk was incarcerated briefly at Jefferson Barracks, Missouri, before the government transferred him, along with his son and his other lieutenants, to Fortress Monroe in Virginia.[28]

One enterprising author took the opportunity of the Black Hawk War not only to question American imperial policy but also to wonder at the admiration that so many Americans held for Bonaparte. The opinion piece seems to have originated in the *New York Daily Advertiser* and was reprinted along the East Coast. The author began with a brief outline of Napoleon's "despotic dominion" over the nations of Europe and his imprisonment on St. Helena, a place "so far remote that he could never again disturb their peace, or endanger their safety." Given the magnitude of Bonaparte's crimes, the author professed to be astonished that there continued to be outrage among Americans at the supposed "hardship and injustice of the case." The author then turned to Black Hawk, treating him rather sympathetically and describing him as the "brave and warlike" leader of a people who had gradually lost most of their territory and who "probably thought the time was not far distant when they should be called upon to part with the remainder." They had only commenced the war in a "fit of desperation," explained the author. In an act analogous to that of the British after Waterloo, upon the conclusion of hostilities, the American government had determined to "remove this uncivilized hero to a place of security, where he could be kept and guarded . . . to ensure the tranquility of the inhabitants upon the distant borders of the United States."[29]

After outlining the two events, the author came to the crux of his argument. "We do not," he wrote, "recollect having seen the slightest remark of disapprobation from any quarter, of the manner in which this Indian Bonaparte has been treated by his conquerors." The author pointed out at length the similarities for his readers. "If Black Hawk was cruel, so was Bonaparte; if Black Hawk was treacherous and vindictive, so was Bonaparte; if Black Hawk was disposed to disturb the peace, and shed the blood of those who stood in the way of his ambition, so was Bonaparte." The two cases were essentially the same, he wrote, except in one way. "Black Hawk doubtless considered himself as fighting for his own and his nation's rights." On the other hand, the author pointed out, "Bonaparte was not even a native of France—ambition was the motive of all his conduct, and his renown grew out of the most bloody wars, and the prosecution of the most extraordinary system of military oppression and tyranny." The issue ultimately went to character. "We have no doubt that Black Hawk's moral principles, tried by the savage standard," the author noted, "were of a higher cast than Bonaparte's, when estimated by the rules of civilization and Christianity." While the author did not reject American expansion per se, he did artfully call out American imperial hypocrisy when it came to Bonaparte.[30]

Another nation that resisted removal was the Seminole people of central Florida. The Seminole were a tribal amalgamation of Creeks who had been driven off their lands by Andrew Jackson in 1815, bands of various Indigenous peoples native to Florida, and escaped slaves from Alabama and Georgia. After months of bitter infighting among the Seminole over how to respond to the demands of the government, a removal treaty was signed by one Seminole band in March 1833. However, this treaty was not accepted as binding by the rest of the Seminole nation. In 1835 tensions came to a head when a government official was killed and fighting erupted. The War Department sent federal troops to enforce the treaty, but they quickly found that the Florida swamps and the tenacity of Seminole leaders such as Osceola had turned the war into a bloody, disease-ridden quagmire where decisive victory was all but impossible. Despite optimistic pronouncements from the various army commanders who were placed in charge of the operation, the war dragged on into 1842, when the government simply declared the war over.[31]

Democrats in Congress tried to make the best of the embarrassing, protracted conflict. Some pointed to the heroism of the American soldier. In 1838, Senator Franklin Pierce of New Hampshire assured his colleagues, "Here is an exhibition of bravery, of cool determined courage, and patient endurance not surpassed in the history of warfare." Of course, there was only one standard by which to measure such courage, and that was Bonaparte's own troops. Pierce continued, noting that in Florida "there was nothing to excite individual ambition; there was no bridge of Lodi; no battle of Wagram, of Lutzen; no 'sun of Austerlitz' had arisen to excite them onward; the watchword was not glory, but my *country and my duty*." Pierce wanted to assure Americans that the heroism of their soldiers had exceeded those of even Bonaparte since his troops had been motivated by ambitious dreams of glory and the excitement of the moment, while American soldiers in Florida were held in the ranks by far more patriotic notions of duty and country.[32]

Others excused failure by drawing on the history of Bonaparte which all Americans knew. A Democratic representative from Georgia named Hopkins Hosley reminded his countrymen that, "The sands of Egypt and the snows of Russia conquered the armies of Napoleon, and the climate of Florida, equally unfavorable to military operations, conquered the forces of the United States." If even Bonaparte's armies could be halted by external forces such as geography and climate, surely that same principle could also excuse the failures of American forces in such a dismal area of operations. By blaming the environment and calling to mind the greatest army Americans knew, Holsey was absolving American troops for their failures and refusing to acknowledge the determination and courage of the Seminole resistance.[33]

When he was called to account in the press for his failures in Florida, one senior officer exploded in frustration with his own open letter to the American public. He had done his best to prosecute the war he insisted, but the "party scribbling" policymakers in Washington had insisted on implementing their "visionary plans of operation according to the Napoleon tactics!!" These, he sarcastically admitted, were "excellent for operations against troops of civilized nations," but, of course, as every American ought to know, they were "fruitless for wilderness swamps against savages." Ultimately, that was the rub. Frontier raids and counterinsurgency campaigns in dismal swamps were simply not what most Americans connected to Bonaparte. Nevertheless, the few Americans who did use Napoleon as a yardstick for American imperialism during the Indian Removal period set in place rhetoric that would be picked up and expanded upon a decade later in Mexico when the United States could fight its own Napoleonic-style campaigns against a new, rival Napoleon.[34]

The Debate over Texas

The outbreak of the Texas Revolution in 1835 set the United States and Mexico on a long, slow, slide toward war. Shortly after gaining its independence from Spain in 1821, the Mexican government had attempted to populate its northern state of Coahuila y Tejas in an effort to create a buffer that would keep both land-hungry Americans and restless Comanche raiders from the core regions of central Mexico. Enticed by promises of cheap land and low taxes, thousands of American families swarmed into the area and largely ignored government demands that they become Mexican citizens, acknowledge the Roman Catholic church, and, perhaps most galling, abandon slavery. By 1836, American-descended families outnumbered the Hispanic Tejanos population by ten to one. For over a decade, the perennially unstable Mexican government turned a blind eye to their marginally loyal northern province. In 1835, however, the military hero Antonio López de Santa Anna took the reins of political power. The charismatic Santa Anna, who had been on nearly every side of every political issue facing the young Mexican republic, abrogated the liberal 1824 Constitution and established a personal dictatorship. His intention was to create a more centralized national state, but this did not sit well with Mexican states that had become used to virtual self-government under the Mexican liberals. Santa Anna's policies set off a series of revolts throughout Mexico, including in Texas.[35]

After successfully dealing with uprisings in Zacatecas and Coahuila, Santa Anna led an army into Texas, where he quickly defeated rebels at the towns of Goliad and San Antonio—including a famous last stand at a mission called the Alamo. A few months later, however, a Texan force under

Sam Houston surprised and virtually annihilated the overstretched Mexican army at the Battle of San Jacinto. Santa Anna himself was captured in the aftermath of the battle and was forced to acknowledge the independent Republic of Texas as a condition of his release—a statement that the Mexican Congress refused to acknowledge, as it had been made under duress. Following their victory at San Jacinto in 1836, the newly formed and cash-strapped Republic of Texas quickly applied for admission into the United States. In response, the Mexican government warned that any American interference with what they still saw as a rebellious province would be viewed as an act of war. Congress deadlocked on the issue, and the future of Texas consumed the debate over American expansion for the next decade.[36]

As they had in the cases of Louisiana and Florida, both expansionists and their opponents took to the newspapers to debate their positions. Some expansionists—almost all Jacksonian Democrats—were ready for a war over Texas immediately. They saw a conflict with Mexico to be an acceptable risk, and many were positively anxious for a military conflict in which they could truly take up the military mantel of Napoleon rather than chasing Seminole warriors through the swamps of Florida. They appealed to the American sense of militarism infused with Napoleonic glory that William Channing and William Ladd had so strongly condemned. Texans assured their northern cousins that they could "plant the American Eagle" over the Mexican presidential palace as easily as "Napoleon replaced his conquering banner on the turrets of Vendome." In a similar fashion a few years later, the editor of the *New York Herald* assured his readers that they need fear no war with Mexico. After all, he explained, the United States had a population of twenty million souls who were "as fearless, as brave, and as passionately fond of glory . . . as the French under Napoleon."[37]

Another expansionist argument that utilized Bonaparte during this slide toward war was more understated, but it deserves careful examination. It played on the old trope of expansion in the name of national security. Without a real Bonaparte threatening their western border, expansionists had to invent one. This they did, partly without even trying to do so. Santa Anna himself laid most of the groundwork for them when he began to accept the moniker "Napoleon of the West." It is unknown when or where this nickname was first applied or by whom, but it was well established at least by the time of his elevation to president and dictator in 1835. There were numerous variations on this theme that littered the papers. Some of the more common were "Napoleon of the South," "Napoleon of the Americas," and "Napoleon of Mexico." This was a helpful image for Santa Anna to present to Mexican citizens looking for a strong nationalist leader. Indeed, it was not unlike the American linking of Andrew Jackson to Bonaparte. Some Americans were even willing to grant Santa Anna some Napoleonic legitimacy—at least at first. "He is," wrote one editor, "unquestionably a man of consummate abilities. He has always heretofore been successful in his enterprises—he subdued a nation to his sway and became the Napoleon of Mexico." However, a powerful Mexico led by a military strongman on the western border could be a threat—just as Napoleon had been in 1803. Once Santa Anna became a threat, Americans turned his Napoleonic pretensions into a weapon.[38]

Democratic expansionists used Santa Anna's use of the Napoleon sobriquet to chip away at his claims to the legacy of Bonaparte. A letter written from Vera Cruz on June 22, 1835, and published in several American papers, for example, described in graphic detail Santa Anna's attack on the Zacatecas rebels. According to the letter, men, women, and children had been butchered in the streets. The sovereignty of the Zacatecas state was destroyed, the author continued, and the "torch of rational liberty" and self-government had been extinguished. His pen dripping with sarcasm, the author attributed this victory over defenseless women and children to that "singular hero of the Americas, the Napoleon of this continent." The vivid picture painted by this letter showed no glorious military conquest to defeat enemy armies and to break the chains of monarchy, only the intentional and irrational slaughter of civilians and the destruction of liberty. In the eyes of Americans who admired Napoleon, such an image showed the falseness of Santa Anna's claim to the true military and democratic legacy of Bonaparte.[39]

Santa Anna's embarrassing failures in the Texas revolt also badly compromised his claims to the military mantel of Napoleon. Not only was his execution of prisoners at Goliad and the Alamo widely publicized and condemned, but the embarrassing rout of his army at San Jacinto was quite un-Napoleonic. Virtually every paper in America printed some variation of Santa Anna's surrender in which the Mexican dictator tells Sam Houston, "The man who conquered the Napoleon of the South was born to no common destiny." Next to the story, the editor of the *New Bedford Gazette* snidely put into words what many Americans were thinking: "A pretty fellow to call himself a Napoleon who was caught napping . . . and whose highest pretentions to military fame consisted in having slaughtered unarmed prisoners." It is important to note that the editor stated that it was Santa Anna who called himself the Napoleon of the South. In other words, Santa Anna had not actually earned such comparisons. Such language highlighted the counterfeit nature of such a lofty claim.[40]

After his humiliating defeat at the hands of the Texans, the moniker "Napoleon" when applied to Santa Anna by American papers was always preceded by "the so-called" or "the self-styled," which delegitimized his claims to greatness and made him vulnerable in a military sense. In the minds of many Americans, Santa Anna was no real Napoleon, simply a military despot aping the real legacy of the actual hero. When Santa Anna returned to power in Mexico in 1842, most Americans were probably unsurprised and sympathetic when they read in their papers that the Republic of Texas was strongly considering a preemptive attack to conquer Mexico to the Isthmus of Panama. To justify this course, the Texans called for an "appeal to the God of Battles for a redress of the grievances" given them by the "self-styled Napoleon of the West." By appropriating Santa Anna's appropriation of Napoleon, Americans and their Texas cousins made him into a counterfeit who had all of Bonaparte's political ambition, but none of his imperial or military greatness.[41]

Those opposed to the annexation of Texas—almost all of them Whigs—drew on years of anti-Bonaparte rhetoric to make their case. Some made arguments that differed little from those made by their fathers against the Louisiana Purchase. For example, one letter to the editor of the *Philadelphia Enquirer* responded to threats from the Texans to conquer Mexico. "If we embrace Texas for fear she will conquer Mexico and become a powerful rival we shall only act upon a policy which knows no limits and is always fatal to those who undertake it as proved by . . . Napoleon." This was virtually the same argument made by the editor of the *American Citizen* writing against Coriolanus in 1803. That is, the fear of a powerful neighbor—whether Mexico or Texas—was no excuse for imperialism and set a dangerous precent. Other Whigs adopted well-worn arguments about legitimacy and constitutionality. In a paragraph that could have been lifted from a paper in 1803, the editor of the *Richmond Whig* argued against annexation by pointing out that there was no provision in the constitution for the incorporation of foreign territory into the union. In fact, he continued, even Jefferson had admitted as much during the purchase of Louisiana and only made the deal at the "order of Bonaparte, at whose name the whole world grew pale, but none grew so pale as Thomas Jefferson." Such arguments, however, were stale and had little power among a population who did not remember Napoleon's imperial ambitions in North America.[42]

Some Whigs tried to incorporate aspects of Bonaparte's new, positive, imperial image into their anti-annexation rhetoric. For example, on May 23, 1844, the freshman senator from New Jersey, Jacob Miller, warned, "This Texan treaty belongs to the code of Napoleon. Its object is dominion and its only sanction the sword." On one hand, this statement rejected Bonaparte as a worthy imperial example. On the other hand, Miller did see a difference between the expansion of the United States and that of Napoleon's empire. "Napoleon first won the country by open, manly war," Miller explained, "whilst we, pursuing a less hazardous course, steal into the country under the cover of a treaty and then having the nine points possession in our favor, make war upon Mexico for our title." Miller, in attempting to use the accepted martial image of Bonaparte, made "open, manly warfare" preferable to expansion through treaty. This was not entirely new since Federalists had complained about negotiating for New Orleans rather than simply seizing it in 1802. The key difference was that in 1803, Federalists had demanded aggressive action to protect the United States from Bonaparte's imperial ambitions, whereas Miller was suggesting that the imperial identity of the United States did not live up to the Napoleonic model of martial manhood.[43]

Another Whig attempt to use the positive imperial image of Napoleon occurred in the June 27, 1844, edition of the *Boston Courier*. An author writing under the name "Franklin" argued that when Napoleon conquered kingdoms and empires, he had always "employed the spoils of victory for nobler purposes than piling up dollars and counting them." He had stimulated the spread of science, established commercial programs that encouraged economic growth for all Europe, and, in the Napoleonic Code had, "laid the foundation for the greatest moral reform since that began at Bethlehem." High praise indeed. "Conquest, in such hands and so used," Franklin mused, "has something to palliate, if not ennoble it." On the other hand, he snorted, American conquest "by land jobbers and stock brokers can have no redeeming qualities." As bizarre as it might sound to modern ears, Franklin was using the new imperial identity of Napoleon as a yardstick. He held the Bonapartist empire up as mechanism for spreading liberal principles and portrayed American imperialism as a vulgar project whose motivation was merely economic exploitation. In a remarkable inversion, both Franklin and Miller argued against the annexation of Texas by arguing that the expansion of the United States was not enough like that of Napoleonic France.[44]

The election of the expansionist Democrat James K. Polk led to the annexation of Texas by the United States in late 1845. War did not come immediately, but a simmering border dispute between the two republics made war a matter of time. Mexico considered the Nueces River the southern border of Texas, and the United States maintained that the boundary was 150 miles farther south along the Rio Grande. After failing in a half-hearted attempt to secure purchase of the disputed territory, Polk ordered an army under Zachary Taylor into the disputed area. In April 1846, a border skirmish occurred in which several American soldiers were killed. Polk used the incident to ask for a declaration of war from Congress, which he got on May 13. With war declared, new arguments had to be mustered. War, after all, did not necessarily mean conquest along a Napoleonic model. Both anti-imperialists and their rivals attempted to shape and describe the conduct of the war within Bonaparte's new, positive, imperial image.[45]

Conquering Mexico by Anecdote

As their armies prepared to invade Mexico, Americans debated the strategic conduct of the United States' first major war of expansion. As they did, they used a new rhetorical method best described as argument by anecdote. Both Whigs and Democrats appealed to the military authority of Napoleon through a short story or a saying. These stories usually came from what they had read about Bonaparte in their volumes of anecdote books and biographies. Another rich source was *Napoleon's Military Maxims*. This was a compilation of pithy Napoleon quotations and critical commentary about the principles of warfare that had conveniently been published in the United States for the first time in 1845. The emergence of these arguments shows that the basic premise of Bonaparte as a military genius was accepted even by those who rejected his imperial model. Yet, Americans found that they could not even agree on the military lessons of Bonaparte.[46]

These arguments by anecdote first emerged in discussions of grand strategy. For anti-imperialists, the most effective national policy would limit American objectives and fight an aggressive defensive war within the bounds of Texas. This, said one commentator, was the "humane" method preferred by Napoleon for breaking up mobs: "Fire balls first to let the enemy learn our seriousness and feel our power, then burn blank cartridges afterwards, if necessary, to stimulate his haste in retreat." In other words, live ammunition should only be used in an initial encounter, and then blank cartridges afterward to limit unnecessary bloodshed. Translated to a strategic scale, this author wanted the United States to use as little force as necessary in the coming war by fighting defensively. Other, more aggressive armchair generals argued that such a policy was foolish—and frankly un-Napoleonic. Rather than fighting a limited conflict on the frontiers of Texas, said an author writing as "St. Mark," the United States ought to "fight with Mexico as Napoleon fought with Europe, by striking at her capitals." Most other commentators agreed with this assessment.[47]

One imperialist argued that Americans ought to take Napoleonic strategy to its logical conclusion in his argument by anecdote. He opened with a quote from a Bonaparte biography in which the French emperor orders his artillery to fire on his Russian and Austrian forces as they flee from the Austerlitz battlefield across a frozen river. The impact of the cannon shot breaks the ice and drowns thousands of enemy soldiers. This anecdote, the author claimed, showed that the United States should adopt a severe military policy in its war with Mexico to terminate the conflict quickly. "War is war, the world over," he concluded darkly. "Napoleon had his way and we have ours for carrying it forward, but ours, no less than his, aims at one simple object—conquest and destruction." This imperialist found in his study of Bonaparte that violence was an inherent part of empire building, and he embraced it.[48]

Recruiting citizen soldiers to carry out these Napoleonic strategies proved less difficult than agreeing on the methods themselves. To supplement the small regular army, Congress called for 65,000 volunteers to serve in state-sponsored units. During the during the War of 1812, recruitment had been a challenge for the national government, especially in New England where anti-Bonapartist sentiment was deepest. At least initially, the government faced no such problem when it came to recruiting young men to invade Mexico. The state of Tennessee had 30,000 men lined up at the recruiting stations to fill a state quota of 3,000. Pennsylvania and Ohio had to turn away whole companies of men because they could not arm them fast enough. Even anti-expansionist Whigs complained that their young men had been caught up in a Democratic war. Historians have pointed to jingoistic patriotism, romantic ideas about adventure and glory, and social advancement as causes for this sudden enthusiasm for imperial conquest.[49]

It bears remembering how closely these reasons for enlistment were tied into the glorious war narratives woven by Scott and other Napoleon biographers during the two decades leading up to the war. As William Ladd had feared, American youths had learned that war was an exciting adventure full of martial valor from military histories of Napoleon. Only months before war was declared, for example, Americans were treated to J. T. Headley's best-selling *Napoleon and His Marshals*. In his introduction, Headley admitted that his critics would "object to books of this kind as fostering the spirit of war by stimulating a love of glory." But, he shrugged, if history was to be "abjured of battles," it would be very boring indeed. Still, Headley was not simply a warmonger. He continued by pointing out that a love of glory was actually an antidote against vulgar commercialism in "this age of dollars and cents." Headley openly held up Napoleon and his commanders as the "stern republicans" who defended "liberty against despotism—equal rights against privilege." Perhaps with William Channing's essay in mind, Headley argued that glory won in defense of such laudable principles was carried on by the "direct command of Heaven," as opposed to imperial struggles fought for mere economic advantage.[50]

Watching the Massachusetts regiments marching off to the war, the Whig editor of the *Boston Evening Transcript* tried to understand their motivation. Many of them, he concluded, who "remember the campaigns of Napoleon, and the honors bestowed upon his brave soldiery, may be expecting promotion according to their fearlessness in the war, their daring exploits, and what might seem to be their dauntless courage in defying death." "The romantic and chivalrous among them," the editor went on, are "filled with ideas of glory," and they "expect to rise . . . from rank to rank crowned in each affray with new distinctions—a brilliant rise from a short battle!" The editor was probably not wrong; he was likely seeing the results of young Americans reading countless Napoleonic biographies and military histories. As they marched off to invade a sister republic, the volunteers carried muskets on their shoulders and dreams of taking on the mantle of Napoleonic greatness in their heads.[51]

As the war intensified in 1846 and 1847, the arguments on the home front that surrounded it expanded their focus to matters of American imperial policy rather than grand military strategy. Both sides continued to use Napoleon as their standard for national conduct, and both continued to come to different conclusions about the legacy of Bonaparte and what it meant to the imperial future of the United States.

The great debate began shortly after war was declared and was clearly illustrated by a set of articles in the *New Bedford Mercury*. On June 5, 1846, the *Mercury* printed a letter to the editor along with the editor's reply. The unnamed correspondent wrote passionately in favor of both the annexation of Texas and the war with Mexico. He briefly cited international law to justify American actions on the border. Yet, he doubted that the editors would take that authority, and so he quoted even higher authorities: God and Bonaparte. "When Napoleon was crowned King of Italy," he wrote, "upon putting on the iron crown of Charlemagne, he is purported as saying emphatically, 'God has placed his crown upon my head, and woe to the man that touches it.'" "God," the correspondent continued, "has given us Texas to the Del Norte, and woe to the foreign nation, prince, or potentate that should interfere with it." In this, the author followed the pattern of using Bonaparte's imperial example as a positive yardstick for American expansion into Mexico.[52]

The *Mercury*'s editor quickly responded. "How unhappy the illustration drawn from Napoleon," he wrote back, apparently shocked that that his correspondent did not rightly understand the history of Bonaparte. "That iron crown of Lombardy was to him a crown of thorns—it bore him to the ground and crushed him. So will this Texas be a thorn in the side of the union." The editor continued with a condemnation of invoking God into a debate on national expansion. "Impious and shortsighted man," he wrote, as if to Bonaparte directly, "how short was the time you wore that crown . . . you died in exile without crown or hope." The editor concluded forcefully, "We are told that God has given Texas to the Rio Bravo as he gave Italy to Napoleon! Sad parallel! May it never be carried out." Both men brought Bonaparte into the debate on expansion, expecting the other to acknowledge his authority in matters of imperial expansion, yet they could not agree on what the legacy of Napoleon actually meant. One saw the story of Bonaparte as one of divinely inspired expansion, the other saw it as a warning against hubris.[53]

A similar exchange took place a little over a year later. This time, an anti-expansionist writing as an "Old Farmer" fired the first shots in the

National Intelligencer. The Old Farmer was gravely concerned about the phrase "manifest destiny," which, since 1845, had come to epitomize the liberal ideology of American expansion. Even the iconic phrase itself had Napoleonic overtones when one considers how closely "destiny" was associated with Bonaparte through the work of Scott. The Old Farmer admitted that might have been "the 'manifest destiny' of Bonaparte to conquer half of Europe"; however, he continued, "it was also his 'manifest destiny' to die in miserable exile on the rock of St. Helena." Instead of national delusions, he continued, it would be far better for the United States to adopt the policy of San Marino. This tiny ancient republic nestled in the mountains of Italy had, when offered additional territory and artillery by Napoleon during his Italian campaign, politely accepted the cannons but refused the territory because they did not wish to "engage in the miserable folly of attempting to govern people without their consent."[54]

Three days later, a delightfully sarcastic reply by an author only identified as "X" appeared in the *Baltimore Sun*. "We are told," the author began, "Napoleon had a great respect for the Republic of San Marino." That may have been true, he continued, but this was so only because it was such a small and insignificant place that it probably did not even appear on most French maps. It was really a silly notion, X snorted, to expect the United States, a great republic, to draw lessons from a republic with an army of "twenty-four soldiers commanded by a Lieutenant, . . . and two corporals." Indeed, X concluded, "I have strong doubts whether the army of San Marino will ever cross the Alps . . . [as] they were crossed by Napoleon unless they are provided with Austrian or French passports." In other words, for X the lesson of the story of San Marino was to be more like the great Napoleon and less like the insignificant San Marino. Both the Old Farmer and X took the exact same story from the history of Napoleon and came to completely opposite conclusions about what it meant to America's imperial identity.[55]

The Foreignness of Mexico

While Americans fought each other in the papers, the war dragged on. In September 1846 American forces under Zachary Taylor seized the northern city of Monterrey. Farther south, another American army under Winfield Scott took the port of Vera Cruz in early 1847. By June, Scott's forces had fought their way inland to the outskirts of Mexico City, and Taylor had won a decisive victory against Mexican forces at the Battle of Buena Vista. Despite losing every battle, the Mexican government steadfastly refused to come to the negotiating table. Many Whigs looked for ways to force a conclusion to the war without the acquisition of territory by appealing to the imperial image of Bonaparte as a warning against imperial overextension—both geographically and nationally. Like William Ladd had done a decade earlier, they did this by asking their audience to consider the less glorious aspects of Bonaparte's imperial career but cautiously avoided besmirching the accepted image of Napoleon as a military genius or a liberal imperialist. At the same time, they updated Ladd's argument by returning to very old arguments made by the Federalists that portrayed the Mexican environment and people as outside the bounds of America's natural limits.[56]

The first such articles appeared in the summer of 1846, and they gathered strength in October of that year as Americans learned of the tenacious Mexican resistance in Monterrey. "A war with a Government and a war with a People are two very different things," warned the editor of the *North American*. He cited Bonaparte's early successes in Italy as an example of the former and his disastrous occupation of Spain as an example of the latter. The defense of Monterrey, he argued, demonstrated that the American war against Mexico was one against a people rather than a government and would likely have the same disastrous conclusion. Six months later, the *National Intelligencer* elaborated on this basic theme. "In Europe, Napoleon conquered other countries because the population made no resistance after the regular army was defeated," the editor explained. "The two hostile armies met as prizefighters, and the country was the stake which belonged to the victors." On the other hand, he continued, "an invading army is unable to conquer any nation where all the people are hostile and opposed to them. Spain is a memorable example of this." In America's present war, he wrote grimly, it was important to remember that in the case of Spain, "Napoleon had possession of her capital and all her strongholds, with 300,000 veteran troops, the country compact and not one fifth the extent of what we propose to overrun." Even holding an enemy's capital could not overturn the bounds of America's demographic natural boundaries.[57]

Mexico, in other words, was a country of people foreign to the United States and unwilling to be assimilated. Some anti-expansionists made this case in racial rather than political ways. They portrayed the Mexican people as racially unassimilable into republican government. For example, one editor in the *National Era* accused the Democrat press of trying to outdo Headley's *Napoleon and His Marshals* by making heroes out of "Taylor and his Generals." The editor found this unseemly since there was little Napoleonic glory in winning victories over a "half-breed, mongrel race" of Mexicans. However, as this article shows, making the demographic boundaries about racial rather than political boundaries undermined the deeply held desire of so many Americans to find Napoleonic glory on the battlefield. By making their argument in a way that did not diminish the martial glory of Napoleon, most Whigs hoped to reach an audience who accepted Bonaparte's imperial model, while still putting Mexico beyond the demographic boundaries of the United States.[58]

Some of Napoleon's other campaigns offered similar opportunities for anti-expansionists to score rhetorical points by encouraging Americans to see Bonaparte's imperial project through the lens of geographic—natural—boundaries. In a speech to the Lowell Institute, one anti-expansionist asked his audience to consider seriously the "natural difficulties to be overcome in our war against Mexico." It was protected by impenetrable mountains, deadly diseases, and unbearable heat. "Man cannot war against nature," he stated flatly, and not even the greatest general of them all was exempt from this maxim. "Napoleon could scatter the Mamelukes like chaff before the wind, but fled from the burning sands of Egypt and from the desolation of the pestilence," he argued. "Of the 500,000 men who went to war with him against the climate of Russia," he went on, "but 40,000 came staggering back." He left his audience with a sobering thought. "Mexico has the mountains of Switzerland, the snows of Russia, and a sicklier sunshine than ever bathed Napoleon's banners." Mexico, in other words, was not only a country of foreign, unassimilable people, but also one that was geographically foreign to the United States and thus outside its natural boundaries. By portraying Napoleon as having been defeated by geographical factors beyond the natural frontiers of France—an element beyond even his control—the author simultaneously acknowledged the martial image of Bonaparte while warning Americans about the inherent dangers of adopting an imperial identity that carried them beyond their own natural frontiers.[59]

Even the eventual taking of Mexico City in the fall of 1847 did little to mollify the basic anti-expansionist argument that acknowledged the military authority of Bonaparte while painting the people and geography of Mexico as inherently foreign to the United States. As Whig anti-expansionists quickly pointed out, Joseph Bonaparte had sat on the Spanish throne in Madrid for years without ending the insurgency. The most famous anti-expansionist speech of the conflict drew on this vein and was given by a weary and saddened Henry Clay. The head of the Whig Party had lost a son in the war, and he noticed the worrisome parallels between American imperialism and that of Napoleon. Clay pointed out to his audience that even Napoleon and his "colossal power" had been unable to subjugate the Spanish people into a foreign system of rule. For Clay—always a supporter of good relations between the Latin American republics and the United States—Mexico was a foreign place that could not be justly or wisely incorporated into the American empire.[60]

Other anti-imperialists reminded anyone who would listen that Napoleon had taken Moscow in 1812 before encountering the Russian winter and the Russian Cossacks. One of these wrote to the *National Intelligencer* shortly after learning of Mexico City's fall to Scott's army. "How long has it been since Bonaparte attempted to conquer Russia?" he asked his audience rhetorically. He continued by reminding his readers that in the beginning of Bonaparte's Russian campaign, "his success was prodigious." Yet, he wrote ominously, history and nature soon turned against even Napoleon when he reached too far. "The city of Mexico may prove the Moscow of our Conquerer [sic]," he concluded. Whether it was Clay or this anonymous writer, while Napoleon's military glory was unquestionable, Napoleon's true imperial legacy was a warning against overreach into areas beyond the natural boundaries of empire.[61]

Expansionists scoffed at the dire predictions of the Whigs. With the war turning in the favor of the United States, they found that comparing American victories to those of their great hero was an easy way to connect their own imperial success to the military manhood embodied in their image of Bonaparte's empire. At one 1847 Independence Day gathering in Virginia, an orator gave a speech that was typical of hundreds more given on the same day across the nation. "The daring and impetuous charge at Palo Alto, the dreadful storming of Monterey, and the heady fight along the terrible pass of the Cerro Gordo," he began, "bring forcibly to mind the desperate valor displayed at Jena, Saragossa, Wagram, and Arcola." "Yet, when the disparity of troops and other disadvantages are considered," he continued, "the impartial judgment of the world must decide that the fame of the imperial eagles of Napoleon, splendid as it is, must yield to the far reflected luster and dazzling glories of American arms acquired in these memorable and brilliant fields of victory." For this speaker, it was military victories in Mexico that had at last proved beyond question that the American empire had finally eclipsed the great empire of Napoleon.[62]

In the closing months of the war anti-expansionists tried desperately to respond to the argument suggested by the Virginia orator above. As they did, they found that they had to separate Napoleon's military prowess from his imperial identity in the minds of their fellow countrymen. One pleaded with an "immense gathering" of Whigs in New York at the end of 1847. Sounding like countless expansionists, he told the cheering crowd, "Our troops have fought bravely—none ever fought better—they have achieved victories that would have conferred honor on Napoleon Bonaparte." This connected American martial manhood to Napoleon's martial identity. He then, however, tried to separate the bravery of Americans from the idea of imperial conquest. "We need no more battles to prove the valor of American soldiers," he insisted. What he meant was that there was no need to engage in imperial conquest to prove American manhood.[63]

Anti-expansionists were fighting a losing battle by the end of 1847. Expansionists tended to understand their victory as a triumph of liberal imperialism, but they understood this in different ways. A few expansionists held onto an older, violent, and immoral imperial identity of Napoleon. One imperialist, for example, asked his audience to contrast the American invasion of Mexico with those of Napoleon forty years prior. Whereas Bonaparte had turned the continent into a "charnel house" and created an "ocean of blood, rapine, murder and monstrosity from Moscow to Gibraltar," the American invasion of Mexico "illuminated the minds of her people, long held in military bondage and civil tyranny." Much more common, however, were valedictories that saw American imperialism as the continuation of Napoleon's own liberal model. One correspondent to the *Baltimore Sun* likened the American invasion of Mexico to Bonaparte's reorganization of the Holy Roman Empire. Those who decried the American invasion, he wrote with mock astonishment, had apparently "never read of the French campaign in Germany, which was a terrible infliction upon the country, but at the same time a means of spreading liberal principles and improvements in every branch of social life." If Mexico lost half its territory in the war but gained a republican education from its conqueror, he maintained, "she would have paid a low price of tuition." These two writers used two different versions of Bonaparte's imperial image to construct America's own imperial identity as a republican empire of liberty.[64]

While anti-expansionists were unable to prevent the war, they were ultimately successful in forcing Polk to accept a more moderate peace treaty than he would have liked. It is impossible to know the precise effect that the anti-expansionist rhetoric built around Bonaparte had on the end of the conflict. The Treaty of Guadalupe Hidalgo, which finally ended the war in 1848, forced Mexico to surrender only its northern territories. These areas were far less populated than the southern provinces, which may suggest that the Whig argument that the people of Mexico were simply outside the natural boundaries of the United States had found its mark. It is also possible that by 1848 enough American political leaders had come to believe that while they had gone to war in search of a glorious Austerlitz-like victory, they were on the brink of falling into an interminable, bloody, Spanish insurgency in a foreign land clearly beyond America's natural imperial frontiers. Such fears may have prompted them to accept a partial victory. [65]

On the other hand, it is entirely possible that anti-expansionists were hurt by their own dire rhetoric. Ultimately, none of their grim prophecies came to fruition. Unlike Napoleon's Russian adversaries, the Mexicans did not burn their capital. Though a few guerilla bands did form and caused some casualties among the invaders, they never represented a true national resistance movement. Indeed, many Americans were surprised at how accommodating Mexicans were to their occupiers. Disease and desertion plagued the American forces, but in the end, an outnumbered American army had marched hundreds of miles into Mexico across sun-burned deserts and treacherous mountains to take an enemy capital without losing a battle. This certainly had as much to do with Mexican political and economic chaos as it did with the prowess of the American soldier or America's liberal imperial destiny, but expansionists did not realize that, nor did they care. After all, the war for them was not only about territorial expansion. It was also about taking up the mantel of Napoleonic imperial glory. In both cases, the expansionists had much to celebrate.[66]

The Triumph of Napoleon

On May 30, 1848, the Treaty of Guadalupe Hidalgo went into effect, at last giving the United States a claim to having fulfilled Napoleon's dream of building a great North American empire. Anti-expansionists had to admit that they had lost the argument. Perhaps what galled them more than losing was that so many people of the United States did not even seem repentant about their aggressive imperialism. In fact, they celebrated it. As the volunteers from the Mexican War returned home, they were feted and honored as the glorious Napoleonic heroes that they had set out to be. It was all too much for a wag writing in the *Berkshire County Whig* who bitterly found humor in the situation. "The Mexican battles surpass even the famous fights of Napoleon in the opportunities they furnish for the sudden manufacture of fame, to order," he quipped. "If half the swords which have been presented to men who have seen the elephant in Mexico, as a reward for their deeds of prowess shall be beaten into plowshares at the termination of the war, we may look for great things in agriculture."[67]

Thanks to the flood of literature sympathetic to Bonaparte that arrived on American bookshelves after his death, by 1830 the common American understanding of Napoleon as a treacherous and ambitious imperial despot had broken down. It was replaced by a new romanticized image of Bonaparte as a military genius and liberal imperialist. Some Americans fought back valiantly against this new Napoleonic legacy by warning their fellow countrymen against the dangerous militarism and unchecked ambition that never lay far below the surface of Napoleon's character. For over a decade, the contest over the Napoleonic legacy played out in the discourse of American empire between Jacksonian Democrats and the Whig opposition. By 1845, however, those Americans who rejected the revisionist legacy of Napoleon were on the defensive. The debates over the annexation of Texas and the resulting Mexican-American War demonstrated the practical effects of such thinking. By the end of the conflict, Americans had used Bonaparte's softened imperial image to create their own imperial identity as a liberal empire of liberty with a continental mission to spread American democracy.

CONCLUSION

Napoleon's Dream

A British traveler was rather shocked at American manners when he visited the United States in 1862. "All Americans have an intense admiration for Napoleon," he sniffed disdainfully, and to make matters worse, "they seldom scruple to express their regret that he was beaten at Waterloo." During the late 1850s, enthusiasm for Bonaparte reached its peak in the United States. After 1855, visitors to virtually any bookshop in America could purchase John S. Abbott's two-volume *History of Napoleon Bonaparte*. This wildly popular account written by the New England minister turned biographer ended with the revealing comment: "Napoleon, in death has become the victor over all his foes. Every generous heart now does homage to his lofty character. . . . His noble fame is every day extending." Abbott was only the latest in a long tradition of antebellum Bonaparte biographers who had turned the emperor into a democratic military hero and his empire into a mechanism to spread human freedom. Even more, however, Abbott's biography represented Napoleon's final triumph over anti-expansionists such as William Channing and William Ladd. Not only did Abbott hold up Bonaparte as a military hero and as a positive imperial example, but he also held up his "lofty character" as worthy of emulation. The turn from the rapacious, bloody, imperial tyrant of 1803 was, at last, complete.[1]

If they had looked hard enough, our hypothetical visitors to the book shop might have also found a little book called *The Deck and Port Songster*, which was an entire volume of laudatory tunes about the French emperor. Upon opening the book to page sixty-five, they would have found one ditty titled "Napoleon's Dream." The song's narrator described falling asleep and visiting St. Helena, where he is welcomed by Napoleon. When he finds that the dreamer is an American, Bonaparte brightens and reminds his visitor of his glorious victories in defense of freedom:

> On the plains of Marengo I tyranny hurl'd
> And wherever my banner the eagle unfurrl'd
> Twas the standard of freedom all over the world!

As the dreamer awakens, he hears Bonaparte's final words ringing in his ears, "Liberty soon ov'r the world shall be seen." The message of this dream combined with Abbot's biography could not have been clearer to American readers. Napoleon had passed on his dream of a global empire of liberty to the United States.[2]

Yet, before the United States could expand further, the nation tore itself apart over the issue of slavery. In mid-1862, Abbott wrote a letter to his publisher with an offer to capitalize on the ongoing military conflict. "At the close of this war there will be a million and a half of young men, who, from their life in the camp, will be particularly interested in Military History," he explained. Abbott continued with some self-promotion, "*The Life of Napoleon*, in that respect, stands preeminent." Given those two facts, Abbott wanted to publish a one-volume edition of his previous work that would be cheaper and more accessible to young men just home from the war. After all, he reminded the publisher, "Napoleon is popular with the masses."[3]

Abbott, though self-promoting, was not wrong. Like their fathers before them, Americans north and south discussed their Civil War military service in terms of Bonaparte. During the first eighteen months of the war, for example, numerous promising officers such as P. G. T. Beauregard and George B. McClellan found themselves heralded as the next Napoleon by the media and by their soldiers. Indeed, McClellan had even been a leading member of West Point's officially sanctioned Napoleon Club and had presented several papers on Bonaparte's campaigns to his fellow officers and cadets. Early in the war, one officer explained to his local newspaper that the duty of an army officer was to lead from the front. For evidence, he pointed to the greatest officer he knew. "Napoleon in person was obliged to lead his bravest men over the bridge of Lodi, and again at Arcola, and at Waterloo," he stated. Furthermore, he continued, "at the last grand charge of the Old Guard he felt the dire necessity of leading them himself, and he rushed to their head, but his officers seized him and forced him back." This had been a mistake. "Had they left him to follow his instinct," the officer mused, "he might have turned the fortune of the day." These brief examples show that at the onset of the war, at least, Civil War soldiers expected their officers to be the Napoleon they had read about in the biographies of Scott, Headley, and Abbott.[4]

They also expected their campaigns to be like those they had read about in countless Napoleonic military histories. Upon learning that a massive United States army was closing in on the Confederate capital of Richmond in early 1862—an army led by that "Young Napoleon," George B. McClellan—a Confederate diplomat in Brussels wrote an encouraging letter to his secretary of state that drew courage from the history of a familiar figure. "If any of our fellow citizens . . . should be disposed to entertain anxiety toward the final result," he began, "let them find fresh courage in recalling to mind the disasters incurred at Moscow by the greatest captain of modern times." His letter went on for another three pages describing in detail the awful calamities that befell the French army in Russia, which he had read about in a recently published memoir. Sounding like an anti-expansionist of ten years earlier, he finally concluded, "It is daily becoming more and more evident . . . that a fate yet more terrible is awaiting the would-be conquerors of the Confederate States, under the burning sun and in the death bringing swamps of the South."[5]

Yet, by the midpoint of the war, references to Napoleon had become far less frequent. A variety of factors was likely to blame. Probably the biggest cause was that the romantic ideas about military life that young men had learned from Scott, Headley, Abbott, and others did not hold up to the reality they experienced during the war. During the winter of 1864–65, for example, one soldier woke up to eighteen inches of snow and noted in his diary, "wading through the deep snow reminds me of a picture that I have often seen, 'Napoleon Bonaparte before Moscow.'" Yet, he continued wearily, "duty must be attended to, no matter what the weather may be." This soldier, and many more like him found that the reality of military life was not nearly so grand as they had been led to believe.[6]

It was not just camp life that did not live up to expectations. Virtually all of the officers who had been labeled as the new Napoleon fell woefully short of expectations. Dashing military men such as George McClellan and P. G. T. Beauregard who promised dramatic victories in the style of

Bonaparte were soon cashiered in favor of other generals, many of whom eschewed the Napoleonic model. In fact, the generals who did the most to bring the war to a successful conclusion seemed to have little to do with the popular perceptions of Bonaparte's martial identity. Ulysses S. Grant and William T. Sherman won their victories through a dogged determination not to lose rather than by glorious, nation-shattering, Austerlitz-style victories. Indeed, those generals who attempted such things usually ended up simply sacrificing the lives of their soldiers to no good result. By the end of the war, Americans had created a new pantheon of their own military heroes who had little to do with Bonaparte. Americans had, in a sense, outgrown the need to measure their military greatness against Napoleon.[7]

The other reason that expansionist rhetoric centered on Bonaparte fell out of favor was that there was no American military expansion between 1850 and 1898. The Gadsden Purchase was obtained from Mexico through treaty in 1853, and Alaska was bought from the Russian empire in 1867, but that was no conquest; those were simply diplomatic transactions. Ambitious plans to seize various parts of Central America or the Caribbean came to naught. Destructive campaigns against the Native peoples of the plains were portrayed as pacification operations within preexisting borders rather than expanding the empire of liberty, and there was little martial glory in conquering Native peoples, unless you lost spectacularly—as George Custer found in 1876. At least one historian has recently written of the end of "manifest destiny" as an imperial ideology by 1872. It was not until the Spanish American War of 1898 that another "real" war of conquest broke out that again allowed Americans to prove their valor. By then, however, most young men compared their battles to their fathers' fights at Gettysburg and Antietam rather than to Napoleon's campaigns.[8]

Americans did not entirely forget Napoleon, of course. In Theodore Roosevelt's famous memoir of his time leading the Rough Riders in Cuba during the Spanish-American War, he described the Spanish forces he encountered as effective guerrilla fighters, but poor soldiers. This, he said, should come as no surprise to any student of history since Spanish soldiers had proved "utterly unable to stand in the open against those of Napoleon's Marshals," but they had proven to be superb partisans who had bled the emperor's armies white. And, according to the French-born literature scholar and social commentator Albert Leon Guérard, when young American doughboys passed through Paris on their way to the Great War in 1917, many were eager to pay a visit to that "great shrine," the sand-bagged tomb of Napoleon. A mild case of "Napoleonitis," he snorted derisively, "is endemic" among young Americans. Yet, it was only a mild case, and Guérard noted in his 1924 book on the Napoleonic legend that America was finally "evolving a legend of her own, much more in harmony with the facts, and much more profitable to the soul, than that of Napoleon."[9]

In many ways, the curtailment of Napoleon as a symbol in the American discourse of empire after the Civil War marks the end of the first phase of American imperialism. Between 1800 and 1850, the image of Napoleon had provided a crucial cultural and political touchstone in the construction of an American imperial identity. The malleability of his imperial image allowed him to be inserted into the American discourse of expansion effectively by imperialists and anti-imperialists alike. Bonaparte's dream of re-creating the French empire in North America allowed American imperialists to justify their own aggressive expansion along the Gulf Coast as defensive measures necessary to national security. At the same time, the American understanding of the Napoleonic system in Europe encouraged an anti-expansion movement that was motivated by the fear of becoming too politically involved with the French empire.

Simultaneously, Napoleon's imperial image provided a yardstick against which Americans could measure their own imperialism. At first, there was common agreement among Americans that Bonaparte's imperial image was a negative one based on insatiable ambition and bloody conquest in violation of natural law, the law of nations, and even rationality. Expansionists argued that, by contrast, the American empire was a peaceful and benign empire of liberty. Anti-expansionists countered by drawing uncomfortable parallels between aggressive American imperialism in North America and Bonaparte's own imperial methods in Europe.

The flood of Napoleon-themed literature that saturated the American market in the two decades after his deposition in 1815 and death in 1821 led to a reimagining of Bonaparte's imperial identity and triggered a reorientation of the imperial identity of the United States. The best-selling works of Barry O'Meara, Walter Scott, and like-minded American biographers reconstructed Napoleon as a model of liberal imperialism whose empire fostered democracy and martial valor. A new generation of Americans internalized this imperial image of Bonaparte and used it to reshape their own imperial identity during the Mexican-American War. By the time the conflict ended in 1848, many Americans imagined their own republican empire as a worthy successor to Napoleon's own.

As the United States continues into the twenty-first-century it is worth taking stock of our national dialogue on imperialism. The US government now has the ability to direct overwhelming force anywhere on the planet in a matter of minutes. American military bases dot the globe. But if the tools and scope of American imperialism have changed, the ideology of imperialism has changed far less. The aftermath of the 9/11 attacks showed that Americans continue to be quick to define nebulous actors as threats to their national security in need of elimination through preemptive war. The Iraq conflict and its many offshoots demonstrate that many Americans continue to believe that aggressive construction of an "empire of liberty" is a worthy goal. As both China and Russia expand their own imperial projects, how the United States should respond to imperialism takes on an increasingly important role in political discussions.

Yet, these recent and ongoing conflicts also show that the ideology of imperialism remains contested. Changes in technology have provided Americans with the unprecedented ability to engage in a discussion about their imperialism. The internet, cellular phones, and social media have largely replaced the newspapers that early Americans read with such alacrity, but they serve the same purpose—to foster a national dialogue. This discourse, however, has become increasingly difficult as Americans seem to lack a common cultural and political measuring stick with which to measure their imperial ambitions. Even Bonaparte occasionally continues to be part of the conversation, though he has lost most of his rhetorical currency. In August 2007, a young army lieutenant serving in Baghdad read an opinion piece by historian Richard Bulliet in the *New York Times*. In the article, which I eagerly read in between endless combat patrols, Bulliet suggested that President George W. Bush might take a lesson from one of the great military captains in history and abandon his stalled Iraq campaign before it proved disastrous. The title of his essay was "Bush and Napoleon."[10]

NOTES

INTRODUCTION

1. Semmes, *John H. B. Latrobe*, 239.
2. Hicks, "Images of Napoleon at Montpelier."
3. Eber Howe, quoted in Appleby, *Inheriting the Revolution*, 27, 81–82; the British also went through a similar process: see Semmel, *Napoleon and The British*.
4. For examples of the "top-down" approach, see P. Onuf, *Jefferson's Empire*; Immerman, *Empire for Liberty*.
5. A. Isenberg and Richards, "Alternative Wests," 4–5; Richards, *Breakaway Americas*, 6–7; also see Minardi, "Pax Americana?"
6. P. Onuf, "Imperialism and Nationalism," 21–22.
7. Larson, "Wisdom Enough to Improve Them," 223–48; Cayton, "Radicals in the Western World," 77–96.
8. P. Onuf, *Jefferson's Empire*, 53–57; Burstein and Isenberg, *Madison and Jefferson*, 387–94.
9. Pasley, *Tyranny of Printers*, 3–5, 85.
10. Pasley, *Tyranny of Printers*, 206–7.
11. "November 11," *Federal Gazette* (Baltimore), November 16, 1796; Esdaile, *Napoleon's Wars*, 49–50; Andrew Jackson to James Robertson, January 11, 1798, in Jackson, *Papers of Andrew Jackson*, 1:165.
12. *Loudon's Register* (New York), July 6, 1797; Shulim, *Old Dominion and Napoleon Bonaparte*, 47–75; also see Cleves, *The Reign of Terror in America*.
13. Englund, *Napoleon*, 126–40.
14. Herring, *From Colony to Superpower*, 82–91.
15. Shulim, *Old Dominion and Napoleon Bonaparte*, 76–109, Elkins and McKitrick, *Age of Federalism*, 676–90.

1. BOUNDARIES

1. Brown, *Address to the Government*, 56.
2. For this chapter and the next one, both DeConte, *This Affair of Louisiana*, and Kukla, *A Wilderness So Immense*, remain standard works on American expansion into Louisiana.
3. Two such ambiguous maps are found in Emmanuel Bowen, *A New and Accurate Map of Louisiana with part of Florida and Canada and the Adjacent Countries* (London, 1752), Library of Congress, LCCN 74693994; and John Senex, *A Map of Louisiana and the River Mississippi* (1721), Library of Congress, LCCN 98685735.
4. Taylor, *American Colonies*, 76–79, 382–94.
5. Taylor, *American Colonies*, 421–33; Herring, *From Colony to Superpower*, 20–23, 32.
6. Nugent, *Habits of Empire*, 48–54, 56.
7. Nugent, *Habits of Empire*, 56–57.
8. Englund, *Napoleon*, 177, 254–55; Lewis, "Tornado on the Horizon," 117–26; Tucker and Henderickson, *Empire of Liberty*, 108–24. Probably the most reprinted article about Bonaparte's North American expedition was "The Fete at Paris," *Daily Advertiser* (Baltimore), January 27, 1802; also see *Newburyport Herald* (Newburyport, MA), December 29, 1801.
9. Esdaile, *Napoleon's Wars*, 105–6, 133–35; Sahlins, "Natural Frontiers Revisited," 1423–51; St. John, "Contingent Continent," 19–20.
10. P. Onuf and N. Onuf, *Federal Union Modern World*, 8–9; Lang, *Foreign Policy*, 15–16.
11. *City Gazette and Advertiser* (Charleston, SC), November 21, 1801.
12. "Political Pie," *Oracle of Dauphin* (Harrisburg, PA), January 19, 1801.
13. *Otsego Herald* (Cooperstown, NY), December 27, 1798; *Virginia Argus* (Richmond, VA), November 24, 1801; the excerpt from the *Federal Gazette* (Baltimore) is quoted in Shulim, *Old Dominion and Napoleon*, 69.
14. No real scholarly work has been done on William Stephens Smith outside of passing references in biographies of John Adams and military histories of the early republic. See, for example, Kohn, *Eagle and Sword*, 233–34, 248, 265–68; Burstein and Isenberg, *Problem of Democracy*, 114, 124.
15. "Communication," *Genius of Liberty* (Morristown, NJ), January 7, 1802; the article appears to have originated in the New York *Morning Chronicle*, though the date is uncertain; as I show later, the Coriolanus articles really gained a wide readership starting in December 1802; see *Morning*

Chronicle (New York, NY), December 20, 1802; *Telegraphe and Daily Advertiser* (Baltimore), December 23, 1802; *New York Spectator,* (New York), December 29, 1802; *Pittsburgh Gazette* (Pittsburgh), January 7, 1803; the Coriolanus letters were discussed as far west as Kentucky in the *Pallidum* (Frankfort, KY), February 17, 1803, as well as in the *Salem Register* (Salem, MA), February 17, 1803, and *Poulson's American Daily Advertiser* (Philadelphia, PA), February 23, 1803.

16. "Communication," *Genius of Liberty.*
17. Ibid.
18. Nugent, *Habits of Empire,* 57–58; Dubois, "Haitian Revolution," 95–110.
19. "From the Gazette de France," *The Times* (New York), June 6, 1802.
20. P. Onuf, "Jefferson, Louisiana and American Nationhood," in Kastor and Weil, *Empires of the Imagination,* 23–33; Lewis, *American Union,* 30; Owsley and Smith, *Filibusters and Expansionists,* 12–13.
21. Nugent, *Habits of Empire,* 60–62; Lewis, "Tornado on the Horizon," 126–28; "For the Guardian of Freedom," *Guardian of Freedom* (Frankfort, KY), March 2, 1803; it took less than a month for the letter to appear in the *Daily Advertiser* (New York), March 25, 1803.
22. "Communication," *Chronicle Express* (New York), December 20, 1802; "Communication," *Chronicle Express,* December 23, 1802; "Communication," *Chronicle Express,* December 27, 1802; *Morning Chronicle* (New York), January 8, 1803; *Morning Chronicle,* January 18, 1803.
23. "President's Message VIII," *American Citizen* (New York), January 13, 1803.
24. "President's Message VIII."
25. "President's Message VIII."
26. "President's Message VIII."
27. "Louisiana," *United States Oracle* (Portsmouth, NH), July 31, 1802; "New Orleans," *Salem Gazette* (Salem, MA), January 4, 1803.
28. "Louisiana," *United States Oracle,* "Louisiana," *American Citizen* (New York), June 16, 1802.
29. "Louisiana," *United States Oracle;* "Extract of a Letter to a Gentleman in Alexandria," *The Balance, and Columbian Repository* (Hudson, NY), June 15, 1802.
30. Lewis, *American Union,* 29–30; Esdaile, *Napoleon's Wars,* 132–39.
31. "For the Washington Federalist," *Washington Federalist* (Washington, DC), February 11, 1803; "For the Balance," *The Balance, and Columbian Repository* (Hudson, NY), February 15, 1803; also see *The Patriot* (Utica, NY), March 7, 1803; *Courier of New Hampshire* (Concord, NH), March 10, 1803.

32. *Alexandria Advertiser and Commercial Intelligencer* (Alexandria, VA), April 12, 1803.
33. "Ross, James (1762–1847)," *Biographical Directory of the United States Congress*, US Congress, Historical Office, http://bioguide.congress.gov; Carson, "Role of Congress," 377–79; US Congress, *Annals of Congress*, 7th Cong., 2nd Sess., 1803, 12:119, 255.
34. "Mr. Ross's Speech," *Morning Gazette* (New York), March 1, 1803.
35. "Speech of Mr. Morris," *New England Palladium* (Boston), April 8, 1803; "Morris, Robert (1734–1806)," *Biographical Directory of the United States Congress*, US Congress, Historical Office, http://bioguide.congress.gov.
36. "Speech of Mr. Morris."
37. "Extract of a Letter," *New York Gazette* (New York), March 4, 1803.
38. "From the New York Herald," *Connecticut Centinel* (Norwich, CT), February 22, 1803; *Daily Advertiser* (New York), April 13, 1801; also see *Poulson's American Daily Advertiser* (Philadelphia), April 13, 1801; *Providence Journal* (Providence, RI), April 22, 1801.
39. "From the Connecticut Courant," *The Patriot* (Utica, NY), March 7, 1803.
40. Levine, "Race and Nation," 332–53; Levine, *Dislocating Race and Nation*, 17–18.
41. Brown, *Address to the Government*. 4–5.
42. Brown, *Address to the Government.*, 7–8; the practice of using the environment to define natural boundaries beyond 1848 is explored in Greenberg, *Manifest Manhood*, 59–78.
43. Brown, *Address to the Government*, 12–15.
44. Brown, *Address to the Government*, 19–28.
45. Brown, *Address to the Government*, 31.
46. Brown, *Address to the Government*, 49.
47. Brown, *Address to the Government*, 49.
48. Brown, *Address to the Government*, 49, 52.
49. Nugent, *Habits of Empire*, 62; Dubois, "The Haitian Revolution," 109–13.
50. Nugent, *Habits of Empire*, 62; Dubois, "The Haitian Revolution," 109–13.

2. COST

1. *Independent Chronicle* (Boston), June 30, 1803; *Republican or Anti-Democrat* (Baltimore), July 4, 1803.
2. G. Ellis, *Napoleonic Empire*, 54–55.
3. Esdaile, *Napoleon's Wars*, 154–208.

4. Treaty between the United States of America and the French Republic, October 17, 1803, in US Department of State, *State Papers and Correspondence*, 253–56; DeConde, *This Affair of Louisiana*, 181.
5. *South Carolina State Gazette* (Charleston, SC), May 19, 1802; *Palladium* article reprinted in, *Evening Post* (New York), October 26, 1802.
6. *The Minerva* (New York, September 10 and 14, 1796).
7. Nugent, *Habits of Empire*, 65.
8. "Fabricius, no. 4," *Columbian Centinel* (Boston), July 23, 1803. Fabricius's fourth essay was the most popular; for example, see *New York Repertory* (New York), July 27, 1803; also see *Columbian Centinel*, "Fabricius, no. 5," July 27; *New York Spectator* (New York), July 20, 1803; *The Patriot* (Stonington, CT), August 22, 1803; *Albany Centinel* (Albany, NY), July 29, 1803.
9. "Fabricius, no. 4," *Columbian Centinel*.
10. "For the Balance, no. 2," *The Balance, and Columbian Repository* (Hudson, NY), August 23, 1803.
11. "For the Balance, no. 3," *The Balance, and Columbian Repository* (Hudson, NY), August 30, 1803; "For the Balance, no. 6," *The Balance, and Columbian Repository*, September 27, 1803.
12. "For the Balance, no. 6"; *The Patriot* (Stonington, CT), August 15, 1803; Dzurec, "Of Salt Mountains," 79–80, 91.
13. *New England Palladium* (Boston), September 11, 1804.
14. "An Address to All the Monarchists," *Political Observatory* (Walpole, NH), August 8, 1804.
15. US Congress, *Annals of Congress*, 8th Cong., 1st Sess., 1803, 13:385–418; Plumer, *William Plumer's Memorandum*, 3–5; Nugent, *Habits of Empire*, 66–68; DeConde, *This Affair of Louisiana*, 189–90; Sanson, "Scouring at the Mortar of the Constitution," 10–12.
16. "Louisiana Title," *Courier of New Hampshire*, November 23, 1803.
17. *New-England Repertory* (Boston), December 11, 1803; *New Hampshire Sentinel* (Keene, NH), November 12, 1803.
18. *Charleston Courier* (Charleston, SC), November 8, 1803.
19. *Middlebury Mercury* (Middlebury, VT), January 11, 1804.
20. *Aurora General Advertiser* (Philadelphia), November 15, 1803.
21. *Senate Executive Journal*, 8th Cong., 1st Sess., 1803, 450; Plumer, *William Plumer's Memorandum*, 13–14.
22. Farnham, "Federal-State Issue," 5–25; Kerber, *Federalists in Dissent*, 41–45.

23. US Congress, *Annals of Congress*, 8th Cong., 1st Sess., 1803, 13:27; Plumer, *William Plumer's Memorandum*, 145; Sanson, "Scouring at the Mortar of the Constitution," 12–14.
24. Quoted in Shulim, *Old Dominion and Napoleon*, 70–71.
25. Ames, *Works of Fisher Ames*, 263–65.
26. Treaty between the United States of America and the French Republic, October 17, 1803, 254; Plumer, *William Plumer's Memorandum*, 7; Kastor, *Nation's Crucible*, 4.
27. *The Repertory* (Boston), February 25, 1806; P. Onuf, *Jefferson's Empire*, 158–; Kastor, "'They Are All Frenchmen,'" in Kastor and Weil, *Empires of the Imagination*, 239–67; *Poulson's American Daily Advertiser* (Philadelphia), October 31, 1803; the idea of "race" as an emerging concern in American imperialism is best explored in Horsman, *Race and Manifest Destiny*; Kastor, *Nation's Crucible*, 28–32.
28. *Poulson's American Daily Advertiser* (Philadelphia), October 28, 1803; *Kennebec Gazette* (Augusta, ME), November 1, 1804.
29. *Evening Post* (New York), January 2, 1804, but extremely widely reprinted throughout the nation. For example, the *American Citizen, Morning Chronicle, Daily Advertiser,* and *Mercantile Advertiser* (all of New York) all published the announcement on January 3, 1804—the *New York Herald* and the *Republican Watchtower* (New York) published it on January 4, 1804, and the *New York Spectator* finally published it on January 5. By January 4, 1804, the announcement had spread south to Pennsylvania, Maryland, Delaware, and even Virginia; see *Aurora General Advertiser* (Philadelphia); the *Carlisle Gazette* (Carlisle, PA); *Maryland Herald* (Hagerstown, MD), *Mirror of the Times* (Wilmington, DE), and *Virginia Argus* (Richmond, VA). It took nearly a week for the first major Boston paper, the *Independent Chronicle* to publish the piece on January 9, 1804, the same day as *The Minerva* (Raleigh, NC) and the *Charleston Courier* (Charleston, SC). Over the next few days, many other papers in every part of the nation published either responses to the declaration or the declaration itself. See *New Jersey Journal* (Elizabethtown, NJ), January 10, 1804; *National Aegis* (Worcester, MA), January 11, 1804; *Connecticut Gazette* (New London, CT), January 11, 1804; *Political Observatory* (Walpole, NH), January 14, 1804; *Providence Gazette* (Providence, RI), January 14, 1804; *The Reporter* (Battleboro, VT), January 16, 1804; and finally, the *Farmer's Gazette* (Sparta, GA), January 20, 1804.
30. *New York Repertory* (New York), March 16 and 23, 1804; Vernet, "More Than Symbolic," 133–44.

31. Gouverneur Morris to Henry Livingston, December 4, 1803, in Morris, *Life of Gouverneur Morris*, 3:192; US Congress, *Annals of Congress*, 8th Cong., 1st Sess., 1803, 13:1058–59; Brown, *Address to the Government*, 52.
32. US Congress, *Annals of Congress*, 8th Cong., 2nd Sess., 1805, 13:1608–21; Kastor, *Nation's Crucible*, 57–61; Vernet, *Strangers on Their Native Soil*, 68–74; Kastor, "Motives of Particular Urgency," 823.
33. John Gurley to the Post Master General, July 14, 1804, and William Claiborne to the Secretary of State, October 3, 1804, in US Department of State,, *Territorial Papers*, 9:263, 305; Kastor, *Nation's Crucible*, 56–67.
34. *Republican Watchtower* (New York), September 5, 1804.
35. *Republican Watchtower*, September 5, 1804.
36. "An Act to Enable the President of the United States to Take Possession of the Territories Ceded by France," *Statutes at Large of the United States of America, 1789–1873*, 8th Cong., 1st Sess., October 31, 1803, 2:245.
37. "An Act Erecting Louisiana into Two Territories and Providing for the Government Thereof," *Statutes at Large of the United States of America, 1789–1873*, 8th Cong., 1st Sess., March 26, 1804, 2:283–89; Plumer, *William Plumer's Memorandum*, 145; Kastor, *Nation's Crucible*, 46–52.
38. *The Repertory* (Boston), March 6, 1804.
39. *The Repertory*, March 6, 1804.
40. "Democratic Consistency," *Washington Federalist* (Washington, DC), February 17, 1804.
41. US Congress, *Annals of Congress*, 8th Cong., 1st Sess., 1803, 13: 60.
42. Messer, "From a Revolutionary History," 205–33; Hostetler, "David Ramsay and Louisiana," 134–46; *Carolina Gazette* (Charleston, SC), May 18, 1804; *The Times* (Alexandria, VA), May 25, 1804. By June 6, the speech had reached the national capital, *The National Intelligencer* (Washington, DC), June 6, 1804; ten days later it was printed in New York, *American Citizen* (New York), June 16, 1804; the same day it was printed in New Hampshire, *Political Observatory* (Walpole, NH), June 16, 1804; about a week later, the oration was printed in Massachusetts, *The Sun* (Pittsfield, MA), June 23, 1804; the oration continued to be published at least through October; see the *American Mercury* (Hartford, CT) October 4, 1804.
43. Ramsay, *Oration on the Cession*, 4, 6–7.
44. Ramsay, *Oration on the Cession*, 7.
45. Ramsay, *Oration on the Cession*, 6–7.
46. Ramsay, *Oration on the Cession*, 8–10.
47. *Daily Advertiser* (New York), January 1, 1805.

3. ALLIES

1. "Short Answers to Short Questions," *Federal Republican* (Baltimore), April 7, 1813, Wood, *Empire of Liberty*, 684–89.
2. "Short Answers to Short Questions," *Federal Republican* (Baltimore), April 7, 1813.
3. Stagg, *Borderlines in Borderlands*, 57–58.
4. Tucker and Hendrickson, *Empire of Liberty*, 137–44, 155, 219–20.
5. DeConde, *This Affair of Louisiana*, 227–30; *Journal of the United States Senate*, 9th Cong., 1st Sess., December 3, 1805, 4–8.
6. US Congress, *Annals of Congress*, 9th Cong., 1st Sess., 1805–6, 15:18–19, 946–93, 1117–44; "An Act Making Provision for Defraying Any Extraordinary Expenses Attending the Intercourse between the United States and Foreign Nations," in US Congress, *Statutes at Large*, 9th Cong., 1st Sess., February 13, 1806, 2:349–50.
7. *The Repertory* (Boston), April 15, 1806.
8. Bailyn, *Ideological Origins*, 57–60; P. Onuf and N. Onuf, *Federal Union, Modern World*, 70–71.
9. *Portland Gazette and Maine Advertiser* (Portland, ME), April 21, 1806.
10. "Bonaparte's Money," *Post Boy* (Windsor, VT), April 22, 1806; *Hampshire Federalist* (Springfield, MA), April 29, 1806.
11. *Hampshire Federalist* (Springfield, MA), April 29, 1806.
12. James Akin, "The Prairie Dog Sickened at the Sting of the Hornet," 1806, Library of Congress, http://lccn.loc.gov/2002708977; Dzurec, "Of Salt Mountains," 99–102; Quimby, "Political Art of James Akin," 67–68; *New York Gazette* (New York), May 12, 1806.
13. *New York Gazette* (New York), May 12, 1806; the same article was also printed in the *Gazette of the United States* (Philadelphia), May 19, 1806.
14. G. Ellis, *Napoleonic Empire*, 54–56, 109–10.
15. N. Isenberg, *Fallen Founder*, 272.
16. N. Isenberg, *Fallen Founder*, 282–310; Andrew Jackson to Daniel Smith, November 12, 1806, in Jackson, *Papers of Andrew Jackson*, 2:117–19.
17. N. Isenberg, *Fallen Founder*, 311–16.
18. For examples of early Napoleonic accusations against Burr, see *Kennebec Gazette* (Augusta, ME), February 13, 1801; and *Hampshire Gazette* (Northampton, MA), January 14, 1801; *The Enquirer* (Richmond, VA), December 11, 1806; *The Aurora General Advertiser* (Philadelphia), December 12, 1806; *Suffolk Gazette* (Sag Harbor, NY), December 12, 1807.
19. *Universal Gazette* (Washington, DC), June 23, 1808.

20. *New York Gazette* (New York), January 1, 1807; *Western World* (Frankfort, KY), January 8, 1807; *Federal Republican* (Baltimore), May 31, 1810.
21. Goldsmith, *Secret History of the Court*, 345-52.
22. Goldsmith, *Secret History of the Court*, 1-3; Kerber, *Women of the Republic*, 54-55; Belkin, *Revolutionary Mothers*, 138-39, 179.
23. Goldsmith, *Secret History of the Court*, 351-52.
24. Leary, "Thomas Branagan," 333-35.
25. Branagan, *Political and Theological Disquisitions*, 34-35.
26. Branagan, *Political and Theological Disquisitions*, 90-91, 123-26.
27. Esdaile, *Napoleon's Wars*, 302-3, 308-9.
28. Esdaile, *Napoleon's Wars*, 321-22; Englund, *Napoleon*, 340-42.
29. *North American and Mercantile Advertiser* (Baltimore), September 14, 1808.
30. *North American and Mercantile Advertiser* (Baltimore), September 14, 1808; Burstein, *Lincoln Dreamt He Died*, 64, 189-90.
31. For one of many examples, see *The Republican Watchtower* (New York), December 25, 1807.
32. *The Repertory* (Boston), January 5, 1808.
33. *New York Spectator* (New York), March 5, 1808.
34. *Spooner's Vermont Journal* (Windsor, VT), March 21, 1808; *Commercial Advertiser* (New York), April 4, 1808; *Litchfield Gazette* (Litchfield, CT), April 27, 1808. The article circulated as far south as Virginia; see the *Alexandria Advertiser* (Alexandria, VA), April 21, 1808.
35. *Spooner's Vermont Journal*, March 21, 1808.
36. *The Repertory* (Boston), January 1, 1808; *North American and Mercantile Advertiser* (Baltimore), August 19, 1808.
37. *American Citizen* (New York), July 10, 1809.
38. *The Monitor* (Washington, DC), July 28, 1808; *Newburyport Herald* (Newburyport, MA), December 30, 1808.
39. *Virginia Patriot* (Richmond, VA), August 7 and 17, 1810; *Hagerstown Gazette* (Hagerstown, MD), September 25, October 2 and 9, 1810; also see *The Sun* (Pittsfield, MA), August 18, 1810.
40. *Alexandria Daily Gazette* (Alexandria, VA), August 11, 1810.
41. *Virginia Patriot* (Richmond, VA), August 7, 1810.
42. *Hagerstown Gazette*, September 25, October 2 and 9, 1810.
43. *Hagerstown Gazette*, September 25, October 2 and 9, 1810.
44. *Hagerstown Gazette*, October 9, 1810.
45. Stagg, *Borderlines in Borderlands*, 61-62; Scallions, "Rise and Fall," 196; Nugent, *Habits of Empire*, 104.
46. Nugent, *Habits of Empire*, 105-7; see also Davis, *Rouge Republic*.

47. Stagg, *Borderlines in Borderlands*, 74–76.
48. Stagg, *Borderlines in Borderlands*, 75–77; Scallions, "Rise and Fall," 214–17; Watson, "Conquerors, Peacekeepers or Both?," 72–73; Kastor, "Motives of Particular Urgency," 839–40. The proclamation of annexation was widely reprinted throughout the United States. The first printing was in the *National Intelligencer* (Washington, DC), December 6, 1810; by December 12, 1810, newspapers in Boston were printing and commenting on not only the president's proclamation but also his occupation orders to Claiborne; for example, see *The Repertory* (Boston), December 14, 1810.
49. *The Repertory* (Boston), December 18, 1810; large portions of the article were reprinted in other papers. For example, see the *Hampshire Federalist* (Springfield, MA), December 20, 1810.
50. *The Repertory* (Boston), December 18, 1810.
51. *Newport Mercury* (Newport, RI), February 2, 1811; *Federal Republican* (Baltimore), February 4, 1811.
52. *The Enquirer* (Richmond, VA), May 27, 1806; Lang, *Foreign Policy*, 27–28, 34–36, 56.
53. *The Old Colony Gazette* (New Bedford, MA), December 14, 1810; *The Repertory* (Boston), December 14, 1810.
54. *Old Colony Gazette*, December 14, 1810.
55. *Old Colony Gazette*, December 14, 1810.
56. *The New Hampshire Patriot* (Concord, NH), January 1, 1811.
57. Stagg, *Borderlines in Borderlands*, 90–93; also see Cusick, *Other War of 1812*.
58. Nugent, *Habits of Empire*, 113–17; Owsley and Smith, *Filibusters and Expansionists*, 80–81.
59. The original *Charleston Courier* article has not survived, though subsequent printings show that it was printed on April 2, 1812; the article was picked up by the *Alexandria Daily Gazette* (Alexandria, VA), April 10, 1812; also see *Norfolk Gazette* (Norfolk, VA), April 13, 1812; *Hagerstown Gazette* (Hagerstown, MD), April 21, 1812; *The Star* (Raleigh, NC), April 24, 1812.
60. The first printing of this proclamation seems to have been in the *Federal Republican* (Baltimore), October 11, 1811. The story reached Virginia and New England on the next day; see *Alexandria Daily Gazette* (Alexandria, VA), October 12, 1811; *Columbian Phoenix* (Providence, RI), October 12; *Centinel of Freedom* (Newark, NJ), October 12, 1811; *Connecticut Herald* (New Haven, CT), October 15, 1811; *American Watchman* (Wilmington, DE), October 16, 1811; *Massachusetts Spy* (Worcester, MA), October 16,

1811; *National Intelligencer* (Washington, DC), October 17, 1811; *The Enquirer* (Richmond, VA), October 18, 1811; *Farmer's Repository* (Charlestown, VA), October 18, 1811; *Plattsburgh Republican* (Plattsburgh, NY), October 25, 1811; *The Reporter* (Lexington, KY), October 26, 1811; *Washington Statesman* (Lexington, KY), November 2, 1811.
61. *Alexandria Daily Gazette* (Alexandria, VA), December 19, 1811.
62. *Alexandria Daily Gazette*, December 19, 1811.
63. "Nestor no. III," *Commercial Advertiser* (New York), January 22, 1812; also see *New York Spectator* (New York), January 25, 1812.
64. "Nestor no. IV," *Commercial Advertiser* (New York), January 23, 1812.
65. "Nestor no. IV."
66. Stagg, *Mr. Madison's War*, 110–13.
67. Stagg, *Mr. Madison's War*, 205–6, 342–43; Nugent, *Habits of Empire*, 83–85; Burstein and Isenberg, *Madison and Jefferson*, 507–9, 513–15, 546–47.
68. *Poulson's American Daily Advertiser* (Philadelphia, PA), April 16, 1812. *Commercial Advertiser* (New York), June 19, 1812.
69. *National Intelligencer* (Washington, DC), January 5, 1813; Governor Strong's speech was simultaneously printed in the *Newburyport Herald* (Newburyport, MA), February 1, 1814, and the *Salem Gazette* (Salem, MA), February 1, 1814; also see *Berkshire Reporter* (Pittsfield, MA), February 10, 1814, and the *Connecticut Herald* (New Haven, CT), February 8, 1814.
70. *Newport Mercury* (Newport, RI), April 11, 1812; *Rhode Island American* (Providence, RI), August 11, 1812.
71. Stagg, *Mr. Madison's War*, 411–19, 427–28, 485–87, 495; Burstein and Isenberg, *Madison and Jefferson*, 538–39; Howe, *What Hath God Wrought*, 15–16.

4. DEMOCRACY

1. F. Ellis, *History of Columbia Country*, 381; *New York Statesman* (Albany, NY), December 19, 1820. Van Buren was baptized with the Dutch version of his name: Maartin; and Napoleon Frenchified "Buonaparte" to "Bonaparte" during the early days of the Revolution.
2. Shulim, *Old Dominion and Napoleon Bonaparte*, 155–58; *Independent Chronicle* (Boston), August 14, 1809; *Boston Gazette* (Boston), September 4, 1809.
3. Esdaile, *Napoleon's Wars*, 460–528.
4. Robertson, *Impartial History*, iii.

5. *Patriot and Evening Advertiser* (Baltimore), January 31, 1815; Anderson and Cayton, *Dominion of War*, 233–34.
6. Owsley, *Struggle for the Gulf Borderlands*, 178–80.
7. *Rhode Island Republican* (Newport, RI), April 12, 1815; *True American* (Bedford, PA), May 4, 1815; Frost, *Pictorial Life of Andrew Jackson*, 345; for similar sentiments also see Cobbett, *Life of Andrew Jackson*, 107; Eaton and Smith, *Memoirs of Andrew Jackson*, 247; Ward, *Andrew Jackson*, 155, 183.
8. Englund, *Napoleon*, 426–27, 431, 439.
9. *Hampshire Gazette* (Northampton, MA), August 23, 1815; Englund, *Napoleon*, 444–45; Ocampo, *Emperor's Last Campaign*, 27–28.
10. *National Advocate* (New York), April 27, 1815. Rumors that Napoleon had left Elba circulated for several days before they were confirmed by the *National Advocate* on April 27. A day later the other New York papers picked up the story: for example, the *Mercantile Advertiser* (New York), April 28, 1815. By April 29, the story had traveled south of the Mason Dixon line: *Baltimore Patriot* (Baltimore), April 29, 1815; and into New England: *Columbian Register* (New Haven, CT), April 29, 1815. After about a week, the story slowed down as other (more objective) reports started to appear, but the original story continued to be printed, probably because of the dramatic flavor; see, for example, *Virginia Patriot* (Richmond, VA), May 3, 1815; *Albany Argus* (Albany, NY), May 5, 1815; *Portland Gazette and Maine Advertiser* (Portland, ME), May 8, 1815; *Geneva Gazette* (Geneva, NY), May 10, 1815. The story reached the Deep South approximately two weeks after its original printing; see the *Augusta Herald* (Augusta, GA), May 11, 1815. A day later, the story reached the far west when it was printed in the *Argus of Western America* (Frankfort, KY), May 12, 1815.
11. Andrew Jackson to Edward Livingston, May 17, 1815, in Jackson, *Papers of Andrew Jackson*, 3:357.
12. "The 'Usurper' and the 'Legitimate,'" *Vermont Republican* (Windsor, VT), November 11, 1815.
13. William Charles, *Louis XVIII Climbing the Mât de Cocagne*, 1815, American Antiquarian Society, reference no. 152935.
14. Caldwell, *Oration Commemorative of American Independence*, 54–55. For similar examples see Custis, *Celebration of the Russian Victories*; Tillinghast, *Oration, Pronounced before the Citizens*.
15. *Courier, and Mercantile Directory* (New York), January 16, 1815.
16. *Hampshire Gazette* (Northampton, MA), August 23, 1815.

17. Remini, *Andrew Jackson*, 341–65; Owsley and Smith, *Filibusters and Expansionists*, 141–63; Anderson and Clayton, *Dominion of War*, 232–33.
18. Owsley and Smith, *Filibusters and Expansionists*, 152–59; Nugent, *Habits of Empire*, 121–23; Anderson and Clayton, *Dominion of War*, 237–38.
19. Edel, *Nation Builder*, 147–54; Lewis, *American Union*, 121–24; Weeks, "John Quincy Adam's 'Great Gun,'" 25–26.
20. Remini, *Andrew Jackson*, 369–74; Anderson and Clayton, *Dominion of War*, 238–46.
21. US Congress, *Annals of Congress*, 15th Cong., 2nd Sess., 1818, 13:631–55.
22. US Congress, *Annals of Congress*, 15th Cong., 2nd Sess., 1818, 13:647; Remini, *Andrew Jackson*, 371–74.
23. US Congress, *Annals of Congress*, 15th Cong., 2nd Sess., 1818, 13:653–55; Geyl, *Napoleon*, 21–24.
24. US Congress, *Annals of Congress*, 15th Cong., 2nd Sess., 1818, 13:697–98.
25. "Cession of Florida," *Providence Patriot* (Providence, RI), July 28, 1819.
26. "Napoleon and Franklin," 339–44.
27. "Napoleon and Franklin," 339–44.
28. "Funeral Honors to Bonaparte," *Easton Gazette* (Easton, MD), November 24, 1821.
29. Casper, *Constructing American Lives*, 27, 81–82.
30. Wilentz, *Rise of American Democracy*, 4–5, 792.
31. Howe, *What Hath God Wrought*, 203–11; Wilentz, *Rise of American Democracy*, 240–57.
32. Burstein, *Sentimental Democracy*, xvii.
33. O'Meara, *Memoirs of the Military*, 17; Tarbox, *Mocking Bird*, 63.
34. Ireland, *Napoleon Anecdotes*, 120–21; though the version I used was a British edition, newspaper advertisements show that the set was being sold in the United States as early as 1823; for other such works also see Howe, *Sketches Designed to Do Good*; American Sunday School Union, *Napoleon Bonaparte*; An American, *Anecdotes of the Emperour Napoleon*.
35. Scott's work was conveniently made available to Americans in a variety of condensed editions, of which the most useful is Scott, *Life of Napoleon Bonaparte*, 665–66; Fuller, *These Sad but Glorious Days*, 120.
36. O'Meara, *Memoirs of the Military*, 150; Ireland, *Napoleon Anecdotes*, 58–59; Scott, *Life of Napoleon Bonaparte*, 149; Tocqueville, *Democracy in America*, 618–19.
37. O'Meara, *Napoleon in Exile*; Andrew Jackson to William Fulton, December 21, 1823, in Jackson, *Papers of Andrew Jackson*, 5:329.

38. O'Meara, *Napoleon in Exile*, 1:228, 261–62, 316–17; Abbot, *History of Napoleon Bonaparte*, 1:175
39. Hazlitt, *Life of Napoleon*; Lockhart, *History of Napoleon Bonaparte*; *Philadelphia Inquirer* (Philadelphia), June 10, 1831; for a popular American reply to Scott see Grimshaw, *Life of Napoleon*.
40. Vail, *History of the McGuffey Readers*, 3–7; Mosier, *Making the American Mind*, 43.
41. McGuffey, *McGuffey's Eclectic Third Reader*, 159–61.
42. The idea that fiction could have a profound impact on foreign policy is not a new one; see Kaplan, "Romancing the Empire," 659–90; Scott, *Life of Napoleon Bonaparte*, 314; *Barre Gazette* (Barre, MA), October 21, 1842; *Salem Gazette* (Salem, MA), December 14, 1832; for Napoleon as a romantic hero, also see Johannsen, *To the Halls*, 75–78.
43. Emerson, "Napoleon," 219–20.
44. Emerson, "Napoleon," 226–27; 230–31.
45. Emerson, "Napoleon," 224, 228.
46. Emerson, "Napoleon," 234–35, 237–40.
47. Emerson, "Napoleon," 247.
48. Ward, *Andrew Jackson*, 182–85.
49. Scott, *Life of Napoleon*, 663–64; Frost, *Pictorial Life of Andrew Jackson*, 148–49; Cobbett, *Life of Andrew Jackson*, 62–63; Jeremiah S. Black, *Eulogy on the Life and Character of General Andrew Jackson* (Chambersburg, PA, 1845), 14.
50. Lee, *Vindication of the Character*, 19–20.
51. Marielle Brie Marielle, "Joseph Bonaparte in America," Emperor Napoleon I's Authentic Saint Helena Eau de Cologne, Le Blog, January 6, 2021, https://blog.napoleon-cologne.fr/en/joseph-bonaparte-in-america/; the first place this story appeared in print seems to have been "President Jackson's Model," *Salem Gazette* (Salem, MA), July 31, 1832.
52. *Congressional Globe*, 25th Cong. 1st Sess., 1837, 5:221.
53. Anthony Imbert, *The Model of a Republican President*, 1834, National Museum of American History, DL.60.3356.
54. *New York Herald* (New York), March 7, 1837.

5. GLORY

1. Howe, *What Hath God Wrought*, 744–45. To give a sense of the geographic range of this story, which originated in a now lost copy of *The Tropic* (New Orleans, LA) see *Richmond Whig* (Richmond, VA), July 11

1846; *The Guard* (Holly Springs, MS), July 22, 1846; *Hillsborough Recorder* (Hillsborough, NC), July 23, 1846; *Juliet Signal* (Joliet, IL), July 28, 1846; *Wisconsin Herald* (Lancaster, WI), September 19, 1846. The story was immortalized after the war in Wynkoop, *Anecdotes and Incidents*, 22–23.

2. Karen Weaver (Palo Alto Battlefield National Military Park), email to the author, July 1, 2022.
3. Howe, *What Hath God Wrought*, 582–83, 706.
4. *Register of Debates*, 20th Cong., 1st Sess., 1828, vol. 4, part 2, 1616.
5. Howe, *Making the American Self*, 5–13.
6. Greenberg, *Manifest Manhood*, 9–14.
7. Howe, *What Hath God Wrought*, 373–74; Wilentz, *Rise of American Democracy*, 364–65.
8. Biddle, *Eulogium on Thomas Jefferson*, 33, 49.
9. Biddle, *Eulogium on Thomas Jefferson*, 49–53.
10. Weld, *Pictorial Life of George Washington*, iii; Edgar Allen Poe, "A Chapter on Autography," *Graham's Magazine* 19, no. 6 (December 1841): 280.
11. Weld, *Pictorial Life of George Washington*, 200–215.
12. Weld, *Pictorial Life of George Washington*, 205–6.
13. Channing, *Remarks on the Character*; Adams, *Diary of Charles Francis Adams*, 2:182, 188, 343; Chase, *Salmon P. Chase Papers*, 1:10.
14. Channing, *Remarks on the Character*, 4, 6–7.
15. Channing, *Remarks on the Character*, 8–9, 31–32.
16. Channing, *Remarks on the Character*, 20, 25–28.
17. Channing, *Remarks on the Character*, 14, 22–25, 33–36; Scott, *Life of Napoleon*, 355.
18. Channing, *Remarks on the Character*, 32–34.
19. Channing, *Remarks on the Character*, 50–51.
20. Sadly, for such a remarkable individual, no scholarly work has been done on Ladd since the cursory treatment in Watkins, "William Ladd," 112–14.
21. Channing, *Remarks on the Character*.
22. Ladd, *Howard and Napoleon Compared*.
23. Ladd, *Howard and Napoleon Compared*, 12–13.
24. Ladd, *Howard and Napoleon Compared*, 68–78; Ségur, *History of the Expedition*, 1:iii–iv.
25. Prucha, *Great Father*, 64–72, Hämäläinen, *Indigenous Continent*, 385–409.
26. *Register of Debates*, 21st Cong., 1st Sess., 1830, 353–54.
27. The article originally from the *New York Observer* was reprinted as "History of the Indian Bill no.5," *Connecticut Courant* (Hartford, CT), September 21, 1830.

28. Prucha, *Great Father*, 90–92; Hämäläinen, *Indigenous Continent*, 397–98.
29. "Bonaparte and Black Hawk," *Phenix Gazette* (Alexandria, VA), May 3, 1833.
30. "Bonaparte and Black Hawk."
31. Prucha, *Great Father*, 83–85; Hämäläinen, *Indigenous Continent*, 389–90, 399–400.
32. *Congressional Globe*, 25th Cong., 2nd Sess., 1838, 6:1031–32.
33. *Register of Debates*, 25th Cong., 1st Sess., 1837, 665.
34. "Gen. Gaine's Letter," *Hudson River Chronicle* (Sing Sing, NY), July 2, 1839.
35. Howe, *What Hath God Wrought*, 658–61; Anderson and Clayton, *Dominion of War*, 264–65.
36. Howe, *What Hath God Wrought*, 663–69; Anderson and Clayton, *Dominion of War*, 266–69.
37. *Houston Telegraph* (Houston, TX), August 12, 1837; *New York Herald* (New York), March 17, 1845.
38. *Saratoga Sentinel* (Saratoga Springs, NY), May 24, 1836; Fowler, *Santa Anna of Mexico*.
39. *Nantucket Inquirer* (Nantucket, MA), July 25, 1835.
40. *New Bedford Gazette* (New Bedford, MA), June 13, 1836.
41. *Weekly Herald* (New York), April 30, 1842.
42. *Philadelphia Inquirer* (Philadelphia), January 1, 1842; *Richmond Whig* (Richmond, VA), May 26, 1845.
43. *National Intelligencer* (Washington, DC), June 10, 1844.
44. *Boston Courier* (Boston), June 27, 1844.
45. Greenberg, *Wicked War*, 95, 99–100, 104.
46. Napoleon I, , *Napoleon's Military Maxims*.
47. "How Shall We Fight?," *Baltimore Sun* (Baltimore), August 23, 1845; *Hartford Times* (Hartford, CT), August 23, 1845; for a similar take see *Barre Gazette* (Barre, MA), May 15, 1846.
48. *National Aegis* (Worcester, MA), May 20, 1846.
49. Stagg, *Mr. Madison's War*, 258–60; Johannsen, *To the Halls*, 10–11, 26–28; Woodworth, *Manifest Destinies*, 157; Greenberg, *Wicked War*, 113–15.
50. Headley, *Napoleon and His Marshals*, 1:iv–vi.
51. *Evening Transcript* (Boston), January 14, 1847.
52. *New Bedford Mercury* (New Bedford, MA), June 5, 1846.
53. *New Bedford Mercury*, June 5, 1846.
54. *National Intelligencer* (Washington, DC), August 6, 1847.
55. *Baltimore Sun* (Baltimore), August 9, 1847.

56. Howe, *What Hath God Wrought*, 772–73, 777, 780–81.
57. *National Intelligencer* (Washington, DC), October 21, 1846, and March 13, 1847.
58. *National Era* (Washington, DC), May 20, 1847; Johannsen, *To the Halls*, 22–23; Greenberg, *Wicked War*, 222, 233; also see Horsman, *Race and Manifest Destiny*, 208–48.
59. *Massachusetts Spy* (Worcester, MA), March 3, 1847; Johannsen, *To the Halls*, 160–62; in the following decade, for an attempt to place the environment of Central America within the natural boundaries of the United States, see Greenberg, *Manifest Manhood*, 59–77.
60. *National Intelligencer* (Washington, DC), September 14, 1847. For only a few sample articles see *The Liberator* (Boston), October 15, 1847; *The Emancipator* (Boston), May 26, 1847; *Boston Recorder* (Boston), December 23, 1847; *Philadelphia Inquirer* (Philadelphia), November 24, 1847.
61. "When Shall We Have Peace?" *National Intelligencer* (Washington D.C.), September 14, 1847.
62. *Alexandria Daily Gazette* (Alexandria, VA), July 29, 1847.
63. *New York Spectator* (New York), December 23, 1847.
64. *The Sun* (Baltimore), May 26, 1847; *Cleveland Plain Dealer* (Cleveland, OH), October 16, 1847.
65. Greenberg, *Wicked War*, 215–16, 262–63.
66. Johannsen, *To the Halls*, 172–73; Greenberg, *Wicked War*, 203, 206, 209, 211.
67. *Berkshire County Whig* (Pittsfield, MA), March 30, 1848.

CONCLUSION

1. Fremantle, *Three Months*, 121; Abbott, *History of Napoleon Bonaparte*, 2:666.
2. *Deck and Port Songster*, 65–66.
3. John C. Abbott to Henry Bill, November 6, 1862, in J. C. S. Abbott Letters (1833–67), American Antiquarian Society.
4. There were dozens of officers who received the sobriquet of Napoleon, and I have only chosen the two most well-known examples: Williams, *PGT Beauregard*; Sears, *George McClellan*; Post, *Soldiers' Letters from Camp*, 40.
5. A. Dudley Mann to Judah P. Benjamin, July 15, 1862, US War Department, *Official Records*, series 2, 3:456–59.
6. Linderman, *Embattled Courage*, 156–58; Lynch, *Civil War Diary*, 141.

7. McPherson *Battle Cry of Freedom* (Oxford University Press, 1988), 516, 569–70.
8. Nugent, *Habits of Empire*, 218, 276–77; Daniel Burge, *Failed Vision of Empire*, 16–17.
9. Roosevelt, *Rough Riders*, 166; Guérard, *Reflections on the Napoleonic Legend*, 101.
10. Richard Bulliet, "Bush and Napoleon," *New York Times*, online edition, August 2, 2007, http://www.nytimes.com/2007/08/02/opinion/02iht-ed bulliet.1.6957129.html?_r=0.

BIBLIOGRAPHY

PRIMARY SOURCES

Newspapers

Albany Argus (Albany, NY)
Albany Centinel (Albany, NY)
Alexandria Advertiser (Alexandria, VA)
Alexandria Advertiser and Commercial Intelligencer (Alexandria, VA)
Alexandria Daily Gazette (Alexandria, VA)
American Citizen (New York, NY)
American Mercury (Hartford, CT)
American Watchman (Wilmington, DE)
Argus of Western America (Frankfort, KY)
Augusta Herald (Augusta, GA)
Aurora General Advertiser (Philadelphia, PA)
The Balance, and Columbian Repository (Hudson, NY)
Baltimore Patriot (Baltimore, MD)
Baltimore Sun (Baltimore, MD)
Barre Gazette (Barre, MA)
Berkshire County Whig (Pittsfield, MA)
Berkshire Reporter (Pittsfield, MA)
Boston Courier (Boston, MA)
Boston Gazette (Boston, MA)
Boston Recorder (Boston, MA)
Carlisle Gazette (Carlisle, PA)
Carolina Gazette (Charleston, SC)
Centinel of Freedom (Newark, NJ)
Charleston Courier (Charleston, SC)
Chronicle Express (New York, NY)

City Gazette and Advertiser (Charleston, SC)
Cleveland Plain Dealer (Cleveland, OH)
Columbian Centinel (Boston, MA)
Columbian Phoenix (Providence, RI)
Columbian Register (New Haven, CT)
Commercial Advertiser (New York, NY)
Connecticut Centinel (Norwich, CT)
Connecticut Courant (Hartford, CT)
Connecticut Gazette (New London, CT)
Connecticut Herald (New Haven, CT)
Courier, and Mercantile Directory (New York, NY)
Courier of New Hampshire (Concord, NH)
Daily Advertiser (Baltimore, MD)
Daily Advertiser (New York, NY)
Easton Gazette (Easton, MD)
The Emancipator (Boston, MA)
The Enquirer (Richmond, VA)
Evening Post (New York, NY)
Evening Transcript (Boston, MA)
Farmer's Gazette (Sparta, GA)
Farmer's Repository (Charlestown, VA)
Federal Gazette (Baltimore, MD)
Federal Republican (Baltimore, MD)
Gazette of the United States (Philadelphia, PA)
Geneva Gazette (Geneva, NY)
Genius of Liberty (Morristown, NJ)
The Guard (Holly Springs, MS)
Guardian of Freedom (Frankfort, KY)
Hagerstown Gazette (Hagerstown, MD)
Hampshire Federalist (Springfield, MA)
Hampshire Gazette (Northampton, MA)
Hartford Times (Hartford, CT)
Hillsborough Recorder (Hillsborough, NC)
Houston Telegraph (Houston, TX)
Hudson River Chronicle (Sing Sing, NY)
Independent Chronicle (Boston, MA)
Juliet Signal (Joliet, IL)
Kennebec Gazette (Augusta, ME)
The Liberator (Boston, MA)

Litchfield Gazette (Litchfield, CT)
Loudon's Register (New York, NY)
Maryland Herald (Hagerstown, MD)
Massachusetts Spy (Worcester, MA)
Middlebury Mercury (Middlebury, VT)
The Minerva (Dedham, MA)
The Minerva (Raleigh, NC)
Mirror of the Times (Wilmington, DE)
The Monitor (Washington, DC)
Morning Chronicle (New York, NY)
Morning Gazette (New York, NY)
Nantucket Inquirer (Nantucket, MA)
National Advocate (New York, NY)
National Aegis (Worcester, MA)
National Era (Washington, DC)
National Intelligencer (Washington, DC)
New Bedford Gazette (New Bedford, MA)
New Bedford Mercury (New Bedford, MA)
Newburyport Herald (Newburyport, MA)
New England Palladium (Boston, MA)
New-England Repertory (Boston, MA)
New Hampshire Patriot (Concord, NH)
New Hampshire Sentinel (Keene, NH)
New Jersey Journal (Elizabethtown, NJ)
Newport Mercury (Newport, RI)
New York Gazette (New York, NY)
New York Herald (New York, NY)
New York Repertory (New York, NY)
New York Spectator (New York, NY)
New York Statesman (Albany NY)
Norfolk Gazette (Norfolk, VA)
North American and Mercantile Advertiser (Baltimore, MD)
Old Colony Gazette (New Bedford, MA)
Oracle of Dauphin (Harrisburg, PA)
Otsego Herald (Cooperstown, NY)
The Pallidum (Frankford, KY)
Patriot (Utica, NY)
The Patriot (Stonington, CT)
Patriot and Evening Advertiser (Baltimore, MD)

Phenix Gazette (Alexandria, VA)
Philadelphia Inquirer (Philadelphia, PA)
Pittsburgh Gazette (Pittsburgh, PA)
Plattsburgh Republican (Plattsburgh, NY)
Political Observatory (Walpole, NH)
Portland Gazette and Maine Advertiser (Portland, ME)
Post Boy (Windsor, VT)
Poulson's American Daily Advertiser (Philadelphia, PA)
Providence Journal (Providence, RI)
Providence Patriot (Providence, RI)
The Repertory (Boston, MA)
The Reporter (Lexington, KY)
Republican or Anti-Democrat (Baltimore, MD)
Republican Watchtower (New York, NY)
Richmond Whig (Richmond, VA)
Rhode Island American (Providence, RI)
Rhode Island Republican (Newport, RI)
Salem Gazette (Salem, MA)
Salem Register (Salem, MA)
Saratoga Sentinel (Saratoga Springs, NY)
South Carolina State Gazette (Charleston, SC)
Spooner's Vermont Journal (Windsor, VT)
The Star (Raleigh, NC)
Suffolk Gazette (Sag Harbor, NY)
The Sun (Pittsfield, MA)
Telegraphe and Daily Advertiser (Baltimore, MD)
The Times (Alexandria, VA)
True American (Bedford, PA)
United States Oracle (Portsmouth, NH)
United States Chronicle (Providence, RI)
Universal Gazette (Washington, DC)
Vermont Republican (Windsor, VT)
Virginia Argus (Richmond, VA)
Virginia Patriot (Richmond, VA)
Washington Federalist (Washington, DC)
Washington Statesman (Lexington, KY)
Weekly Herald (New York, NY)
Western World (Frankfort, KY)
Wisconsin Herald (Lancaster, WI)

Napoleonic Biographies & Literature

Abbot, John S. C. *A History of Napoleon Bonaparte*. 2 vols. New York, 1855.
An American. *Anecdotes of the Emperour Napoleon, and His Times*. Buffalo, NY, 1840.
An American. *The Campaigns of Napoleon Buonaparte*. Boston, 1834.
Channing, William E. *Remarks on the Character of Napoleon Bonaparte Occasioned by the Publication of Scott's Life of Napoleon*. New York, 1831.
The Deck and Port Songster: Being a Choice Collection of Bonaparte and Sea Songs. New York, 1855.
Emerson, Ralph Waldo. "Napoleon, or Man of the World." In *Representative Men: Seven Lectures*, 219–53. Boston, 1850.
Goldsmith, Lewis. *A Secret History of the Court and Cabinet of St. Cloud*. 4th ed. New York, 1807.
Grimshaw, William. *The Life of Napoleon*. Philadelphia, 1829.
Hazlitt, William. *The Life of Napoleon*. 7 vols. Philadelphia, 1828.
Headley, J. T. *Napoleon and His Marshals*. 2 vols. New York, 1846.
Ireland, William H. ed., *The Napoleon Anecdotes: Illustrating the Mental Energies of the Late Emperor of France*. 6 vols. London, 1822–23.
Lockhart, J. G. *The History of Napoleon Buonaparte*. 2 vols. New York, 1833.
Napoleon I. *Military Maxims of Napoleon*. Translated by J. Akerly. New York, 1845.
"Napoleon and Franklin." *U.S. Literary Gazette* 3, no. 9 (February 1, 1826): 339–44.
O'Meara, Barry. *Napoleon in Exile, or A Voice from St. Helena*. 2 vols. Philadelphia, 1822.
O'Meara, Barry. *Memoirs of the Military and Political Life of Napoleon Bonaparte*. 2 vols. Hartford, CT, 1822.
Robertson, Hume. *An Impartial History of the Life of Napoleon Bonaparte*. Philadelphia, 1808.
Scott, Walter. *The Life of Napoleon Bonaparte*. Philadelphia, 1839.
Schlabrendorf, Gustov von. *Bonaparte and the French People under His Consulate*. New York, 1804.
Ségur, Philipe-Paul Comte de. *History of the Expedition of Russia Undertaken by the Emperor Napoleon in 1812*. 2 vols. New York, 1858.

Children's Books

American Sunday School Union. *Napoleon Bonaparte: Sketches from His History Adapted for the Young*. Philadelphia 1845.
Howe, Henry. *Sketches Designed to Do Good*. Cincinnati, OH, 1846.

Ladd, William. *Howard and Napoleon Compared in Eight Dialogues.* Hallowell, NH, 1838.

McGuffey, William H. *William H. McGuffey's Third Eclectic Reader.* Cincinnati, OH, 1836.

Tarbox, Increase. *The Mocking Bird, and Other Stories.* New York, 1855.

Weld, Horatio Hastings. *Pictorial Life of George Washington: Embracing Anecdotes, Illustrative of His Character.* Philadelphia, 1846.

Pamphlets

Branagan, Thomas. *Political and Theological Disquisitions on the Signs of the Times.* Trenton, NJ, 1807.

Brown, Charles Brockden. *An Address to the Government of the United States on the Cession of Louisiana to the French and the Late Breach of Treaty by the Spanish.* Philadelphia, 1803.

Caldwell, Charles. *An Oration Commemorative of American Independence Delivered before the Washington Benevolent Society of Pennsylvania.* Philadelphia, 1814.

Custis, George Washington Parke. *The Celebration of the Russian Victories.* Georgetown, Washington, DC. 1813.

Tillinghast, Joseph L. *An Oration, Pronounced before the Citizens of Pawtuxet.* Providence, RI, 1814.

Other Published Primary Sources

Adams, Charles Francis. *Diary of Charles Francis Adams.* 2 vols. Edited by Aïda DiPace Donald and David Donald. Harvard University Press, 1964.

Ames, Fisher. *The Works of Fisher Ames.* Boston, 1809.

Biddle, Nicholas. *Eulogium on Thomas Jefferson.* Philadelphia, 1827.

Black, Jeremiah S. *Eulogy on the Life and Character of General Andrew Jackson.* Chambersburg, PA, 1845.

Chase, Salmon P. *The Salmon P. Chase Papers.* Vol. 1. Edited by John Niven. Kent State University Press, 1993.

Cobbett, William. *Life of Andrew Jackson.* New York, 1836.

Eaton, John, and Jerome van Crowninshield Smith. *Memoirs of Andrew Jackson.* Philadelphia, 1834.

Fremantle, Arthur L. *Three Months in the Southern States.* New York, 1864.

Frost, John. *A Pictorial Life of Andrew Jackson.* Philadelphia, 1836.

Fuller, Margret. *These Sad but Glorious Days: Dispatches from Europe, 1846–1850.* Edited by Larry Reynolds and Susan Belaco Smith. Yale University Press, 1991.

BIBLIOGRAPHY   211

Jackson, Andrew. *The Papers of Andrew Jackson*. 11 vols. Edited by Harold Moser, et al. Knoxville: University of Tennessee Press, 1980–2019.
Lee, Henry. *A Vindication of the Character and Public Services of Andrew Jackson*. Boston, 1828.
Lynch, Charles. *The Civil War Diary of Charles Lynch, 18th Connecticut Volunteers*. Hartford, CT: Case, Lockwood & Brainard, 1915.
Morris, Gouverneur. *The Life of Gouverneur Morris with Selections from His Correspondence*. Edited by Jared Sparks. 3 vols. Boston, 1832.
Plumer, William. *William Plumer's Memorandum of the Proceedings in the United States Senate, 1803–1807.* Edited by Everett Brown. Macmillan, 1923.
Post, Lydia Minturn, ed. *Soldiers Letters from Camp, Battlefield, and Prison*. New York, 1865.
Ramsay, David. *An Oration on the Cession of Louisiana to the United States*. Charleston, NC, 1804.
Roosevelt, Theodore. *The Rough Riders*. New York, 1899.
Toqueville, Alexis de. *Democracy in America*. Translated by Harvey Mansfield and Delba Winthrop. University of Chicago Press, 2000.
Wynkoop, J.M. *Anecdotes and Incidents: Comprising Daring Exploits, Personal and Amusing Adventures of the Officers and Privates of the Army and Thrilling Incidents of the Mexican War*. Pittsburgh, 1848.

Government Records

US Congress. *Annals of the Congress of the United States, 1789–1824*. 42 vols. Washington, DC, 1834–56.
US Congress. *Congressional Globe*. 46 vols. Washington, DC, 1834–73.
US Congress. *Register of Debates*. 14 vols. Washington, DC, 1824–37.
US Congress. *Statutes at Large of the United States of America, 1789–1873*. 32 vols. Washington, DC, 1845–74.
US Department of State. *State Papers and Correspondence Bearing upon the Purchase of the Territory of Louisiana*. Washington D.C., 1903.
US Department of State. *Territorial Papers of the United States*. Vol. 9. Edited by Clarence Edwin Carter. Washington, DC, 1940.
US War Department, *The Official Records of the War of the Rebellion: A Compilation of the Official Records of the Union and Confederate Navies*. 30 vols. Washington, DC, Government Printing Office. 1894–1922.

Archival Sources

J. C. S. Abbott Letters (1833–67). American Antiquarian Society. Worcester, MA.
Prints and Photographs Division. Library of Congress. Washington, DC.

SECONDARY SOURCES

Anderson, Fred, and Andrew Cayton. *The Dominion of War: Empire and Liberty in North America, 1500–2000.* Viking Press, 2005.

Appleby, Joyce. *Inheriting the Revolution: The First Generation of Americans.* Harvard University Press, 2001.

Bailyn, Bernard. *The Ideological Origins of the American Revolution.* Rev. ed. Harvard University Press, 1992.

Belkin, Carol. *Revolutionary Mothers: Women in the Struggle for America's Independence.* Vintage Press, 2006.

Blaakman, Michael, Amy Conroy Krutz, and Noelani Arista, eds. *The Early Imperial Republic: From the American Revolution to the U.S.-Mexican War.* University of Pennsylvania Press, 2023.

Burstein, Andrew. *Lincoln Dreamt He Died: The Midnight Visions of Remarkable Americans from Colonial Times to Freud.* St. Martin's Press, 2013.

Burstein, Andrew. *Sentimental Democracy: The Evolution of America's Romantic Self-Image.* Hill and Wang, 1999.

Burstein, Andrew, and Nancy Isenberg, *Madison and Jefferson.* Random House, 2010.

Burge, Daniel J. *A Failed Vision of Empire: The Collapse of Manifest Destiny, 1845–1872.* University of Nebraska Press, 2022.

Carson, David. "The Role of Congress in the Acquisition of the Louisiana Territory," *Louisiana History* 26, no. 4 (1985): 369–83.

Casper, Scott. *Constructing American Lives: Biography and Culture in Nineteenth-Century America.* University of North Carolina Press, 1999.

Clayton, Andrew. "Radicals in the Western World: The Federalist Conquest of Trans-Appalachia." In *Federalists Reconsidered,* edited by Doron S. Ben-Atar and Barbara B. Olberg. University Press of Virginia, 1998.

Cleves, Rachel Hope. *The Reign of Terror in America: Visions of Violence from Anti-Jacobinism to Anti-Slavery.* Cambridge University Press, 2009.

Cusick, James. *The Other War of 1812: The Patriot War and the Invasion of East Florida.* University of Georgia Press, 2003.

Davis, William. *The Rouge Republic: How Would-Be Patriots Waged the Shortest Revolution in American History.* Houghton Mifflin, 2011.

DeConde, Alexander. *This Affair of Louisiana.* Scribner, 1976.

Dubois, Laurent. "The Haitian Revolution and the Sale of Louisiana." In Kastor and Weil, *Empires of the Imagination.*

Dzurec, David. "Of Salt Mountains, Prairie Dogs, and Horned Frogs: The Louisiana Purchase and the Evolution of Federalist Satire, 1803–1812." *Journal of the Early Republic* 35, no. 1 (Spring 2015): 79–108.

Edel, Charles. *Nation Builder: John Quincy Adams and the Grand Strategy of the Republic.* Harvard University Press, 2014.
Elkins, Stanley, and Eric McKitrick, *The Age of Federalism: The Early American Republic, 1788–1800.* Oxford University Press, 1993.
Ellis, Franklin. *A History of Columbia County, New York.* Philadelphia, 1878.
Ellis, Geoffrey. *The Napoleonic Empire.* 2nd ed. Palgrave Macmillan, 2003.
Englund, Steven. *Napoleon: A Political Life.* Harvard University Press, 2004.
Esdaile, Charles. *Napoleon's Wars: An International History.* Penguin, 2007.
Farnham, Thomas. "The Federal-State Issue and the Louisiana Purchase." *Louisiana History* 6, no. 1 (Winter, 1965): 5–25.
Fowler, Will. *Santa Anna of Mexico.* University of Nebraska Press, 2007.
Geyl, Pieter. *Napoleon: For and Against.* Translated by Olive Renier. Penguin Books, 1976.
Greenberg, Amy S. *Manifest Manhood and the Antebellum Empire.* Cambridge University Press, 2005.
Greenberg, Amy S. *A Wicked War: Polk, Clay, Lincoln, and the 1846 Invasion of Mexico.* Alfred Knopf, 2012.
Guérard, Albert Leon. *Reflections on the Napoleonic Legend.* Charles Scribner, 1924.
Guyatt, Nicholas. "Imperialism in the American Imagination." In Blaakman, Conroy-Krutz, and Arista, *Early Imperial Republic.*
Hämäläinen, Pekka. *Indigenous Continent: The Epic Contest for North America.* Liveright Press, 2022.
Herring, George C. *From Colony to Superpower: U.S. Foreign Relations since 1776.* Oxford University Press, 2008.
Hicks, Hilarie M. "Images of Napoleon at Montpelier." Research report, November 7, 2019. Montpelier Foundation, Orange, VA, MRD-S 48202.
Horsman, Reginald. *Race and Manifest Destiny: The Origins of American Racial Anglo-Saxonism.* Harvard University Press, 1981.
Hostetler, Michael. "David Ramsay and Louisiana: Time and Space in the Adolescent Rhetoric of America." *Western Journal of Communication* 70, no. 2 (April 2006): 134–46.
Howe, Daniel Walker. *Making the American Self: Jonathan Edwards to Abraham Lincoln.* Oxford University Press, 1997.
Howe, Daniel Walker. *What Hath God Wrought: The Transformation of America.* Oxford University Press, 2007.
Immerman, Richard H. *Empire for Liberty: A History of American Imperialism from Benjamin Franklin to Paul Wolfowitz.* Princeton University Press, 2010.
Isenberg, Andrew C., and Thomas Richards, Jr. "Alternative Wests: Rethinking Manifest Destiny." *Pacific Historical Review* 86, no. 1 (February 2017): 4–17.

Isenberg, Nancy. *Fallen Founder: The Life of Aaron Burr.* Viking, 2007.

Isenberg, Nancy, and Andrew Burnstein. *The Problem of Democracy: The Presidents Adams Confront the Cult of Personality.* Penguin, 2019.

Johannsen, Robert W. *To the Halls of the Montezumas: The Mexican War in the American Imagination.* Oxford University Press, 1985.

Kaplan, Amy. "Romancing the Empire: The Embodiment of American Masculinity in the Historical Novel of the 1890s." *American Literary History* 2, no. 4 (Winter 1990): 659–90.

Kastor, Peter J. "'Motives of Particular Urgency': Local Diplomacy in Louisiana." *William and Mary Quarterly* 58, no. 4 (October 2001): 819–48.

Kastor, Peter J. *The Nation's Crucible: The Louisiana Purchase and the Making of America.* Yale University Press, 2004.

Kastor, Peter J. "'They Are All Frenchmen': Background and Nation in an Age of Transformation." In Kastor and Weil, *Empires of the Imagination.*

Kastor, Peter J., and François Weil, eds. *Empires of the Imagination: Transatlantic Histories of the Louisiana Purchase.* University of Virginia Press, 2009.

Kerber, Linda. *Federalists in Dissent: Imagery and Ideology in Jeffersonian America.* Reprint. Cornell University Press, 1980.

Kerber, Linda. *Women of the Republic: Intellect and Ideology.* University of North Carolina Press, 1997.

Kohn, Richard H. *Eagle and the Sword: The Federalists and the Creation of the Military Establishment in America, 1783–1802.* Free Press, 1975.

Kukla, Jon. *A Wilderness So Immense: The Louisiana Purchase and the Destiny of America.* Alfred Knopf, 2003.

Lang, Daniel. *Foreign Policy in the Early Republic: The Law of Nations and the Balance of Power.* Louisiana State University Press, 1985.

Larson, John Lauritz. "Wisdom Enough to Improve Them: Government, Liberty and Inland Waterways in the Rising American Empire." In *Launching the "Extended Republic": The Federalist Era,* edited by Ronald Hoffman and Peter J. Albert. University Press of Virginia, 1996.

Leary, Lewis. "Thomas Branagan: Republican Rhetoric and Romanticism in America." *Pennsylvania Magazine of History and Biography* 77 no. 3 (July 1953): 332–52.

Levine, Robert. *Dislocating Race and Nation: Episodes in Nineteenth Century Literary Nationalism.* University of North Carolina Press, 2008.

Levine, Robert. "Race and Nation in Brown's Louisiana Writings of 1803." In *Revising Charles Brockden Brown: Culture, Politics and Sexuality in the Early Republic,* edited by Phillip Barnard, Mark Kamrath, and Stephen Shapiro, 332–53. University of Tennessee Press, 2004.

Lewis, James E., Jr., *The American Union and the Problem of Neighborhood: The United States and the Collapse of the Spanish Empire, 1783–1829*. University of North Carolina Press, 1998.

Lewis, James E., Jr., "A Tornado on the Horizon: The Jefferson Administration, the Retrocession Crisis and the Louisiana Purchase." In Kastor and Weil, *Empires of the Imagination*.

Lindermann, Gerald. *Embattled Courage: The Experience of Combat in the American Civil War*. Free Press, 1989.

McPherson, James M. *Battle Cry of Freedom: The Civil War Era*. Oxford University Press, 1988

Messer, Peter. "From a Revolutionary History to a History of Revolution: David Ramsay and the American Revolution." *Journal of the Early Republic* 22, no. 2 (Summer 2002): 205–33.

Minardi, Margot. "Pax Americana? The Imperial Ambivalence of American Peace Reformers." In Blaakman, Conroy-Krutz, and Arista, *Early Imperial Republic*.

Mosier, Richard D. *Making the American Mind: Social and Moral Ideas in the McGuffey Readers*. Columbia University Press, 1947.

Nugent, Walter. *Habits of Empire: A History of American Expansion*. Vintage, 2009.

Ocampo, Emilo. *The Emperor's Last Campaign: A Napoleonic Empire in America*. University of Alabama Press, 2009.

Onuf, Peter. "Imperialism and Nationalism in the Early American Republic." In *Empire's Twin: U.S. Anti-Imperialism from the Founding Era to the Age of Terrorism*, edited by Ian Tyrell and Jay Sexton. Cornell University Press, 2015.

Onuf, Peter. "Jefferson, Louisiana and American Nationhood." In Kastor and Weil, *Empires of the Imagination*.

Onuf, Peter. *Jefferson's Empire: The Language of American Nationhood*. University of Virginia Press, 2000.

Onuf, Peter, and Nicholas Onuf. *Federal Union, Modern World: The Law of Nations in an Age of Revolutions*. Madison House, 1993.

Owsley, Frank L., Jr. *The Struggle for the Gulf Borderlands: The Creek War and the War of 1812*. University of Alabama Press, 1981.

Owsley, Frank L., Jr., and Gene Smith. *Filibusters and Expansionists: Jeffersonian Manifest Destiny, 1800–1821*. University of Alabama Press, 1997.

Pasley, Jeffrey. *The Tyranny of Printers: Newspaper Politics in the Early American Republic*. University of Virginia Press, 2002.

Prucha, Francis Paul. *The Great Father: The United States Government and the American Indians*. Abridged ed. University of Nebraska Press, 1986.

Quimby, Maureen O'Brien. "The Political Art of James Akin." *Winterthur Portfolio* 7 (1972): 59–112.

Remini, Robert. *Andrew Jackson and the Course of American Empire.* Harper and Row, 1977.

Richards, Thomas, Jr. *Breakaway Americas: The Unmanifest Future of the Jacksonian United States.* Johns Hopkins University Press, 2020.

Sahlins, Peter. "Natural Frontiers Revisited: France's Boundaries since the Seventeenth Century." *American Historical Review* 95, no. 5 (December 1990): 1423–51.

Sanson, Jerry. "'Scouring at the Mortar of the Constitution': Louisiana and the Fundamental Law of the United States." *Louisiana History* 48, no. 1 (Winter 2007): 5–24.

Scallions, Cody. "The Rise and Fall of the Original Lone Star State: Infant American Imperialism Ascendant in West Florida." *Florida Historical Quarterly* 90, no. 2 (Fall 2011): 193–220.

Sears, Steven. *George McClellan: The Young Napoleon.* DeCapro Press, 1999.

Semmel, Stuart. *Napoleon and the British.* Yale University Press, 2004.

Semmes, John Edward. *John H. B. Latrobe and His Times.* Norman-Remington, 1917.

Shulim, Joseph. *The Old Dominion and Napoleon Bonaparte: A Study in American Opinion.* Columbia University Press, 1952.

Smith-Rosenberg, Carroll. *This Violent Empire: The Birth of an American National Identity.* University of North Carolina Press, 2010.

Stagg, J. C. A. *Borderlines in Borderlands: James Madison and the Spanish-American Frontier.* Yale University Press, 2009.

Stagg, J. C. A. *Mr. Madison's War: Politics, Diplomacy, and Warfare in the Early American Republic.* Princeton University Press, 1983.

St. John, Rachel. "Contingent Continent: Spatial and Geographic Arguments in the Shaping of the Nineteenth-Century United States." *Pacific Historical Review* 86, no. 1 (February 2017): 18–49.

Taylor, Alan. *American Colonies: The Settling of North America.* Penguin, 2001.

Tucker, Robert W., and David C. Hendrickson. *Empire of Liberty: The Statecraft of Thomas Jefferson.* Oxford University Press, 1990.

Vail, Henry H. *A History of the McGuffey Readers.* Burrows Brothers, 1911.

Vernet, Julien. "More Than Symbolic: Pierre Clément de Laussat's Municipal Council and Louisianan Protest against American Territorial Government." *French Colonial History* 4 (2003): 133–44.

Vernet, Julien. *Strangers on Their Native Soil: Opposition to United States Governance in Louisiana's New Orleans Territory.* University of Mississippi Press, 2013.

Ward, John William. *Andrew Jackson: Symbol for an Age.* Reprint. Oxford University Press, 1981.
Watkins, Martin. "William Ladd: Peacemaker." *World Affairs* 114, no. 4 (Winter 1951): 112–14.
Watson, Samuel. "Conquerors, Peacekeepers or Both? The U.S. Army and West Florida." *Florida Historical Quarterly* (Summer 2013): 69–105.
Weeks, Williams E. "John Quincy Adams's 'Great Gun' and the Rhetoric of American Empire." *Diplomatic History* 14, no. 1 (Winter 1990): 25–42.
Wilentz, Sean. *The Rise of American Democracy: Jefferson to Lincoln.* W. W. Norton, 2005.
Williams, T. Harry. *PGT Beauregard: Napoleon in Gray.* Reprint. Louisiana State University Press, 1995.
Wood, Gordon. *Empire of Liberty: A History of the Early Republic.* Oxford University Press, 2009.
Woodworth, Steven E. *Manifest Destinies: America's Westward Expansion and the Road to the Civil War.* Alfred A. Knopf, 2010.

INDEX

Page numbers in italics refer to figures in the text.

Abbott, John: *History of Napoleon Bonaparte*, 130–31, 181–83
abolitionism, 82
Adams, Charles Francis, 153
Adams, John, 9, 18
Adams, John Quincy, 119, 126–27, 140, 153
Adams-Onís Treaty (1819), 119–20, 123
Akin, James: "The Prairie Dog Sickened at the Sting of the Hornet" (satirical cartoon), 75–76, *75*
Alabama, 70, 90, 92, 118, 139, 162. *See also* Mobile
Alaska, 184
Alexander I, Emperor, 100
Alexander the Great, 8
Alexandria Advertiser, 28
Alexandria Daily Gazette, 101
alliances, 95–96
Ambrister, Robert, 119, 121
American Antiquarian Society, 131
American Citizen, 23–26, 32, 88, 167
American Civil War. *See* Civil War
American navy, 104
American Peace Society, 157
American Philosophical Society, 150
American Revolution. *See* War for Independence

Ames, Fisher, 54
"An Address to All the Monarchists" (pamphlet), 48
Anglo-American Jay Treaty (1796), 9
anti-expansionists/anti-imperialists, 39, 52, 73, 86–109, 149, 159, 169–79, 183; dire rhetoric of, 178, 185; Napoleon's final triumph over, 181; Whigs as, 170–71, 175–78. *See also* Federalists; Whig Party
anti-militarism, 156–59
Appalachian Mountains, 13, 19, 26
Arbuthnot, Alexander George, 119, 121
Aurora, The, 78, 84
Aurora General Advertiser, 51
Australia, 45
Austria, 42, 54

Balance, The, 26
balance of power, 16, 20, 47–48; states in the Americas in a, 92; Vattelian, 96, 122
Baltimore, 106
Baltimore Patriot and Evening Advertiser, 111
Baltimore Sun, 173, 177
Barbary Coast pirates, 45
Barre Gazette, 135

Batavian Republic, 77, 83
Baton Rouge, 92–93. *See also* Louisiana
Battle of Antietam (1862), 184
Battle of Austerlitz (1806), 77, 108, 134, 145, 163, 170, 184
Battle of Bad Axe (1832), 161
Battle of Buena Vista (1847), 174
Battle of Gettysburg (1863), 184
Battle of Horseshoe Bend (1814), 118
Battle of Lutzen (1813), 163
Battle of New Orleans (1815), 111–13, 118, 139
Battle of Palo Alto (1846), 145–46
Battle of San Jacinto (1836), 165
Battle of Wagram (1809), 145, 163
Battle of Waterloo (1815), 3, 108, 113, 141, 145, 162, 181–83
Bavaria, 96
Bayard, Richard, 141–42
Beauregard, P. G. T., 182–84
Belgium, 41
Berkshire County Whig, 179
Biddle, Nicholas, 149–52, 154
Black Hawk, 161–62; character of, 162
Black Hawk War (1831–32), 161
Bonaparte, Joseph, 84, 87, 141–42, 176
Bonaparte, Napoleon: Alpine crossing of, 132–33, *134*, 135; American view of violence and tyranny of, 4, 35, 106, 110–11, 116–17, 141, 147, 154, 159, 162, 177, 181; character of, 127–29, 135–38, 142, 162; death of, 109, 143, 146; democratic legitimacy of the reign of, 114–16; democratic self-construction of, 135–37; dreams of North American empire of, 14, 25–27, 35, 38, 50–52, 65, 69, 77–90, 97, 101, 110, 118, 125, 168, 185; and the early Republic, 7–10; engraving that shows how most Americans imagined Napoleon's return from exile on Elba in 1815 (1875), *115*; exile to Elba of, 69, 110–11, 113, 115–16, 138, 140, 198n10; exile to St. Helena of, 114, 116, 123, 125, 130, 146, 161, 173; expansionist appetite of, 17, 22–25, 27, 30, 33, 37, 39, 66; as First Consul, 10–11, 14–19, 23, 28–45, 51, 56–61, 65, 70, 104, 111, 155; full-length portrait of, *2*; as liberal imperialist, 150, 159, 174, 179, 185; mid-nineteenth-century lithograph of, *146*; morally ambiguous imperial policies of, 50; name change in the early days of the French Revolution of, 197n1; and the rhetoric of 1812, 103–6; three biographies of, 1–2; tomb of, 185; two statues of, 1; as usurper, 62, 69, 88; as the wily Corsican, 80–83, 86. *See also* France; Napoleonic Wars

borders: dangerous irrational, 92; East Florida and West Florida with ill-defined international, 119; Enlightenment concept of national, 15; interpretation of American and Spanish, 70, 113; "intrigues of France" and disputes regarding American, 105–6; of Louisiana, 12–14, 120, 188n3; vagueness between the United States and Mexico regarding, 90–91; war scare on the border of Texas and Louisiana, 78. *See also* natural boundaries
Boston, 40, 44, 61, 97
Boston Courier, 168
Boston Evening Transcript, 171
Boston Gazette, 115
Boston Repertory. See *Repertory, The*
boundaries. See borders
Branagan, Thomas: *Political and Theological Disquisitions on the Signs of the Times Relative to the Present Conquests of France*, 82–83
Breckinridge, Senator John, 63–64
Bringham, Elijah, 105
British empire, 5. *See also* Great Britain
British navy, 15, 38, 42, 68, 72, 78, 85, 88, 93, 104; impressment of American sailors on the high seas by the, 99

Brown, Charles Brockden, 33–38, *34*, 91; "An Address to the Government of the United States on the Cession of the Louisiana Territory to the French and on the Late Breach of Treaty by the Spaniards, including the Translation of a Memorial on the War of St. Domingo, and the Cession of the Mississippi to France" (pamphlet), 11–12, 33–34, 47, 55, 57
Bulliet, Richard: "Bush and Napoleon" (opinion piece), 186
Burr, Aaron, 77–80, 87; as American Napoleon, 79, 194n18
Burr conspiracy, 69, 77–80, 83
Burstein, Andrew, 127
Bush, George W., 186

"Calculator," 45–47, 55, 64
Caldwell, Charles, 116–17
Campbell, Senator George, 57
Canada, 13, 21, 28, 57, 85–86, 101–5; American campaign to annex, 68; American invasion of, 104; French control of, 87, 101
Caribbean, 13; British invasion force in the, 106; French military presence in the, 20–21
Casper, Scott, 2, 125–26
Channing, William Ellery, 152–54, *153*, 165, 181; *Remarks on the Character of Napoleon Bonaparte Occasioned by the Publication of Scott's "Life of Napoleon"* (pamphlet), 152–56, 159, 171
Charles IV, King, 83
Charles V, King, 16
Charleston, 40
Charleston Courier, 50, 100
Chase, Salmon P., 153
Cherokees, 139. *See also* Native peoples
Chesapeake incident (1807), 85
China, 131, 186
Christian Examiner, 152

Civil War, 2, 182–85, 203n4
Claiborne, Governor William, 58, 93–94
Clay, Henry, 120–22, 126–27, 140, 142, 176
Cockburn, Admiral Sir George, 114
"Col. Cent," 74
colonialism: expansion of, 17; French military in Louisiana for, 35–36; settler, 6. *See also* imperialism
Columbian Centinel, 44–45
Comanches, 164. *See also* Native peoples
Commercial Advertiser, 104
Confederation of Rhine, 77
Congress, 29, 53; "An Act Making Provision for Defraying Any Extraordinary Expenses Attending the Intercourse Between the United States and Foreign Nations" (Act of Congress), 72–73, 75–76; debate over the aggressive expansionism of Jackson in the House of Representatives (1819), 120–21, 127; Federalists in the House of Representatives, 49; Jeffersonian-dominated, 98–99; "A Remonstrance of the People of Louisiana Against the Political System Adopted by Congress for Them" (congressional document), 58–59; resolution that provided for the "temporary occupation" of West Florida (1811) of, 98; statute creating the territorial government of Louisiana of, 60; vote to accept the Louisiana treaty in the Senate, 52. *See also* United States
Congress of Vienna (1814–15), 114–15
Connecticut Current, 101
Consulate, 14, 40. *See also* France
Continental Congress, 30, 63
Continental System, 77, 83, 100, 185
Convention of 1800, 10
Corbin, Molly, 81
"Coriolanus," 18–20, 28, 32, 48, 188n15
Courier, and Mercantile Directory, 117

INDEX

Creeks, 118–20, 138–39, 162. *See also* Native peoples
Creek War (1811–13), 118, 139, 141, 159
"Creole," 59
Cuba, 87
Currier, Nathaniel, *134*
Custer, George, 184

Danton, Georges, 15
Dayton, Senator Jonathon, 52
Deck and Port Songster, The (volume of tunes), 181–82
Declaration of Independence, 58
Delaware, 141
democracy: Bonaparte and American, 125–27, 135–38, 144; Bonaparte and French, 128–29, 137; expansion of American, 126; imperial warfare as noble method of spreading freedom and, 131. *See also* liberalism
Democratic Party, 127, 138–42, 169; Jacksonian wing of the, 147–48, 160, 163, 165, 179; as the party of the laborer and the poor farmer left behind by the Market Revolution, 147; policy of using national power and military force to expel Indigenous peoples from their lands to make room for white settlement of the, 138; rejection of the idea of "natural expansion" in the, 138. *See also* United States
D'Enghein, Duc, 121
de Staël, Madam, 121, 142; *Secret History of St. Cloud*, 80–81, 87, 157
de Tocqueville, Alexis, 129–30
Directory, 8–10, 14, 31, 140; Napoleon's usurpation of the, 140. *See also* France
dreams, 84
Duane, William, 84

East Florida, 70, 88, 93, 100, 102, 105; Jackson's full-scale invasion of Spanish, 119; Spanish cession to the United States of, 119. *See also* East Florida rebellion; Florida
East Florida rebellion, 98–100. *See also* East Florida
Easton Gazette, 125
Elliot, Representative James, 51
Emerson, Ralph Waldo: "Napoleon; or the Man of the World" (essay), 135–37
empire: aggressive war for the sake of, 149; American visions of, 4–6, 23–24, 53, 63–67, 86, 108–9, 122–25, 140, 186; authoritarian Napoleonic, 85, 94, 109, 123, 125; fate of the western American, 106–7; French New World, 100, 110; Jacksonian building of, 148; liberal American, 20, 25, 27–28, 33, 149, 178, 185; military victories in Mexico and the American, 177; Spanish New World, 49. *See also* expansion; imperialism
Enlightenment: concept of national borders of the, 15; idea of rational self-interest among rival states of the, 16
Esdaile, Charles, 42
Europe: export of products to, 5; imperial states of, 12; Napoleon's authoritarian empire in, 85, 94, 109, 123, 125; Napoleon's "sister republics" in, 73, 76, 103, 106
expansion: American exceptionalism and, 66; American imperial, 12, 22, 52, 62, 66, 70, 90–91, 117, 122, 124, 144, 178, 184; contest over Bonaparte's image in American discourse over imperial (1835–50), 147; Democratic advocates of, 166; Federalist opposition to expansion linking Bonaparte to American, 53, 66, 70, 72–73, 76, 95–96, 104, 106, 109, 117; Jeffersonian theory of natural, 22, 52, 66, 78–79, 99; Napoleonic, 61, 66, 120–22, 124,

130–31; natural security standpoint and the idea of, 87–88, 106, 108–9, 122, 125, 165; principles of just, 91. *See also* empire; imperialism

"Fabricius," 44–45, 47, 55, 64, 191n8
Federal Gazette, 17
Federalists, 5–7, 18, 29, 48–49, 55–57, 66, 126, 149, 168; anti-expansionist, 69–70, 79, 86–88, 94–96, 99, 102; anti-treaty, 44, 52–53, 60, 62, 64–65; charge of the Madison administration scheming to pervert the entire world order from the, 96; charge of the United States sending tribute to Bonaparte from the, 73–74, 76, 88–89; as divided and decidedly minority party, 42; Franco-phobic, 15, 41, 43, 88–89, 105, 116; as New England elites, 75–76, 116; newspapers of the, 47, 98; political infighting among the, 9; satiric wit of, 74–75; standard rhetoric of the, 87, 117–18. *See also* anti-expansionists/anti-imperialists; United States
Federal Republican, 68, 80, 95; "Short Answers to Short Questions" (article), 68–69
filibustering, 78–79
Florida, 3, 12–13; American acquisition of, 24, 31, 38, 89–90, 92–99, 120, 123; colonial independence movement in, 91; French control of, 30; northern boundary of Spanish, 13; problem of, 85, 88; pro-independence movement in, 92–94; Spanish control of, 69–70, 78, 85, 87, 92–94, 98. *See also* East Florida; Pensacola; Republic of West Florida; Spain; St. Augustine; West Florida
Flournoy, Francis, 22
France, 3, 13–15; Bonaparte's claim to the "ancient limits" of, 20, 22, 27–28; divinely appointed "natural boundaries" of, 24; Republican, 17; restoration of the Bourbons to the throne of, 114–16; revolutionary disorder of, 6. *See also* Bonaparte, Napoleon; Consulate; Directory; French Revolution; Napoleonic Wars; Nice; Paris; retrocession
"Franklin," 168–69
Franklin, Benjamin, 123–24
freedom: as acting independently, 73; imperial warfare as noble method of spreading democracy and, 131. *See also* liberty
French navy, 88
French Revolution, 2, 5–6, 8, 21, 30–31, 197n1. *See also* France
French Revolutionary Wars, 8, 27, 44
Fuller, Margaret, 129
fur-trading posts, 13

Gadsden Purchase (1853), 184
Gazette de France, 21–23, 25
Genoa, 105. *See also* Italy
Georgia, 51, 99, 118, 139, 162–63
Germany, 18, 23, 41
Glar, Martha, 81
Grand Duchy of Warsaw, 77
Grant, Ulysses S., 184
Great Britain, 2, 38, 41, 78; aristocratic order of, 6; French Canada ceded to, 13; liberal imperial system of, 5; Napoleon guaranteeing the United States, Canada, and Nova Scotia for American entry into a war against, 85; Napoleonic war on the North American continent against the United States and, 32; prospects of success for French invasion of, 8; Spanish Florida ceded to, 13. *See also* British empire; War of 1812
Greenberg, Amy, 149

Guérard, Albert Leon: *Reflections on the Napoleonic Legend*, 184–85
Guiana, 18
Gulf Coast, 6, 12–13, 69; American expansion in the, 25, 85, 106, 185; of colonial Florida from the Florida Keys to the Mississippi River, 71
Gulf of Mexico, 14, 90

Halifax, 105. See also Nova Scotia
Hamilton, Alexander, 9, 31–32, 77, 84
Hazlitt, William, 131
Headley, J. T.: *Napoleon and His Marshals*, 171, 175, 183
Holland, 54, 96, 116, 160; conquest of, 100; conspiratorial stories of Napoleon's imperial treachery in, 84, 86; as French client state, 15, 76–77, 105, 120
Holy Roman Empire, 27, 41, 77, 177
Hosley, Representative Hopkins, 163
Houston, Sam, 165–66
Howe, Daniel Walker, 148
Howe, Eber, 2
Hungary, 110

identity: American imperial, 3–4, 12, 66, 94, 106–7, 144, 147, 155, 159, 173, 178, 185; American national, 5; Napoleonic imperial, 130, 156, 159, 185; popular perceptions of Bonaparte's martial, 177, 184. See also ideology
ideology: American foundations of, 43–44, 186; of capitalism and free labor, 126; contested imperialist, 186; naive Jeffersonian, 36–37, 46, 49–50, 56, 65, 86; principles of right and justice in American imperial, 91. See also identity
Imbert, Anthony: "The Model of a Republican President" (lithograph), 142, 143
imperialism, 25–28, 91–92; American, 3–5, 12, 23–27, 33–39, 58–64, 69, 90–92, 98, 109, 131, 142–48, 160, 168–69; end of the first phase (1800–1850) of American, 185; hypocrisy of American, 162; Napoleon as a yardstick for American, 111, 125–26, 164, 185; Napoleonic, 3–4, 41, 50, 54–55, 61–69, 89–91, 102–3, 110, 117, 121–22, 129–35, 146, 151, 175. See also colonialism; empire; expansion
Independence Day, 8, 176
Independent Chronicle, 40–41, 110
India, 8, 131
Indian Removal Act (1830), 160
Indigenous peoples. See Native peoples
individualism, 126; unregulated passions and American, 149; will of the individual as sacrosanct in American, 131, 136–37, 139. See also self-government
industrial revolution, 126; economic cycles of the early, 138
infrastructure: Jacksonian reluctance to pay for improvements in, 148; periphery of the American empire united to its core through public, 148; projects of public, 147
Iraq War, 186
Italy, 96; as French client state, 76, 120; French occupation of Northern, 15, 49, 53–54; Napoleon's victories in, 7–8, 43, 100, 141, 153, 174; Piedmont region of, 27, 41; territory in, 14; transalpine regions of, 18, 27. See also Genoa; Lucca; Naples; Venice
Ives, James, 134

Jackson, Andrew, 8, 66, 78, 106–8, 111–14, 118–22, 126–27, 130, 150; House Military Affairs Committee report condemning actions in Florida of, 120; killing a man in a duel by, 121–22; as military chieftain, 140–43; as "Napoleon of the backwoods," 119, 138–42, 166; political cartoons depicting Andrew Jackson as crude

copy of Napoleon, 143; as president, 142–43
Jackson, Senator James, 51
Jacksonians, 147, 148, 155
Jefferson, Thomas, 2, 15, 18, 38, 42, 45, 49, 59, 61–62, 69, 168; as American expansionist, 70, 86; eulogy for, 149–50; shrewd diplomacy of, 97; West Florida fiasco of, 70–77, 94, 104
Jeffersonian papers, 51
Jeffersonians, 5–10, 29, 37, 41–44, 48, 57, 66, 78, 88–89; defenses of the treaty by the, 52–55, 62–63; expansionist policies of the, 69, 96, 99, 106, 138; as subordinate to the French empire, 73–74; "war hawk" wing of the, 103–4
Jena-Auerstedt, 80, 83
Junot, General Jean-Andoche, 129

Kastor, Peter, 58
Kentucky, 5, 7, 22, 28, 40, 45, 65, 120

Ladd, William, 156–59, 165, 171, 174, 181, 201n20; *Howard and Napoleon Compared in Eight Dialogues*, 157–59
Latin America: good relations between the United States and the republics of, 120, 176; nationalist rebellions against European rule in, 89
Latrobe, John H., 1–2
Laussat, Pierre, 56–57
law: international, 12, 172; Napoleonic imperialism as gross violation of international and moral, 117; natural, 12
Leclerc, Charles, 15, 21
Lee, Henry: *A Vindication of the Character and Public Services of Andrew Jackson* (pamphlet), 140
Le Montieur, 101
Lewis and Clark, 150
liberalism, 55, 58–59; Napoleonic destruction of established privilege as promoting, 109, 125, 130, 138, 143–44, 174. *See also* democracy; liberty
liberty: Americans as architects of a liberal empire of, 52, 125, 178–79, 182, 184–86; economic, 138; Napoleon and the promise of, 43, 54–55, 57, 182; republican, 4, 17, 59. *See also* freedom; liberalism
literature: Jacksonian era, 129; Napoleon-themed, 132–36, 139–41, 151, 185. *See also* popular culture
Livingston, Robert, 46
Lockhart, J. G., 131
Louis XIV, King, 16, 35
Louis XVIII, King, 1, 114–16, 129
Louisiana: administration of, 60–62; American debates over the natural limits of, 13, 33–36; American occupation of, 60–62, 90; army, navy gunboats, and militia from, 94; Federalist fears about the Napoleonic loyalty of the "French" inhabitants of, 102; French control of, 14, 36, 41, 49–50; Napoleonic designs for, 19, 21–22, 26–28, 35–36, 78; Spanish control of, 37, 47, 50, 60, 112; as territory of Frenchmen, 87; western and southern boundaries of Louisiana as largely undefined in map (1805), 65. *See also* Baton Rouge; Louisiana Purchase (1803); New Orleans
Louisiana Purchase (1803), 2–3, 12, 38–67, 98, 106, 150–51, 167, 192n26; benefits of the, 97; debates regarding the, 66, 102; evolution of anti-expansionist rhetoric in the decade following the, 69; Florida as tenuous part of the, 72, 93, 95, 120; objections to the, 49–53; opposition to occupation regarding the, 53–60; Spanish objections to the, 52, 87. *See also* Louisiana; Purchase Treaty (1803)
Louisiana Territory, 11–12

L'Ouverture, Toussaint, 21
Lucca, 105. *See also* Italy
Luxemburg, 41

Madison, James, 1–2, 15, 58, 68–69, 110; as agent of French foreign policy in the Americas, 95, 118; declaration of war against Great Britain asked from Congress by, 104; foreign policy of, 102, 117–18; military annexation of West Florida of, 94–99, 196n48; West Florida as foreign policy crisis for, 93–94
Maine, 7
Malta, 42, 64
manifest destiny, 4; of Bonaparte, 173; as imperial ideology, 184
masculinity, 149; martial, 157, 168; restrained, 157
McClellan, George B., 182–84
McCrea, Jane, 81
McGuffey, William, 132–34
media: debate about the nature of American expansion in the, 3; popular renderings of Bonaparte in the American, 80–84. *See also* newspapers
Memoirs of the Military and Political Life of Napoleon Bonaparte (book), 127–28
Mexican-American War (1846–48), 3, 109, 145–79, 185–86. *See also* Mexico
Mexico, 13–14, 21, 47, 144; colonial independence movement in, 91; France as a buffer between the United States and, 14; as geographically foreign to the United States, 175; liberal 1824 Constitution of, 164; Spanish control of, 78, 87. *See also* Mexican-American War (1846–48); Mexico City; Monterrey
Mexico City, 175. *See also* Mexico
Milan Decree, 85
Miller, Senator James, 168–69
Miner, Charles, 148

Minerva, The, 43
Mississippi, 70, 78, 90, 92; army, navy gunboats, and militia from, 94
Mississippi Crisis (1802–3), 3, 11–39, 41–42, 55, 66, 70, 91, 101
Mississippi River, 5–6, 12–14, 19–31, 37, 47–48, 58, 79, 91, 139, 159–64
Missouri River, 12, 28
Mobile, 94, 98–99. *See also* Alabama
Monitor, The, 88
Monroe, James, 45, 126
Monterrey, 173–74. *See also* Mexico
Morning Chronicle, 23, 188n15
Morris, Senator Gouverneur, 30–31, 38, 57
Moscow, 110, 124, 176, 183. *See also* Russia

Naples, 42. *See also* Italy
"Napoleon and Franklin" (article), 123–24
Napoleon Anecdotes, The (biography), 128
Napoleonic Code, 168
Napoleonic Wars, 15, 40–41, 73, 99–100; catalyst for the resumption of the, 64–65; Egyptian campaign of the, 8–10, 131, 163; end of the, 117; liberal values spread throughout Europe from the, 130, 174; massive invasion of the Russian empire by France and European allies in the, 104, 110, 145, 163, 176, 183; Spain as key British ally during the late, 112; veteran in America of the, 145–46. *See also* Bonaparte, Napoleon; France
Napoleon's Military Maxims (compilation), 169
National Era, 175
National Intelligencer, 79, 173–74, 176
nationalism: French, 158; Latin American, 89
Native peoples, 6; covert British support for anti-expansionist, 99; imperial

expansion into the lands of the, 144; of the Mississippi Valley, 26; pacification operations as campaigns against plains, 184; removal east of the Mississippi River of the, 139, 159–64; as stirred up by Spanish agents along the border with East Florida, 93; uprising on the western fringes of the United States of, 118. *See also* Cherokees; Comanches; Creeks; Seminoles
natural boundaries: American transgression of, 48, 178; attempt to place Central America within American, 203n59; Bonaparte's disregard for, 133, 136; Jeffersonian theory of expansion and, 36–37, 46; of Louisiana, 28; political role of, 47; practice of using the environment to define, 190n42; self-evident language of, 28, 37. *See also* borders
natural rights, 4
"Nestor," 101–3
Netherlands, 41
New Bedford Gazette, 166–67, 172
Newburyport Herald, 88–89
New Hampshire, 52
New Hampshire Patriot, 98
New Jersey, 52, 141
New Orleans, 11–15; American control of, 24, 29, 31–32, 38, 112; American military force to capture, 45, 70, 78, 106, 111–12; closure of American shipping to, 23, 26, 28; crisis over, 17, 20–22, 25; French control of, 21, 30; as natural part of the French empire, 35–36; pro-French municipal council in, 57; Spanish, 21, 26, 29, 35, 70. *See also* Louisiana
Newport Mercury: "Providence Resolves," 105
newspapers: biographies of Napoleon Bonaparte as advertised in American, 125; early American, 2, 27–29;

Federalist, 7–9, 40, 75, 84, 95; Jeffersonian, 84, 97–98; as political weapons, 6–7. *See also* media
New York, 137, 141
New York City, 7, 18
New York Daily Advertiser, 161
New York Daily Tribune, 129
New York Gazette, 75, 80
New York Herald, 143, 165
New York Journal, 27–28
New York Observer, 160
New York Spectator, 86
New York Times, 186
Nice, 41. *See also* France
9/11 attacks, 186
North American and Mercantile Advertiser, 84, 174
Nova Scotia, 85–86, 102, 105; French control of, 101. *See also* Halifax
Nueces River, 169

Ohio, 5, 137, 170
Ohio River, 13–14, 28
Oklahoma, 139
Old Colony Gazette, 97–98
"Old Farmer," 172–73
"Old Soldier, The," 48
O'Meara, Barry: *Napoleon in Exile*, 130–31, 135, 141, 143, 149, 185
Oregon, 70
Osceola, 163
Otsego Herald, 17
Ottoman Egypt, 8–9

Palladium, 43
Paris, 38, 115, 150, 184–85. *See also* France
"Peace": "War Unnecessary and Ruinous" (article), 86–87
Peace of Amiens (1801), 14–16, 21, 41
Peace of Lunéville (1801), 14–16
Pennsylvania, 141, 170. *See also* Philadelphia

Pensacola, 92–94, 98, 102. *See also* Florida
Perdido River, 70, 92, 98, 101
Peru, 47, 49
Philadelphia, 7, 116, 150. *See also* Pennsylvania
Philadelphia Enquirer, 167
Philipe-Paul, General (comte de Ségur): *History of the Expedition to Russia*, 158–59
Pierce, Senator Franklin, 163
Pinckney, Charles, 9
Pinckney Treaty (1795), 14, 22; Spanish violations of the, 44
Plumer, Senator William, 55
Poland, 110
political cartoons, 143; satirical, 75–76, 75
Polk, James K., 169, 178
popular culture: established tropes of American, 81; presentation of Napoleon Bonaparte in American, 146–48, 151, 158, 179, 181–82, 185, 200n42. *See also* literature
Portugal, 83, 100
Poulson's American Daily Advertiser, 104
Providence Patriot, 123
Prussia, 80, 83, 120
Purchase Treaty (1803), 55–56, 58–59, 62. *See also* Louisiana Purchase (1803)

Quasi-War, 9, 18

race, 56; and American imperialism, 192n27
Ramsay, David: *History of the Revolution in South Carolina*, 63–66, 97, 123
Randolph, John, 72
Red Scares, 85
Remini, Robert, 121
Repertory, The, 56–57, 61, 94–95; "Dream" (article), 86
republicanism, 42–44, 56, 61; American imperial identity as expression of, 94
Republican Watchtower, 59

Republic of West Florida, 93–94, 141. *See also* Florida
retrocession, 14–17, 27–28, 49, 70. *See also* France; Spain
Rhode Island, 105
Richmond, 183
Richmond Enquirer, 79, 96
Richmond Whig, 167–68
Rio Grande River, 169
rivers, 15, 28, 70
Robertson, Hume, 111
Rocky Mountains, 12
Roosevelt, Theodore, 184
Ross, Senator James, 29–30, 32
Ross Resolutions, 28–33, 45, 63
Russia, 42, 77, 100, 186; Napoleon's invasion of, 104, 110, 141, 152. *See also* Moscow
"Rusticus": comparison of American imperial conduct to the image of Bonaparte by, 90, 101; and the new world order, 89–92

Saint-Domingue (Haiti), 21–22, 26, 28, 34–36; French invasion of, 33, 35; French loss of control of, 38; population of, 55; successful slave revolt against the French in, 82; veteran French army in, 22, 25, 31, 37
Salem Gazette, 135
San Marino, 173
Santa Anna, Antonio López de, 164–67
Savoy, 41
Scott, Sir Water: *Ivanhoe*, 128, 134; *Life of Napoleon Bonaparte*, 128–36, 139–43, 149–58, 171, 173, 183, 185, 199n35; *Waverly*, 134
Scott, Winfield, 173, 176
self-government, 149. *See also* individualism
selfhood, 148
Seminoles, 118–20, 162–63; raids between American settlers and war

bands of the, 118–19; removal treaty signed by one band of, 162–63. *See also* Native peoples
Seminole War (1835–42), 139, 141, 162–65
Seven Years' War, 13
Sherman, William T., 184
slavery: imperial project of Bonaparte as, 54; Ladd's attempt to undermine African, 156; in newly acquired territories, 147; runaway slaves in Florida, 93; in Saint-Domingue, 38; writing against, 82
Smith, Representative Ballard, 122
Smith, William Stephens, 18–20, 24, 32, 188n14
South Carolina State Gazette, 42–43
Spain, 11–14, 19, 41, 47, 50, 78, 100, 102, 116, 160; ability to restrain American expansion by, 21–22; Bourbon monarchy of, 83–85, 87–88, 92–93, 95; as French client state, 76, 83, 120, 174; French Louisiana ceded to, 13; friction between the United States and, 70, 72; Napoleon's imperial aggression in, 84–85, 152; objection to the American invasion and occupation of territory in East Florida of, 119; as wartime ally of Britain, 112; as wartime ally of France, 72, 95. *See also* Florida; retrocession; Spanish usurpation
Spanish-American War (1898), 184
Spanish navy, 72
Spanish usurpation, 83–85, 88–90, 92–93, 102–3, 106, 176. *See also* Spain
Sprague, Senator Peleg, 160
St. Augustine, 99. *See also* Florida
St. Louis, 13
Strong, Governor Caleb, 105
sugar, 38–39
Sweden, 42
Switzerland, 41, 50, 54; conquest of, 100; conspiratorial stories of Napoleon's imperial treachery in, 84; as French client state, 15, 96, 105; French invasion of republican, 81–82
Syria, 9

Taney, Roger B., 142
Taylor, Zachary, 169, 173–74
technology, 186
Tennessee, 22, 28, 65, 170
Tennessee River, 28
"Ten Thousand Freemen of Connecticut" (article), 32
Texas, 70, 144; annexation by the United States of, 169, 172, 179; application into the United States of the Republic of, 165; debate over, 164–69; famous last stand at a mission called the Alamo in, 164
Texas Revolution, 164
trade, 5–6
Treaty of Campio-Formio (1797), 8
Treaty of Fort Jackson (1814), 118, 121–23, 139
Treaty of Ghent (1814), 106, 112–13, 117–18
Treaty of Guadalupe Hidalgo (1848), 178–79
Treaty of Paris (1783), 12–13, 20, 26
Treaty of San Ildefonso (1800), 49
Treaty of Westphalia (1648), 96

United Nations, 157
United States, 3–6, 85; democracy in the, 125–27; emergence as great imperial power of the, 47–48; expansionist policy of the, 18–20, 23–24, 28, 31–33, 36–37, 40, 46–51; as French client state, 73–77, 96, 118; friction between Spain and the, 70, 72; invasion of British Canada by the, 100; Louisiana as divine indication of the imperial destiny of the, 64; national debt of the, 49; national security of the, 66, 69–70,

United States (*continued*)
73, 85, 89, 92, 97, 103, 106, 108–10, 125; process of democratization in the, 109, 144; stunting by the French of the imperial growth of the, 36; Western Hemisphere not as monopolar world dominated by the, 89. *See also* Congress; Democratic Party; War for Independence; War of 1812; Whig Party

United States Constitution, 58

United States Oracle, 25–26

United States Supreme Court, 139

Universal Gazette, 79

Van Buren, Martin, 108, 142–43, 197n1

Vattel, Emmerich: *The Law of Nations*, 16, 47, 92, 96

Venice, 54, 105. *See also* Italy

"Veritatis Amans," 161

Vermont, 51

Vernet, Julien, 57

violence, 4; of warfare of imperial conquest, 17. *See also* warfare

Virginia Argus, 17

Virginia Patriot, 89

Ward, John William, 139

warfare, 130; as American method of spreading democracy and freedom, 131; "defensive" Napoleonic, 152; martial manhood and imperial, 155–56. *See also* violence

War for Independence, 4–5, 9, 18, 44, 63. *See also* United States

War of 1812, 68–107, 110–11; anti-imperial rhetoric critiquing American conduct in the, 100, 105–6; British offensive in the, 106; declaration of war on Great Britain by the United States to start the, 110; end of the, 117; Federalist opposition to the, 87, 100–101, 104–7, 116–18, 126; recruitment for the, 170; War Hawks of the, 120. *See also* Great Britain; United States

War of the Third Coalition (1803–6), 41

Wars of the First and Second Coalitions (1792–98 and 1799–1802), 15

Washington, George, 2, 63, 84, 152

Washington Federalist, 61–62

Weld, Horatio Hastings: *Pictorial History of George Washington*, 151–52

Western World, 80

West Florida, 68–77, 80, 83, 88, 92–102, 112; seizure from Spain (1811) of, 69, 98–99, 113, 141; series of unsuccessful rebellions by American immigrants (1804–5) in, 72. *See also* Florida

Whig Party, 127, 167, 169, 175–79; and the American self, 147–49; anti-expansionists in the, 170–71, 174; as the party of economic modernity and the growing American middle class, 147. *See also* anti-expansionists/anti-imperialists; United States

Wilkinson, General James, 78, 87, 99

Wittenburg, 96

XYZ Affair (1796), 9, 74

"Yankee Doodle" (song), 74–76

Zacatecas rebels, 166

THE REVOLUTIONARY AGE

Before Manifest Destiny: The Contested Expansion of the Early
United States
Nicholas G. DiPucchio

Revolutionary Diplomacy: Spanish Statecraft and the Birth of the
United States
Thomas E. Chávez

Declarations of Independence: Indigenous Resilience, Colonial Rivalries,
and the Cost of Revolution
Christopher R. Pearl

Dishonored Americans: The Political Death of Loyalists in
Revolutionary America
Timothy Compeau

The American Liberty Pole: Popular Politics and the Struggle for
Democracy in the Early Republic
Shira Lurie

European Friends of the American Revolution
Andrew J. O'Shaughnessy, John A. Ragosta, and Marie-Jeanne
Rossignol, editors

The Tory's Wife: A Woman and Her Family in Revolutionary America
Cynthia A. Kierner

Writing Early America: From Empire to Revolution
Trevor Burnard

Spain and the American Revolution: New Approaches and Perspectives
Gabriel Paquette and Gonzalo M. Quintero Saravia, editors

The American Revolution and the Habsburg Monarchy
Jonathan Singerton

Navigating Neutrality: Early American Governance in the Turbulent Atlantic
Sandra Moats

Ireland and America: Empire, Revolution, and Sovereignty
Patrick Griffin and Francis D. Cogliano, editors

www.ingramcontent.com/pod-product-compliance
Lightning Source LLC
Chambersburg PA
CBHW030620230426

43661CB00053B/2075